Excel Macros

2nd Edition

by Michael Alexander
Microsoft Excel MVP

A Wiley Brand

Excel® Macros For Dummies®, 2nd Edition

Published by: **John Wiley & Sons, Inc.,** 111 River Street, Hoboken, NJ 07030-5774, www.wiley.com

Copyright © 2017 by John Wiley & Sons, Inc., Hoboken, New Jersey

Published simultaneously in Canada

For general information on our other products and services, please contact our Customer Care Department within the U.S. at 877-762-2974, outside the U.S. at 317-572-3993, or fax 317-572-4002. For technical support, please visit https://hub.wiley.com/community/support/dummies.

Wiley publishes in a variety of print and electronic formats and by print-on-demand. Some material included with standard print versions of this book may not be included in e-books or in print-on-demand. If this book refers to media such as a CD or DVD that is not included in the version you purchased, you may download this material at http://booksupport.wiley.com. For more information about Wiley products, visit www.wiley.com.

Library of Congress Control Number: 2017931733

ISBN: 978-1-119-36924-0

ISBN: 978-1-119-36926-4 (ePDF)

ISBN: 978-1-119-36927-1 (ePub)

Manufactured in the United States of America

10 9 8 7 6 5 4 3 2 1

Contents at a Glance

Table of Contents

Introduction

n its broadest sense, a *macro* is a sequence of instructions that automates some aspect of Excel so that you can work more efficiently and with fewer errors. You might create a macro, for example, to format and print a month-end sales report. After you develop the macro, you can execute it to perform many time-consuming procedures automatically.

Macros are written in VBA, which stands for Visual Basic for Applications. VBA is a programming language developed by Microsoft and a tool used to develop programs that control Excel.

Excel programming terminology can be a bit confusing. For example, VBA is a programming language but also serves as a macro language. What do you call something written in VBA and executed in Excel? Is it a macro or is it a program? Excel's Help system often refers to VBA procedures as *macros*, so this is the terminology used in this book.

You'll also see the term *automate* throughout this book. This word means that a series of steps are completed automatically. For example, if you write a macro that adds color to some cells, prints the worksheet, and then removes the color, you have automated those three steps.

You're probably aware that people use Excel for thousands of different tasks. Here are just a few examples:

>> Keeping lists of things, such as customer names and transactions

>> Budgeting and forecasting

>> Analyzing scientific data

>> Creating invoices and other forms

>> Developing charts from data

The list could go on and on. The point is simply that Excel is used for a wide variety of tasks, and everyone reading this book has different needs and expectations regarding Excel. One thing most readers have in common, however, is the need to automate some aspect of Excel, which is what macros (and this book) are all about.

About This Book

This book approaches the topic of Excel macros with the recognition that programming VBA takes time and practice — time that you may not have right now. In fact, many analysts don't have the luxury of taking a few weeks to become expert at VBA. So instead of the same general overview of VBA topics, this book provides some of the most commonly used real-world Excel macros.

Each section in the book outlines a common problem and provides an Excel macro to solve the problem — along with a detailed explanation of how the macro works and where to use it.

Each section presents the following:

>> The problem

>> The macro solution

>> How the macro works

After reading each section, you'll be able to

>> Immediately implement the required Excel macro

>> Understand how the macro works

>> Reuse the macro in other workbooks or with other macros

The macros in this book are designed to get you up and running with VBA in the quickest way possible. Each macro tackles a common task that benefits from automation. The idea here is to learn through application. This book is designed so that you can implement the macro while getting a clear understanding of what the macro does and how it works.

Foolish Assumptions

I make three assumptions about you as the reader:

>> You've installed Microsoft Excel 2007 or a higher version.

>> You have some familiarity with the basic concepts of data analysis, such as working with tables, aggregating data, creating formulas, referencing cells, filtering, and sorting.

>> You have an Internet connection so you can download the sample files, found at www.dummies.com/go/excelmacros.

Icons Used in This Book

TIP

Tip icons cover tricks or techniques related to the current discussion.

REMEMBER

Remember icons indicate notes or asides that are important to keep in mind.

WARNING

Warning icons hold critical information about pitfalls you will want to avoid.

Beyond the Book

In addition to the material in the print or e-book you're reading, this product comes with more online goodies:

>> **Sample files:** Each macro in this book has an associated sample file that enables you to see the macro working and to review the code. You can use the sample files also to copy and paste the code into your environment (as opposed to typing each macro from scratch). Download the sample files at:

www.dummies.com/go/excelmacros

Each macro in this book has detailed instructions on where to copy and paste the code. In general terms, you open the sample file associated with the macro, go to the Visual Basic Editor (by pressing Alt+F11), and copy the code. Then you go to your workbook, open the Visual Basic Editor, and paste the code in the appropriate location.

REMEMBER

TIP

Note that in some macros, you need to change the macro to suit your situation. For example, in the macro that prints all workbooks in a directory (see Chapter 4), you point to the C:\Temp\ directory. Before using this macro, you must edit it to point to your target directory.

If a macro is not working for you, most likely a component of the macro needs to be changed. Pay special attention to range addresses, directory names, and any other hard-coded names.

>> **Cheat sheet:** The cheat sheet offers shortcut keys that can help you work more efficiently in Excel's Visual Basic Editor. You can find the cheat sheet by visiting www.dummies.com and searching for "Excel Macros Cheat Sheet".

Where to Go from Here

If you're completely new to Excel macros, start with Part 1 (Chapters 1 – 3) to get the fundamentals you'll need to leverage the macros in this book. There, you will gain a concise understanding of how macros and VBA work, along with the basic foundation you need to implement the macros provided in this book.

If you've got some macro experience and want to dive right into the macro examples, feel free to peruse Chapters 4 – 9 and search for the task or macro that looks interesting to you. Don't worry. Each macro example stands on its own within its own section that gives you all the guidance you need to understand and implement the code in your own workbook.

Visit Part 2 if you're interested in macros that automate common workbook and worksheet tasks to save time and gain efficiencies.

Explore Part 3 to find macros that navigate ranges, format cells, and manipulate the data in your workbooks.

If you want to find macros that work with PivotTables, charts, and emails, thumb through the macros in Part 4 where you will discover macros that automate redundant PivotTable and chart tasks, as well as macros that send emails and connect to external data sources.

Don't forget to hit Part 5 for some useful tips and advice on how to get the most out of your new macro skills.

Here are some final things to keep in mind while working with the macros in this book:

>> **Any file that contains a macro must have the .xlsm file extension.** See the section on macro-enabled file extensions in Chapter 1 for more information.

>> **Excel does not run macros until they are enabled.** As you implement these macros, you and your customers must comply with Excel's macro security measures. See the section in Chapter 1 on macro security in Excel for details.

>> **You cannot undo macro actions.** When working in Excel, you can often undo the actions you've taken because Excel keeps a log (called the undo stack) recording your last 100 actions. However, running a macro automatically destroys the undo stack, so you can't undo the actions you take in a macro.

>> **You need to tweak the macros to fit your workbook.** Many of the macros reference example sheet names and ranges that you may not have in your workbook. Be sure to replace references like "Sheet 1" or Range("A1") with the sheet names and cell addresses you are working with in your own workbooks.

1

Holy Macro Batman!

Chapter **1**

Macro Fundamentals

A macro is essentially a set of instructions or code that you create to tell Excel to execute any number of actions. In Excel, macros can be written or recorded. The key word here is recorded.

Recording a macro is like programming a phone number into your cell phone. You first manually dial and save a number. Then when you want, you can redial those numbers with the touch of a button. Just as on a cell phone, you can record your actions in Excel while you perform them. While you record, Excel gets busy in the background, translating your keystrokes and mouse clicks to written code (also known as Visual Basic for Applications (VBA)). After a macro is recorded, you can play back those actions anytime you want.

In this chapter, you'll explore macros and learn how you can use macros to automate your recurring processes to simplify your life.

Why Use a Macro?

The first step in using macros is admitting you have a problem. Actually, you may have several problems:

» **Problem 1 - Repetitive tasks:** As each new month rolls around, you have to make the donuts (that is, crank out those reports). You have to import that data.

You have to update those PivotTables. You have to delete those columns, and so on. Wouldn't it be nice if you could fire up a macro and have those more redundant parts of your dashboard processes done automatically?

» **Problem 2 - You're making mistakes:** When you go hand-to-hand combat with Excel, you're bound to make mistakes. When you're repeatedly applying formulas, sorting, and moving things around manually, there's always that risk of catastrophe. Add to that the looming deadlines and constant change requests, and your error rate goes up. Why not calmly record a macro, ensure that everything is running correctly, and then forget it? The macro is sure to perform every action the same way every time you run it, reducing the chance of errors.

» **Problem 3 - Awkward navigation:** You often create reports for an audience that probably has a limited knowledge of Excel. It's always helpful to make your reports more user-friendly. Macros can be used to dynamically format and print worksheets, navigate to specific sheets in your workbook, or even save the open document in a specified location. Your audience will appreciate these little touches that help make perusal of your workbooks a bit more pleasant.

Macro Recording Basics

To start recording your first macro, you need to first find the Macro Recorder, which is on the Developer tab. Unfortunately, Excel comes out of the box with the Developer tab hidden — you may not see it on your version of Excel at first. If you plan to work with VBA macros, you'll want to make sure that the Developer tab is visible. To display this tab

1. **Choose File ⇨ Excel Options.**

2. **In the Excel Options dialog box, select Customize Ribbon.**

3. **In the list box on the right, place a check mark next to Developer.**

4. **Click OK to return to Excel.**

Now that you have the Developer tab showing in the Excel Ribbon, you can start up the Macro Recorder by selecting Record Macro from the Developer tab. This activates the Record Macro dialog box, as shown in Figure 1-1.

FIGURE 1-1:
The Record
Macro dialog box.

Here are the four parts of the Record Macro dialog box:

>> **Macro Name:** This should be self-explanatory. Excel gives a default name to your macro, such as Macro1, but you should give your macro a name more descriptive of what it actually does. For example, you might name a macro that formats a generic table as FormatTable.

>> **Shortcut Key:** Every macro needs an event, or something to happen, for it to run. This event can be a button press, a workbook opening, or in this case, a keystroke combination. When you assign a shortcut key to your macro, entering that combination of keys triggers your macro to run. This is an optional field.

>> **Store Macro In:** This Workbook is the default option. Storing your macro in This Workbook simply means that the macro is stored along with the active Excel file. The next time you open that particular workbook, the macro is available to run. Similarly, if you send the workbook to another user, that user can run the macro as well (provided the macro security is properly set by your user — more on that later in this chapter).

>> **Description:** This is an optional field, but it can come in handy if you have numerous macros in a spreadsheet or if you need to give a user a more detailed description about what the macro does.

With the Record Macro dialog box open, follow these steps to create a simple macro that enters your name into a worksheet cell:

1. **Enter a new single-word name for the macro to replace the default Macro1 name.**

   A good name for this example is MyName.

2. **Assign this macro to the shortcut key Ctrl+Shift+N.**

   You do this by entering uppercase N in the edit box labeled Shortcut Key.

3. **Click OK.**

   This closes the Record Macro dialog box and begins recording your actions.

4. **Select any cell on your Excel spreadsheet, type your name into the selected cell, and then press Enter.**

5. **Choose Developer ⇨ Code ⇨ Stop Recording (or click the Stop Recording button in the status bar).**

Examining the macro

The macro was recorded in a new module named Module1. To view the code in this module, you must activate the Visual Basic Editor. You can activate the VB Editor in either of two ways:

>> Press Alt+F11.

>> Choose Developer ⇨ Code ⇨ Visual Basic.

In the VB Editor, the Project window displays a list of all open workbooks and add-ins. This list is displayed as a tree diagram, which you can expand or collapse. The code that you recorded previously is stored in Module1 in the current workbook. When you double-click Module1, the code in the module appears in the Code window.

The macro should look something like this:

```
Sub MyName()
'
' MyName Macro
'
' Keyboard Shortcut: Ctrl+Shift+N
'
    ActiveCell.FormulaR1C1 = "Michael Alexander"

End Sub
```

The macro recorded is a Sub procedure named MyName. The statements tell Excel what to do when the macro is executed.

Notice that Excel inserted some comments at the top of the procedure. These comments are some of the information that appeared in the Record Macro dialog box. These comment lines (which begin with an apostrophe) aren't really necessary, and deleting them has no effect on how the macro runs. If you ignore the comments, you'll see that this procedure has only one VBA statement:

```
ActiveCell.FormulaR1C1 = "Michael Alexander"
```

This single statement causes the name you typed while recording to be inserted into the active cell.

Testing the macro

Before you recorded this macro, you set an option that assigned the macro to the Ctrl+Shift+N shortcut key combination. To test the macro, return to Excel by using either of the following methods:

>> Press Alt+F11.

>> Click the View Microsoft Excel button on the VB Editor toolbar.

When Excel is active, activate a worksheet. (It can be in the workbook that contains the VBA module or in any other workbook.) Select a cell and press Ctrl+Shift+N. The macro immediately enters your name into the cell.

REMEMBER

In the preceding example, notice that you selected the cell to be altered before you started recording your macro. This step is important. If you select a cell while the macro recorder is turned on, the actual cell that you selected is recorded into the macro. In such a case, the macro would always format that particular cell, and it would not be a general-purpose macro.

Editing the macro

After you record a macro, you can make changes to it (although you must know what you're doing). For example, assume that you want your name to be bold. You could re-record the macro, but this modification is simple, so editing the code is more efficient. Press Alt+F11 to activate the VB Editor window. Then activate Module1 and insert the following statement before the End Sub statement:

```
ActiveCell.Font.Bold = True
```

The edited macro appears as follows:

```
Sub MyName()
'
```

```
' MyName Macro
'
' Keyboard Shortcut: Ctrl+Shift+N
'
    ActiveCell.Font.Bold = True

    ActiveCell.FormulaR1C1 = "Michael Alexander"

End Sub
```

Test this new macro, and you see that it performs as it should.

Comparing Absolute and Relative Macro Recording

Now that you've read about the basics of the Macro Recorder interface, it's time to go deeper and begin recording macros. The first thing you need to understand before you begin is that Excel has two modes for recording — absolute reference and relative reference.

Recording macros with absolute references

Excel's default recording mode is in absolute reference. As you may know, the term absolute reference is often used in the context of cell references found in formulas. When a cell reference in a formula is an absolute reference, it does not automatically adjust when the formula is pasted to a new location.

The best way to understand how this concept applies to macros is to try it out. Open the Chapter 1 Sample File.xlsx file and record a macro that counts the rows in the Branchlist worksheet. (See Figure 1-2.)

TIP

The sample dataset used in this chapter can be found on this book's companion website at www.dummies.com/go/excelmacros.

Follow these steps to record the macro:

1. Before recording, make sure cell A1 is selected.

2. Select Record Macro from the Developer tab.

3. Name the macro AddTotal.

4. Choose This Workbook for the save location.

FIGURE 1-2:
Your pre-totaled
worksheet
containing two
tables.

	A	B	C	D	E	F	G	H	I
1		**Region**	**Market**	**Branch**			**Region**	**Market**	**Branch**
2		NORTH	BUFFALO	601419			SOUTH	CHARLOTTE	173901
3		NORTH	BUFFALO	701407			SOUTH	CHARLOTTE	301301
4		NORTH	BUFFALO	802202			SOUTH	CHARLOTTE	302301
5		NORTH	CANADA	910181			SOUTH	CHARLOTTE	601306
6		NORTH	CANADA	920681			SOUTH	DALLAS	202600
7		NORTH	MICHIGAN	101419			SOUTH	DALLAS	490260
8		NORTH	MICHIGAN	501405			SOUTH	DALLAS	490360
9		NORTH	MICHIGAN	503405			SOUTH	DALLAS	490460
10		NORTH	MICHIGAN	590140			SOUTH	FLORIDA	301316
11		NORTH	NEWYORK	801211			SOUTH	FLORIDA	701309
12		NORTH	NEWYORK	802211			SOUTH	FLORIDA	702309
13		NORTH	NEWYORK	804211			SOUTH	NEWORLEANS	601310
14		NORTH	NEWYORK	805211			SOUTH	NEWORLEANS	602310
15		NORTH	NEWYORK	806211			SOUTH	NEWORLEANS	801607

5. **Click OK to start recording.**

At this point, Excel is recording your actions. While Excel is recording, perform the following steps:

1. **Select cell A16 and type Total in the cell.**

2. **Select the first empty cell in Column D (D16) and enter = COUNTA(D2:D15).**

   This gives a count of branch numbers at the bottom of column D. You need to use the COUNTA function because the branch numbers are stored as text.

3. **Click Stop Recording on the Developer tab to stop recording the macro.**

The formatted worksheet should look something like the one in Figure 1-3.

FIGURE 1-3:
Your post-totaled
worksheet.

	A	B	C	D	E	F	G	H	I
1		**Region**	**Market**	**Branch**			**Region**	**Market**	**Branch**
2		NORTH	BUFFALO	601419			SOUTH	CHARLOTTE	173901
3		NORTH	BUFFALO	701407			SOUTH	CHARLOTTE	301301
4		NORTH	BUFFALO	802202			SOUTH	CHARLOTTE	302301
5		NORTH	CANADA	910181			SOUTH	CHARLOTTE	601306
6		NORTH	CANADA	920681			SOUTH	DALLAS	202600
7		NORTH	MICHIGAN	101419			SOUTH	DALLAS	490260
8		NORTH	MICHIGAN	501405			SOUTH	DALLAS	490360
9		NORTH	MICHIGAN	503405			SOUTH	DALLAS	490460
10		NORTH	MICHIGAN	590140			SOUTH	FLORIDA	301316
11		NORTH	NEWYORK	801211			SOUTH	FLORIDA	701309
12		NORTH	NEWYORK	802211			SOUTH	FLORIDA	702309
13		NORTH	NEWYORK	804211			SOUTH	NEWORLEANS	601310
14		NORTH	NEWYORK	805211			SOUTH	NEWORLEANS	602310
15		NORTH	NEWYORK	806211			SOUTH	NEWORLEANS	801607
16	Total			14					

To see your macro in action, delete the total row you just added and play back your macro by following these steps:

1. **Select Macros from the Developer tab.**

2. **Find and select the AddTotal macro you just recorded.**

3. **Click the Run button.**

If all goes well, the macro plays back your actions to a T and gives your table a total. Now here's the thing: No matter how hard you try, you can't make the AddTotal macro work on the second table (G1:I15 in Figure 1-3). Why? Because you recorded it as an absolute macro.

To understand what this means, examine the underlying code. To examine the code, select Macros from the Developer tab to get the Macro dialog box you see in Figure 1-4.

FIGURE 1-4:
The Excel Macro dialog box.

Select the AddTotal macro and click the Edit button. This opens the Visual Basic Editor to show you the code that was written when you recorded your macro:

```
Sub AddTotal()

    Range("A16").Select

    ActiveCell.FormulaR1C1 = "Total"

    Range("D16").Select
```

```
    ActiveCell.FormulaR1C1 = "=COUNTA(R[-14]C:R[-1]C)"

End Sub
```

Pay particular attention to lines 2 and 4 of the macro. When you asked Excel to select cell range A16 and then D16, those cells are exactly what it selected. Because the macro was recorded in absolute reference mode, Excel interpreted your range selection as absolute. In other words, if you select cell A16, that cell is what Excel gives you. In the next section, you take a look at what the same macro looks like when recorded in relative reference mode.

Recording macros with relative references

In the context of Excel macros, relative means relative to the currently active cell. So you should use caution with your active cell choice — both when you record the relative reference macro and when you run it.

First, make sure the Chapter 1 Sample File.xlsx file is open. Then, use the following steps to record a relative-reference macro:

To download the Chapter 1 Sample file, visit www.dummies.com/go/excelmacros.

REMEMBER

1. Select the Use Relative References option from the Developer tab, as shown in Figure 1-5.

2. Before recording, make sure cell A1 is selected.

3. Select Record Macro from the Developer tab.

4. Name the macro AddTotalRelative.

5. Choose This Workbook for the save location.

6. Click OK to start recording.

7. Select cell A16 and type Total in the cell.

8. Select the first empty cell in Column D (D16) and type = COUNTA(D2:D15).

9. Click Stop Recording on the Developer tab to stop recording the macro.

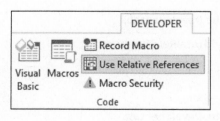

FIGURE 1-5:
Recording a macro with relative references.

At this point, you have recorded two macros. Take a moment to examine the code for your newly created macro.

Select Macros from the Developer tab to open the Macro dialog box. Here, choose the AddTotalRelative macro and click Edit.

Again, this opens the Visual Basic Editor to show you the code that was written when you recorded your macro. This time, your code looks something like the following:

```
Sub AddTotalRelative()

    ActiveCell.Offset(15, 0).Range("A1").Select

    ActiveCell.FormulaR1C1 = "Total"

    ActiveCell.Offset(0, 3).Range("A1").Select

    ActiveCell.FormulaR1C1 = "=COUNTA(R[-14]C:R[-1]C)"

End Sub
```

Notice that there are no references to any specific cell ranges at all (other than the starting point "A1"). Let's take a quick look at what the relevant parts of this VBA code really mean.

Notice that in line 2, Excel uses the Offset property of the active cell. This property tells the cursor to move a certain number of cells up or down and a certain number of cells left or right.

The Offset property code tells Excel to move 15 rows down and 0 columns across from the active cell (in this case, A1). There's no need for Excel to explicitly select a cell as it did when recording an absolute reference macro.

To see this macro in action, delete the total row for both tables and do the following:

1. **Select cell A1.**
2. **Select Macros from the Developer tab.**
3. **Find and select the AddTotalRelative macro.**
4. **Click the Run button.**
5. **Now select cell F1.**
6. **Select Macros from the Developer tab.**

7. Find and select the AddTotalRelative macro.

8. Click the Run button.

Notice that this macro, unlike your previous macro, works on both sets of data. Because the macro applies the totals relative to the currently active cell, the totals are applied correctly.

For this macro to work, you simply need to ensure that

» You've selected the correct starting cell before running the macro.

» The block of data has the same number of rows and columns as the data on which you recorded the macro.

Hopefully, this simple example has given you a firm grasp of macro recording with both absolute and relative references.

Other Macro Recording Concepts

At this point, you should feel comfortable recording your own Excel macros. Here are some of other important concepts you'll need to keep in mind when working with macros.

Macro-enabled file extensions

Beginning with Excel 2007, Excel workbooks were given the standard file extension .xlsx. Files with the .xlsx extension cannot contain macros. If your workbook contains macros and you then save that workbook as an .xlsx file, your macros are removed automatically. Excel warns you that macro content will be removed when saving a workbook with macros as an .xlsx file.

If you want to retain the macros, you must save your file as an Excel Macro-Enabled Workbook. This gives your file an .xlsm extension. The idea is that all workbooks with an .xlsx file extension are automatically known to be safe, whereas you can recognize .xlsm files as a potential threat.

Macro security in Excel 2010

With the release of Office 2010, Microsoft introduced significant changes to its Office security model. One of the most significant changes is the concept of trusted documents. Without getting into the technical minutia, a trusted document is essentially a workbook you have deemed safe by enabling macros.

If you open a workbook that contains macros in Excel 2010, you see a yellow bar message under the Ribbon stating that macros (active content) have, in effect, been disabled.

If you click Enable, it automatically becomes a trusted document. This means you no longer are prompted to enable the content as long as you open that file on your computer. The basic idea is that if you told Excel that you "trust" a particular workbook by enabling macros, it is highly likely that you will enable macros each time you open it. Thus, Excel remembers that you've enabled macros before and inhibits any further messages about macros for that workbook.

This is great news for you and your clients. After enabling your macros just one time, they won't be annoyed at the constant messages about macros, and you won't have to worry that your macro-enabled dashboard will fall flat because macros have been disabled.

Trusted locations

If the thought of any macro message coming up (even one time) unnerves you, you can set up a trusted location for your files. A trusted location is a directory that is deemed a safe zone where only trusted workbooks are placed. A trusted location allows you and your clients to run a macro-enabled workbook with no security restrictions as long as the workbook is in that location.

To set up a trusted location, follow these steps:

1. **Select the Macro Security button on the Developer tab.**

   This activates the Trust Center dialog box.

2. **Click the Trusted Locations button.**

   This opens the Trusted Locations menu (see Figure 1-6), which shows you all the directories that are considered trusted.

3. **Click the Add New Location button.**

4. **Click Browse to find and specify the directory that will be considered a trusted location.**

After you specify a trusted location, any Excel file opened from this location will have macros automatically enabled.

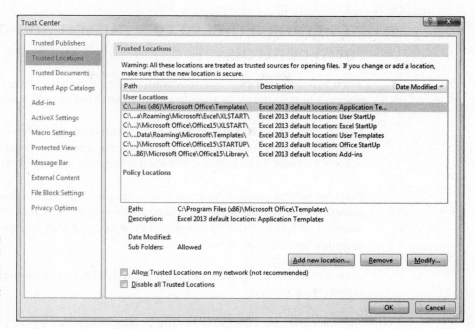

FIGURE 1-6:
The Trusted
Locations menu
allows you to add
directories that
are considered
trusted.

Storing macros in your Personal Macro Workbook

Most user-created macros are designed for use in a specific workbook, but you may want to use some macros in all your work. You can store these general-purpose macros in the Personal Macro Workbook so that they're always available to you. The Personal Macro Workbook is loaded whenever you start Excel. This file, named personal.xlsb, doesn't exist until you record a macro using Personal Macro Workbook as the destination.

To record the macro in your Personal Macro Workbook, select the Personal Macro Workbook option in the Record Macro dialog box before you start recording. This option is in the Store Macro In drop-down list (refer to Figure 1-1).

If you store macros in the Personal Macro Workbook, you don't have to remember to open the Personal Macro Workbook when you load a workbook that uses macros. When you want to exit, Excel asks whether you want to save changes to the Personal Macro Workbook.

REMEMBER

The Personal Macro Workbook normally is in a hidden window to keep it out of the way.

Assigning a macro to a button and other form controls

When you create macros, you may want to have a clear and easy way to run each macro. A basic button can provide a simple but effective user interface.

As luck would have it, Excel offers a set of form controls designed specifically for creating user interfaces directly on spreadsheets. There are several different types of form controls, from buttons (the most commonly used control) to scrollbars.

The idea behind using a form control is simple: You place a form control on a spreadsheet and then assign a macro to it — that is, a macro you've already recorded. When a macro is assigned to the control, that macro is executed, or played, when the control is clicked.

Take a moment to create a button for the AddTotalRelative macro you created earlier. Here's how:

1. **Click the Insert button under the Developer tab. (See Figure 1-7.)**

2. **Select the Button Form Control from the drop-down list that appears.**

3. **Click the location where you want to place your button.**

   When you drop the button control onto your spreadsheet, the Assign Macro dialog box, shown in Figure 1-8, activates and asks you to assign a macro to this button.

4. **Select the macro you want to assign to the button and then click OK.**

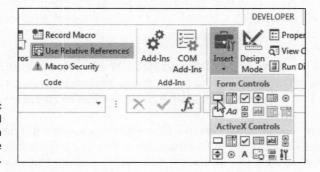

FIGURE 1-7:
You can find the form controls in the Developer tab.

At this point, you have a button that runs your macro when you click it! Keep in mind that all the controls in the Form Controls group (shown in Figure 1-7) work in the same way as the command button, in that you assign a macro to run when the control is selected.

FORM CONTROLS VERSUS ActiveX CONTROLS

Notice the form controls and ActiveX controls in Figure 1-7. Although they look similar, they're quite different. Form controls are designed specifically for use on a spreadsheet, and ActiveX controls are typically used on Excel user forms. As a general rule, you should always use form controls when working on a spreadsheet. Why? Form controls need less overhead, so they perform better, and configuring form controls is far easier than configuring their ActiveX counterparts.

FIGURE 1-8:
Assign a macro to the newly added button.

Placing a macro on the Quick Access Toolbar

You can also assign a macro to a button in Excel's Quick Access Toolbar. The Quick Access Toolbar sits either above or below the Ribbon. You can add a custom button that runs your macro by following these steps:

1. **Right-click your Quick Access Toolbar and select Customize Quick Access Toolbar.**

   This opens the dialog box shown in Figure 1-9.

2. **Click the Quick Access Toolbar button on the left of the Excel Options dialog box.**

3. **Select Macros from the Choose Commands From drop-down list on the left.**

4. Select the macro you want to add and click the Add button.

5. Change the icon by clicking the Modify button.

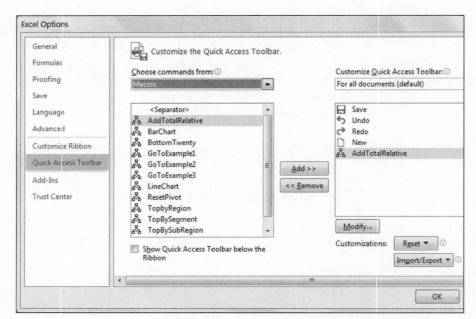

FIGURE 1-9:
Adding a macro
to the Quick
Access Toolbar.

Examples of Macros in Action

Covering the fundamentals of building and using macros is one thing. Coming up with good ways to incorporate them into your reporting processes is another. Take a moment to review a few examples of how macros automate simple reporting tasks.

REMEMBER

Open the Chapter 1 Samples.xlsm file to follow along in the next section. To download the Chapter 1 Sample file, visit www.dummies.com/go/excelmacros.

Building navigation buttons

The most common use of macros is navigation. Workbooks that have many worksheets or tabs can be frustrating to navigate. To help your audience, you can create some sort of a switchboard, like the one shown in Figure 1-10. When a user clicks the Example 1 button, he's taken to the Example 1 sheet.

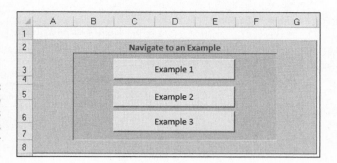

FIGURE 1-10: Use macros to build buttons that help users navigate your reports.

Creating a macro to navigate to a sheet is quite simple.

1. **Start at the sheet that will become your switchboard or starting point.**

2. **Start recording a macro.**

3. **While recording, click the destination sheet (the sheet this macro will navigate to).**

4. **After you click in the destination sheet, stop recording the macro.**

5. **Assign the macro to a button.**

TIP

It's useful to know that Excel has a built-in hyperlink feature, allowing you to convert the contents of a cell into a hyperlink that links to another location. That location can be a separate Excel workbook, a website, or even another tab in the current workbook. Although using a hyperlink may be easier than setting up a macro, you can't apply a hyperlink to form controls (like buttons). Instead of a button, you'd use text to let users know where they'll go when they click the link.

Dynamically rearranging PivotTable data

Macros be used with any Excel object normally used in reporting. For instance, you can use a macro to give your audience a way to dynamically change a pivot table. In the example illustrated in Figure 1-11, macros allow a user to change the perspective of the chart simply by selecting any one of the buttons shown.

Figure 1-12 reveals that the chart is actually a pivot chart tied to a PivotTable. The recorded macros assigned to each button are doing nothing more than rearranging the PivotTable to slice the data using various pivot fields.

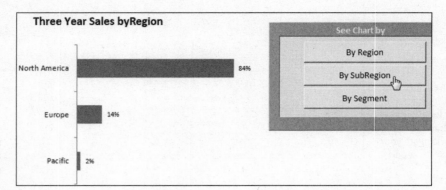

FIGURE 1-11:
This report allows
users to choose
their perspective.

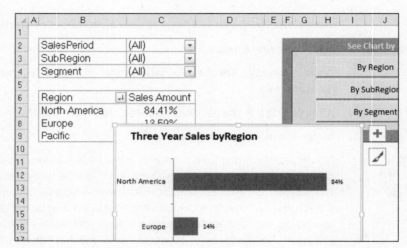

FIGURE 1-12:
The macros
behind these
buttons
rearrange the
data fields in a
PivotTable.

Here are the high-level steps needed to create this type of setup:

1. **Create your PivotTable and a pivot chart.**

2. **Start recording a macro.**

3. **While recording, move a pivot field from one area of the PivotTable to the other. When you're done, stop recording the macro.**

4. **Record another macro to move the data field back to its original position.**

5. **After both macros are set up, assign each one to a separate button.**

You can fire your new macros in turn to see your pivot field dynamically move back and forth.

Offering one-touch reporting options

The last two examples demonstrate that you can record any action that you find of value. That is, if you think users would appreciate a certain feature being auto-mated for them, why not record a macro to do so?

In Figure 1-13, notice that you can filter the PivotTable for the top or bottom 20 customers. Because the steps to filter a PivotTable for the top and bottom 20 have been recorded, users can get the benefit of this functionality without knowing how to do it themselves. Also, recording a specific action allows you to manage risk a bit. That is to say, you'll know that your users will interact with your reports in a method that has been developed and tested by you.

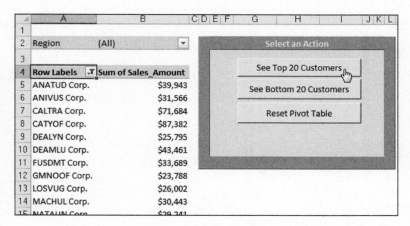

FIGURE 1-13: Offering prerecorded views not only saves time and effort, but it also allows users that don't know how to use advanced features to benefit from them.

This not only saves them time and effort, but it also allows users that don't know how to take these actions to benefit from them.

Figure 1-14 demonstrates how you can give your audience a quick and easy way to see the same data on different charts. Don't laugh too quickly at the uselessness of this example. It's not uncommon to be asked to see the same data different ways. Instead of taking up real estate, just record a macro that changes the Chart Type of the chart. Your clients can switch views to their heart's content.

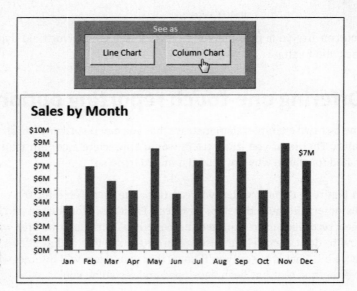

FIGURE 1-14:
You can give
your audience a
choice in how
they view data.

IN THIS CHAPTER

» Understanding Visual Basic Editor
  components

» Working with the Project window

» Using the Code window

» Customizing the Visual Basic Editor

Chapter **2**

Getting Cozy with the Visual Basic Editor

The Visual Basic Editor (VBE) is the environment where all Excel macros are stored and processed. Each workbook you create comes with this interconnected VBE environment free of charge. Even if you never record one macro, the VBE is in the background waiting to be used. When you create a macro, the VBE quietly comes to life ready to process the various procedures and routines you give it.

In this chapter, you'll take your first look behind the curtain to explore the Visual Basic Editor.

Working in the Visual Basic Editor

The Visual Basic Editor is actually a separate application that runs when you open Excel. In order to see this hidden VBE environment, you'll need to activate it. The quickest way to activate the VBE is to press Alt+F11 when Excel is active. To return to Excel, press Alt+F11 again.

You can also activate the VBE by using the Visual Basic command found on Excel's Developer tab.

Figure 2-1 shows the VBE program with some of the key parts identified. Chances are your VBE program window won't look exactly like what you see in Figure 2-1. The VBE contains several windows and is highly customizable. You can hide windows, rearrange windows, dock windows, and so on.

Toolbar

Menu Bar

Code Window

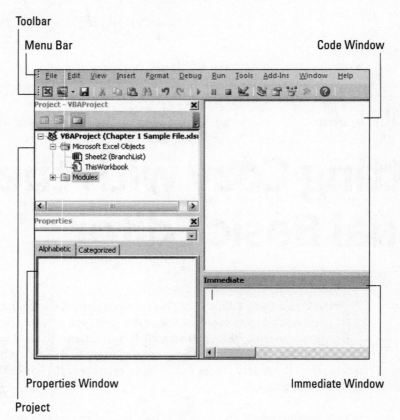

FIGURE 2-1:
The VBE with significant elements identified.

Properties Window

Project

Immediate Window

The VBE menu bar

The VBE menu bar works just like every other menu bar you've encountered. It contains commands that you use to do things with the various components in the VBE. You will also find that many of the menu commands have shortcut keys associated with them.

The VBE also features shortcut menus. You can right-click virtually anything in the VBE and get a shortcut menu of common commands.

The VBE toolbar

The Standard toolbar, which is directly under the menu bar by default, is one of four VBE toolbars available. You can customize the toolbars, move them around, display other toolbars, and so on. If you're so inclined, use the View ⇨ Toolbars command to work with VBE toolbars. Most people just leave them as they are.

The Project window

The Project window displays a tree diagram that shows every workbook currently open in Excel (including add-ins and hidden workbooks). Double-click items to expand or contract them. You'll explore this window in more detail in the "Working with the Project Window" section later in this chapter.

If the Project window is not visible, press Ctrl+R or use the View ⇨ Project Explorer command. To hide the Project window, click the Close button in its title bar. Alternatively, right-click anywhere in the Project window and select Hide from the shortcut menu.

The Code window

A Code window contains VBA code. Every object in a project has an associated Code window. To view an object's Code window, double-click the object in the Project window. For example, to view the Code window for the Sheet1 object, double-click Sheet1 in the Project window. Unless you've added some VBA code, the Code window is empty.

You find out more about Code windows later in this chapter's "Working with a Code Window" section.

The Immediate window

The Immediate window may or may not be visible. If it isn't visible, press Ctrl+G or use the View ⇨ Immediate Window command. To close the Immediate window, click the Close button in its title bar (or right-click anywhere in the Immediate window and select Hide from the shortcut menu).

The Immediate window is most useful for executing VBA statements directly and for debugging your code. If you're just starting out with VBA, this window won't be all that useful, so feel free to hide it and free up some screen space for other things.

Working with the Project Window

When you're working in the VBE, each Excel workbook and add-in that's open is a project. You can think of a project as a collection of objects arranged as an outline. You can expand a project by clicking the plus sign (+) at the left of the project's name in the Project window. Contract a project by clicking the minus sign (−) to the left of a project's name. Or, you can double-click the items to expand and contract them.

Figure 2-2 shows a Project window with two projects listed: a workbook named Book1 and a workbook named Book2.

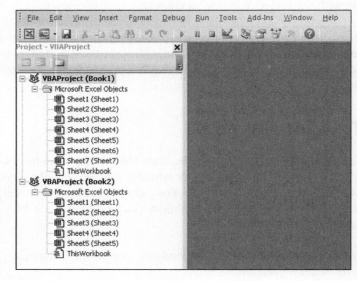

FIGURE 2-2:
This Project window lists two projects. They are expanded to show their objects.

Every project expands to show at least one node called Microsoft Excel Objects. This node expands to show an item for each sheet in the workbook (each sheet is considered an object), and another object called ThisWorkbook (which represents the Workbook object). If the project has any VBA modules, the project listing also shows a Modules node.

Adding a new VBA module

When you record a macro, Excel automatically inserts a VBA module to hold the recorded code. The workbook that holds the module for the recorded macro depends on where you choose to store the recorded macro, just before you start recording.

In general, a VBA module can hold three types of code:

» **Declarations:** One or more information statements that you provide to VBA. For example, you can declare the data type for variables you plan to use, or set some other module-wide options.

» **Sub procedures:** A set of programming instructions that performs some action. All recorded macros are Sub procedures.

» **Function procedures:** A set of programming instructions that returns a single value (similar in concept to a worksheet function, such as Sum).

A single VBA module can store any number of Sub procedures, Function procedures, and declarations. How you organize a VBA module is completely up to you. Some people prefer to keep all their VBA code for an application in a single VBA module; others like to split up the code into several different modules. It's a personal choice, just like arranging furniture.

Follow these steps to manually add a new VBA module to a project:

1. **Select the project's name in the Project window.**

2. **Choose Insert ➪ Module.**

Or you can

1. **Right-click the project's name.**

2. **Choose Insert ➪ Module from the shortcut menu.**

The new module is added to a Modules folder in the Project window (see Figure 2-3). Any modules you create in a given workbook is placed in this Modules folder.

Removing a VBA module

You may want to remove a code module that is no longer needed. To do so, follow these steps:

1. **Select the module's name in the Project window.**

2. **Choose File ➪ Remove *xxx*, where *xxx* is the module name.**

Or

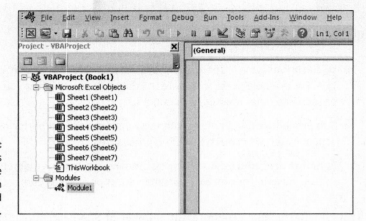

FIGURE 2-3:
Code modules
are visible in the
Project window in
a folder called
Modules.

1. **Right-click the module's name.**

2. **Choose Remove *xxx* from the shortcut menu.**

REMEMBER

You can remove VBA modules, but there is no way to remove the other code modules — those for the Sheet objects, or ThisWorkbook.

Working with a Code Window

As you become proficient with VBA, you spend lots of time working in Code windows. Macros that you record are stored in a module, and you can type VBA code directly into a VBA module.

Minimizing and maximizing windows

Code windows are much like workbook windows in Excel. You can minimize them, maximize them, resize them, hide them, rearrange them, and so on. Most people find it much easier to maximize the Code window that they're working on. Doing so lets you see more code and keeps you from getting distracted.

To maximize a Code window, click the maximize button in its title bar (right next to the X). Or, just double-click its title bar to maximize it. To restore a Code window to its original size, click the Restore button.

Sometimes, you may want to have two or more Code windows visible. For example, you may want to compare the code in two modules or copy code from one module to another. You can arrange the windows manually, or use the Window ⇨ Tile Horizontally or Window ⇨ Tile Vertically commands to arrange them automatically.

You can quickly switch among code windows by pressing Ctrl+Tab. If you repeat that key combination, you keep cycling through all the open Code windows. Pressing Ctrl+Shift+Tab cycles through the windows in reverse order.

Minimizing a Code window gets it out of the way. You can also click the window's Close button in a Code window's title bar to close the window completely. (Closing a window just hides it; you won't lose anything.) To open it again, just double-click the appropriate object in the Project window. Working with these Code windows sounds more difficult than it really is.

Getting VBA code into a module

Before you can do anything meaningful, you must have some VBA code in the VBA module. You can get VBA code into a VBA module in three ways:

>> Use the Excel macro recorder to record your actions and convert them to VBA code.

>> Enter the code directly.

>> Copy the code from one module and paste it into another.

You have discovered the excellent method for creating code by using the Excel macro recorder. However, not all tasks can be translated to VBA by recording a macro. You often have to enter your code directly into the module. Entering code directly basically means either typing the code yourself or copying and pasting code you have found somewhere else.

Entering and editing text in a VBA module works as you might expect. You can select, copy, cut, paste, and do other things to the text.

A single line of VBA code can be as long as you like. However, you may want to use the line-continuation character to break up lengthy lines of code. To continue a single line of code (also known as a statement) from one line to the next, end the first line with a space followed by an underscore (_). Then continue the statement on the next line. Here's an example of a single statement split into three lines:

```
Selection.Sort Key1:=Range("A1"), _

Order1:=xlAscending, Header:=xlGuess, _

Orientation:=xlTopToBottom
```

This statement would perform exactly the same way if it were entered in a single line (with no line-continuation characters). Notice that the second and third lines of this statement are indented. Indenting is optional, but it helps clarify the fact that these lines are not separate statements.

The VBE has multiple levels of undo and redo. If you delete a statement that you shouldn't have, use the Undo button on the toolbar (or press Ctrl+Z) until the statement appears again. After undoing, you can use the Redo button to perform the changes you've undone.

Ready to enter some real, live code? Try the following steps:

1. **Create a new workbook in Excel.**
2. **Press Alt+F11 to activate the VBE.**
3. **Click the new workbook's name in the Project window.**
4. **Choose Insert ➪ Module to insert a VBA module into the project.**
5. **Type the following code into the module:**

```
Sub GuessName()

    Dim Msg as String

    Dim Ans As Long

    Msg = "Is your name " & Application.UserName & "?"

    Ans = MsgBox(Msg, vbYesNo)

    If Ans = vbNo Then MsgBox "Oh, never mind."

    If Ans = vbYes Then MsgBox "I must be clairvoyant!"

End Sub
```

6. **Make sure the cursor is located anywhere within the text you typed and press F5 to execute the procedure.**

TIP

The VBE has its own set of shortcut keys you can use to quickly fire a command using your keyboard. F5 is a shortcut for the Run ➪ Run Sub/UserForm command. For more VBE shortcut keys, check out the Cheat Sheet by visiting www.dummies. com and search for "Excel Macros For Dummies Cheat Sheet" in the Search box.

When you enter the code listed in Step 5, you might notice that the VBE makes some adjustments to the text you enter. For example, after you type the Sub statement, the VBE automatically inserts the End Sub statement. And if you omit the space before or after an equal sign, the VBE inserts the space for you. Also, the VBE changes the color and capitalization of some text. This is all perfectly normal. It's just the VBE's way of keeping things neat and readable.

If you followed the previous steps, you just created a VBA Sub procedure, also known as a macro. When you press F5, Excel executes the code and follows the instructions. In other words, Excel evaluates each statement and does what you told it to do. You can execute this macro any number of times — although it tends to lose its appeal after a few dozen executions.

This simple macro uses the following concepts:

- » Defining a Sub procedure (the first line)
- » Declaring variables (the Dim statements)
- » Assigning values to variables (Msg and Ans)
- » Concatenating (joining) a string (using the & operator)
- » Using a built-in VBA function (MsgBox)
- » Using built-in VBA constants (vbYesNo, vbNo, and vbYes)
- » Using an If-Then construct (twice)
- » Ending a Sub procedure (the last line)

As mentioned previously, you can copy and paste code into a VBA module. For example, a Sub or Function procedure that you write for one project might also be useful in another project. Instead of wasting time reentering the code, you can activate the module and use the normal copy-and-paste procedures (Ctrl+C to copy and Ctrl+V to paste). After pasting it into a VBA module, you can modify the code as necessary.

Customizing the VBA Environment

If you're serious about becoming an Excel programmer, you'll spend a lot of time with VBA modules on your screen. To help make things as comfortable as possible, the VBE provides quite a few customization options.

When the VBE is active, choose Tools ➪ Options. You'll see a dialog box with four tabs: Editor, Editor Format, General, and Docking. Take a moment to explore some of the options found on each tab.

The Editor tab

Figure 2-4 shows the options accessed by clicking the Editor tab of the Options dialog box. Use the option in the Editor tab to control how certain things work in the VBE.

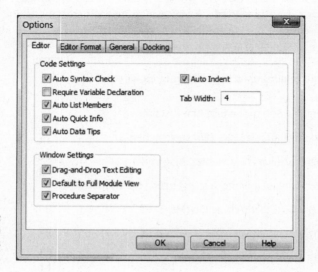

FIGURE 2-4:
The Editor tab in the Options dialog box.

The Auto Syntax Check option

The Auto Syntax Check setting determines whether the VBE pops up a dialog box if it discovers a syntax error while you're entering your VBA code. The dialog box tells roughly what the problem is. If you don't choose this setting, VBE flags syntax errors by displaying them in a different color (red by default) from the rest of the code, and you don't have to deal with any dialog boxes popping up on your screen.

The Require Variable Declaration option

If the Require Variable Declaration option is set, VBE inserts the following statements at the beginning of each new VBA module you insert:

Option Explicit

Changing this setting affects only new modules, not existing modules. If this statement appears in your module, you must explicitly define each variable you use. Using a Dim statement is one way to declare variables.

The Auto List Members option

If the Auto List Members option is set, VBE provides some help when you're entering your VBA code. It displays a list that would logically complete the statement you're typing. This is one of the best features of the VBE.

The Auto Quick Info option

If the Auto Quick Info option is selected, VBE displays information about functions and their arguments as you type. This is similar to the way Excel lists the arguments for a function as you start typing a new formula.

The Auto Data Tips option

If the Auto Data Tips option is set, VBE displays the value of the variable over which your cursor is placed when you're debugging code. This is turned on by default and often quite useful. There is no reason to turn this option off.

The Auto Indent setting

The Auto Indent setting determines whether VBE automatically indents each new line of code the same as the previous line. Most Excel developers are keen on using indentations in their code, so this option is typically kept on.

TIP

By the way, you should use the Tab key to indent your code, not the spacebar. Also, you can use Shift+Tab to "unindent" a line of code. If you want to indent more than just one line, select all lines you want to indent and then press the Tab key.

The VBE's Edit toolbar (which is hidden by default) contains two useful buttons: Indent and Outdent. These buttons let you quickly indent or "unindent" a block of code. Select the code and click one of these buttons to change the block's indenting.

The Drag-and-Drop Text Editing option

The Drag-and-Drop Text Editing option, when enabled, lets you copy and move text by dragging and dropping with your mouse.

The Default to Full Module View option

The Default to Full Module View option sets the default state for new modules. (It doesn't affect existing modules.) If set, procedures in the Code window appear as a single scrollable list. If this option is turned off, you can see only one procedure at a time.

The Procedure Separator option

When the Procedure Separator option is turned on, separator bars appear at the end of each procedure in a Code window. Separator bars provide a nice visual line between procedures, making it easy to see where one piece of code ends and where another starts.

The Editor Format tab

Figure 2-5 shows the Editor Format tab of the Options dialog box. With this tab, you can customize the way the VBE looks.

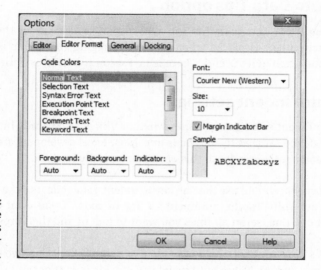

FIGURE 2-5:
Change the way VBE's looks with the Editor Format tab.

The Code Colors option

The Code Colors option lets you set the text color and background color displayed for various elements of VBA code. This is largely a matter of personal preference. Personally, most Excel developers stick with the default colors. But if you like to change things up, you can play around with these settings.

The Font option

The Font option lets you select the font that's used in your VBA modules. For best results, stick with a fixed-width font such as Courier New. In a fixed-width font, all characters are exactly the same width. This makes your code more readable because the characters are nicely aligned vertically and you can easily distinguish multiple spaces (which is sometimes useful).

The Size setting

The Size setting specifies the point size of the font in the VBA modules. This setting is a matter of personal preference determined by your video display resolution and how good your eyesight is.

The Margin Indicator Bar option

This option controls the display of the vertical margin indicator bar in your modules. You should keep this turned on; otherwise, you won't be able to see the helpful graphical indicators when you're debugging your code.

The General tab

Figure 2-6 shows the options available under the General tab in the Options dialog box. In almost every case, the default settings are just fine.

The most important setting on the General tab is Error Trapping. If you are just starting your Excel macro writing career, it's best to leave the Error Trapping set to Break on Unhandled Errors. This ensures Excel can identify errors as you type your code.

FIGURE 2-6:
The General tab of the Options dialog box.

The Docking tab

Figure 2-7 shows the Docking tab. These options determine how the various windows in the VBE behave. When a window is docked, it is fixed in place along one of the edges of the VBE program window. This makes it much easier to identify and locate a particular window. If you turn off all docking, you have a big, confusing mess of windows. Generally, the default settings work fine.

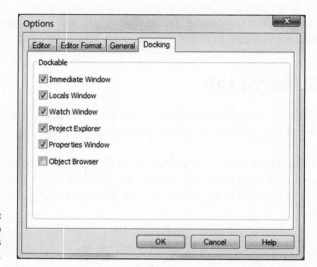

FIGURE 2-7:
The Docking tab
of the Options
dialog box.

Chapter **3**

The Anatomy of Macros

The engine behind macros is VBA (Visual Basic for Applications). When you record a macro, Excel is busy writing the associated VBA behind the scenes. To fully understand macros, it's important to understand the underlying VBA typically used in Excel macros.

This chapter starts you on that journey by giving you a primer on some of the objects, variables, events, and error handlers you will encounter in the macro examples found in this book.

A Brief Overview of the Excel Object Model

Visual Basic for Applications is an object-oriented programming language. The basic concept of object-oriented programming is that a software application (Excel in this case) consists of various individual objects, each of which has its own set of features and uses. An Excel application contains cells, worksheets, charts, PivotTables, drawing shapes — the list of Excel's objects is seemingly endless. Each object has its own set of features, which are called *properties*, and its own set of uses, called *methods*.

You can think of this concept just as you would the objects you encounter every day, such as your computer in your office, your car in your garage, or the refrigerator in your kitchen. Each of those objects has identifying qualities, such as height, weight, and color. They each have their own distinct uses, such as your computer for working with Excel, your car to transport you over long distances, and your refrigerator to keep your perishable foods cold.

VBA objects also have their identifiable properties and methods of use. A worksheet cell is an object, and among its describable features (its properties) are its address, its height, its formatted fill color, and so on. A workbook is also a VBA object, and among its usable features (its methods) are its abilities to be opened, closed, and have a chart or PivotTable added to it.

In Excel you deal with workbooks, worksheets, and ranges on a daily basis. You likely think of each of these "objects" as all part of Excel, not really separating them in your mind. However, Excel thinks about these internally as all part of a hierarchical model called the Excel object model. The Excel object model is a clearly defined set of objects structured according to the relationships between them.

Understanding objects

In the real world, you can describe everything you see as an object. When you look at your house, it is an object. Your house has rooms; those rooms are also separate objects. Those rooms may have closets. Those closets are likewise objects. As you think about your house, the rooms, and the closets, you may see a hierarchical relationship between them. Excel works in the same way.

In Excel, the Application object is the all-encompassing object — similar to your house. Inside the Application object, Excel has a workbook. Inside a workbook is a worksheet. Inside that is a range. These are all objects that live in a hierarchical structure.

To point to a specific object in VBA, you can traverse the object model. For example, to get to cell A1 on Sheet 1, you can enter this code:

```
Activeworkbook.Sheets("Sheet1").Range("A1").Select
```

In most cases, the object model hierarchy is understood, so you don't have to type every level. Entering this code also gets you to cell A1 because Excel infers that you mean the active workbook, and the active sheet:

```
Range("A1").Select
```

Indeed, if you have you cursor already in cell A1, you can simply use the ActiveCell object, negating the need to actually spell out the range.

```
Activecell.Select
```

Understanding collections

Many of Excel's objects belong to collections. Your house sits within a neighborhood, for example, which is a collection of houses called a neighborhood. Each neighborhood sits in a collection of neighborhoods called a city. Excel considers collections to be objects themselves.

In each Workbook object, you have a collection of Worksheets. The Worksheets collection is an object that you can call upon through VBA. Each worksheet in your workbook lives in the Worksheets collection.

If you want to refer to a worksheet in the Worksheets collection, you can refer to it by its position in the collection, as an index number starting with 1, or by its name, as quoted text. If you run these two lines of code in a workbook that has only one worksheet called MySheet, they both do the same thing:

```
Worksheets(1).Select
Worksheets("MySheet").Select
```

If you have two worksheets in the active workbook that have the names MySheet and YourSheet, in that order, you can refer to the second worksheet by typing either of these statements:

```
Worksheets(2).Select
Worksheets("YourSheet").Select
```

If you want to refer to a worksheet called MySheet in a particular workbook that is not active, you must qualify the worksheet reference and the workbook reference, as follows:

```
Workbooks("MyData.xls").Worksheets("MySheet").Select
```

Understanding properties

Properties are essentially the characteristics of an object. Your house has a color, a square footage, an age, and so on. Some properties can be changed — such as the color of your house. Other properties cannot be changed — such as the age of your house.

Likewise, an object in Excel such as the Worksheet object has a sheet name property that can be changed, and a Rows.Count row property that cannot.

You refer to the property of an object by referring to the object, and then the property. For example, you can change the name of your worksheet by changing its Name property.

In this example, you are renaming Sheet1 to MySheet:

```
Sheets("Sheet1").Name = "MySheet"
```

Some properties are read-only, which means that you can't assign a value to them directly — for example, the Text property of cell. The Text property gives you the formatted appearance of value in a cell, but you cannot overwrite or change it.

Understanding methods

Methods are the actions that you can perform against an object. It helps to think of methods as verbs. You can paint your house, so in VBA, that translates to something like

```
house.paint
```

A simple example of an Excel method is the Select method of the Range object:

```
Range("A1").Select
```

Another is the Copy method of the Range object:

```
Range("A1").Copy
```

Some methods have parameters that dictate how the method is applied. For example, you can use the Paste method more effectively by explicitly defining the Destination parameter:

```
ActiveSheet.Paste Destination:=Range("B1")
```

A Brief Look at Variables

Another concept you will see throughout the macros in this book is the concept of *variables*. It's important to dedicate a few words to this concept, as it plays a big part in most of the macros you will encounter here.

You can think of variables as memory containers that you can use in your procedures. There are different types of variables, each tasked with holding a specific type of data.

The common variable types

Some of the common types of variables you will see in this book are

>> **String:** Holds textual data

>> **Integer:** Holds numeric data ranging from -32,768 to 32,767

>> **Long:** Holds numeric data ranging from -2,147,483,648 to 2,147,483,647

>> **Double:** Holds floating point numeric data

>> **Variant:** Holds any kind of data

>> **Boolean:** Holds binary data that returns True or False

>> **Object:** Holds an actual object from the Excel object model

The term used for creating a variable in a macro is "declaring a variable." You do so by entering Dim (abbreviation for dimension), then the name of your variable, then the type. For example:

```
Dim MyText as String

Dim MyNumber as Integer

Dim MyWorksheet as Worksheet
```

Once you create your variable, you can fill it with data. Here are a few simple examples of how you would create a variable, then assign values to them.

```
Dim MyText as String
Mytext = Range("A1").Value

Dim MyNumber as Integer
MyNumber = Range("B1").Value * 25

Dim MyObject as Worksheet
Set MyWorksheet = Sheets("Sheet1")
```

The values you assign to your variables often come from data stored in your cells. However, the values may also be information that you yourself create. It all depends on the task at hand. This notion will become clearer as you go through the macros in this book.

While it is possible to create code that does not use variables, you will encounter many examples of VBA code where variables *are* employed. There are two main reasons for this.

First, Excel doesn't inherently know what your data is used for. It doesn't see numerals, symbols, or letters. It just sees data. When you declare variables with specific data types, you help Excel know how it should handle certain pieces of data so that your macros produce the results you'd expect.

Secondly, variables help by making your code more efficient and easier to understand. For example, suppose you have a number in cell A1 that you are repeatedly referring to in your macro. You could retrieve that number by pointing to cell A1 each time you need it.

```
Sub Macro1()

Range("B1").Value = Range("A1").Value * 5

Range("C1").Value = Range("A1").Value * 10

Range("D1").Value = Range("A1").Value * 15

End Sub
```

However, this would force Excel to waste cycles storing the same number into memory every time you point to cell A1. Also, if you need to change your workbook so that the target number is not in cell A1, but in, let's say, cell A2, you would need to edit your code by changing all the references from A1 to A2.

A better way is to store the number in cell A1 just once. For example, you can store the value in cell A1 in an Integer variable called myValue.

```
Sub WithVariable()

Dim myValue As Integer

myValue = Range("A1").Value

Range("C3").Value = myValue * 5

Range("D5").Value = myValue * 10

Range("E7").Value = myValue * 15

End Sub
```

This not only improves the efficiency of your code (ensuring Excel reads the number in cell A1 just once), it also ensures that you only have to edit one line should the design of your workbook change.

Understanding Event Procedures

Many of the example macros in this book implement code as *event procedures*. In order to fully understand why these examples use event procedures, it's important to get acquainted with events.

An *event* is nothing more than an action that takes place during a session in Excel. Everything that happens in Excel happens to an object through an event. A few examples of events are opening a workbook, adding a worksheet, changing a value in a cell, saving a workbook, double-clicking a cell, and the list goes on.

The nifty thing is that you can tell Excel to run a certain macro or piece of code when a particular event occurs. For example, you may want to ensure that your workbook automatically saves each time it closes. You can add code to the Before-Close workbook event that saves the workbook before it closes.

REMEMBER

Chapter 2 discussed how to create a new VBA module to hold the code you write. However, event procedures are special in that they are not stored in the standard modules discussed in Chapter 2. As you will see in the next few sections, event procedures are stored directly within each object's built-in modules.

Worksheet events

Worksheet events occur when something happens to a particular worksheet, such as when a worksheet is selected, when a cell on the worksheet is edited, or when a formula on a worksheet is calculated. Each worksheet has its own built-in module where you can place your own event procedure.

To get to this built-in module, you can right-click on the worksheet and select the View Code option (see Figure 3-1).

The Visual Basic Editor automatically opens to the built-in module for the worksheet. This module has two drop-down boxes at the top.

Select the Worksheet option in the dropdown on the left. This action automatically selects the SelectionChange event in the dropdown on the right. As you can see in Figure 3-2, this also adds some starter code where you can enter or paste your code.

The idea is to choose the most appropriate event from the Event dropdown for the task at hand. Figure 3-3 illustrates the different events you can choose.

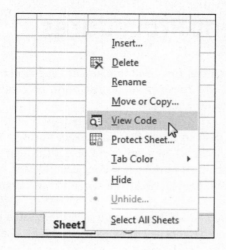

FIGURE 3-1:
Getting to the
built-in module
for a worksheet.

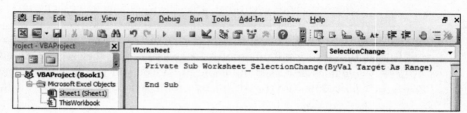

FIGURE 3-2:
The default
SelectionChange
event for the
Worksheet object.

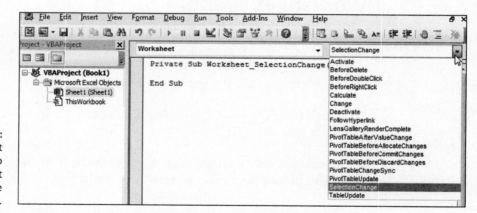

FIGURE 3-3:
Click the Event
dropdown to
choose the most
appropriate
event.

The more commonly used worksheet events are

>> **Worksheet_Change:** Triggers when any data on the worksheet is changed

>> **Worksheet_SelectionChange:** Triggers each time a new cell or object on the
worksheet is selected

- >> **Worksheet_BeforeDoubleClick:** Triggers before Excel responds to a double-click on the worksheet

- >> **Worksheet_BeforeRightClick:** Triggers before Excel responds to a right-click on the worksheet

- >> **Worksheet_Activate:** Triggers when the user moves from another worksheet to this worksheet

- >> **Worksheet_Deactivate:** Triggers when the user moves from this worksheet to another worksheet

- >> **Worksheet_Calculate:** Triggers each time a change on the worksheet causes Excel to recalculate formulas

Workbook events

Workbook events occur when something happens to a particular workbook, such as when a workbook is opened, when a workbook is closed, when a new worksheet is added, or when a workbook is saved. Each workbook has its own built-in module where you can place your own event procedure.

To get to this built-in module, you first need to activate the Visual Basic Editor (press Alt+F11). Then in the Project Explorer menu, right-click on ThisWorkbook, and then choose the View Code option (see Figure 3-4).

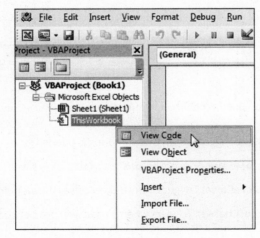

FIGURE 3-4:
Getting to the built-in module for a workbook.

The Visual Basic Editor automatically opens to the built-in module for the workbook. This module has two drop-down boxes at the top.

Select the Workbook option in the dropdown on the left. This action automatically selects the Open event in the dropdown on the right. As you can see in Figure 3-5, this also adds some starter code where you can enter or paste your code.

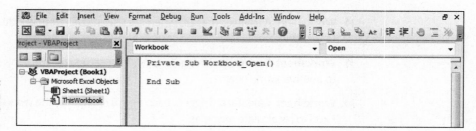

FIGURE 3-5:
The default Open event for the Worksheet object.

The idea is to choose the most appropriate event from the Event dropdown for the task at hand. Figure 3-6 illustrates some of the events you can choose.

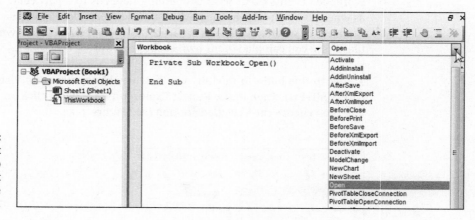

FIGURE 3-6:
Click the Event dropdown to choose the most appropriate event.

The more commonly used Workbook events are

>> **Worksheet_Open:** Triggers when the workbook is opened

>> **Worksheet_BeforeSave:** Triggers before the workbook is saved

>> **Worksheet_BeforeClose:** Triggers before Excel closes the workbook

>> **Worksheet_SheetChange:** Triggers when a user switches between sheets

Error Handling in a Nutshell

In some of the macros in this book, you will see a line similar to this:

```
On Error GoTo MyError
```

This is called an *error handler*. Error handlers allow you to specify what happens when an error is encountered while your code runs.

Without error handlers, any error that occurs in your code prompts Excel to activate a less-than-helpful error message which typically won't clearly convey what actually happened. However, with the aid of error handlers, you can choose to ignore the error or exit the code gracefully with your own message to the user.

There are three types of On Error statements:

>> **On Error GoTo SomeLabel:** The code jumps to the specified label.

>> **On Error Resume Next:** The error is ignored and the code resumes.

>> **On Error GoTo 0:** VBA resets to normal error-checking behavior.

On Error GoTo SomeLabel

There are times when an error in your code means you need to gracefully exit the procedure and give your users a clear message. In these situations, you can use the On Error GoTo statement to tell Excel to jump to a certain line of code.

Take this small piece of code for example. Here, you are telling Excel to divide the value in cell A1 by the value in cell A2, and then place the answer in cell A3. Easy. What could go wrong?

```
Sub Macro1()

Range("A3").Value = Range("A1").Value / Range("A2").Value

End Sub
```

As it turns out, two major things can go wrong. If cell A2 contains a 0, you get a divide by 0 error. If cell A2 contains a non-numeric value, you get a type mismatch error.

To avoid a nasty error message, you can tell Excel that On Error, you want the code execution to jump to the label called MyExit.

In the code below, you see the MyExit label is followed by a message to users that gives them friendly advice rather than a nasty error message. Also note the Exit Sub line before the MyExit label. This ensures that the code simply exits if no error is encountered.

```
Sub Macro1()

On Error GoTo MyExit

Range("A3").Value = Range("A1").Value / Range("A2").Value
Exit Sub

MyExit:
MsgBox "Please Use Valid Non-Zero Numbers"

End Sub
```

On Error Resume Next

Sometimes, you want Excel to ignore an error and simply resume running the code. In these situations, you can use the On Error Resume Next statement.

For example, this piece of code is meant to delete a file called GhostFile.exe from the C:\Temp directory. After the file is deleted, a nice message box tells the user the file is gone.

```
Sub Macro1()

Kill "C:\Temp\GhostFile.exe"

MsgBox "File has been deleted."

End Sub
```

It works great if there is indeed a file to delete. But if for some reason the file called GhostFile.exe does not exist in the C:\Temp drive, an error is thrown.

In this case, you don't care if the file is not there. You were going to delete it anyway. So you can simply ignore the error and move on with the code.

By using the On Error Resume Next statement, the code runs its course whether or not the targeted file exists.

```
Sub Macro1()

On Error Resume Next

Kill "C:\Temp\GhostFile.exe"

MsgBox "File has been deleted."

End Sub
```

On Error GoTo 0

When using certain error statements, it may be necessary to reset the error-checking behavior of VBA. To understand what this means, take a look at this example.

Here, you first want to delete a file called GhostFile.exe from the C:\Temp directory. In order to avoid errors that may stem from the fact that the targeted file does not exist, you use the On Error Resume Next statement. After that, you are trying to do some suspect math by dividing 100/Mike.

```
Sub Macro1()

On Error Resume Next

Kill "C:\Temp\GhostFile.exe"

Range("A3").Value = 100 / "Mike"

End Sub
```

Running this piece of code should generate an error due to the fuzzy math, but it doesn't. Why? Because the last instruction you gave to the code was On Error Resume Next. Any error encountered after that line is effectively ignored.

To remedy this problem, you can use the On Error GoTo 0 statement to resume the normal error-checking behavior.

```
Sub Macro1()

On Error Resume Next

Kill "C:\Temp\GhostFile.exe"

On Error GoTo 0

Range("A3").Value = 100 / "Mike"

End Sub
```

This code ignores errors until the On Error GoTo 0 statement. After that statement, the code goes back to normal error checking where it triggers the expected error stemming from the fuzzy math.

2

Making Short Work of Workbook Tasks

Look at various techniques you can use to manipulate your workbooks.

See how you can leverage macros to automate the creation and duplication of Excel files.

Uncover macros that automate common worksheet tasks.

Explore how you can use macros to protect and back up your Excel workbooks.

Chapter **4**

Working with Workbooks

A workbook is not just an Excel file; it's also an object in Excel's object model (a programming hierarchy that exposes parts of Excel to VBA).

This means that you can reference workbooks through VBA to do cool things like automatically create new workbooks, prevent users from closing workbooks, and automatically back up workbooks.

In this chapter, you explore a few of the more useful workbook-related macros.

Creating a New Workbook from Scratch

You may sometimes want or need to create a new workbook in an automated way. For example, you may need to copy data from a table and paste it into a newly created workbook. The following macro copies a range of cells from the active sheet and pastes the data into a new workbook.

How it works

This macro is relatively intuitive as you read through the lines of the code.

```
Sub Macro1()

'Step 1 Copy the data
    Sheets("Example 1").Range("B4:C15").Copy

'Step 2 Create a new workbook
    Workbooks.Add

'Step 3 Paste the data
    ActiveSheet.Paste Destination:=Range("A1")

'Step 4 Turn off application alerts
    Application.DisplayAlerts = False

'Step 5 Save the newly created workbook
    ActiveWorkbook.SaveAs _
    Filename:="C:\MyNewBook.xlsx"

'Step 6 Turn application alerts back on
    Application.DisplayAlerts = True

End Sub
```

1. In Step 1, you simply copy the data on the "Example 1" sheet ranging from cells B4 to C15.

   The thing to note here is that you are specifying both the sheet and the range by name. This is a best practice when you are working with multiple workbooks open at one time.

2. You are using the Add method of the Workbook object to create a new workbook. This is equivalent to manually choosing File ⇨ New ⇨ Blank Document in the Excel Ribbon.

3. In Step 3, you use the Paste method to send the data you copied to cell A1 of the new workbook. Pay attention to the fact that the code refers to the ActiveSheet object. When you add a workbook, the new workbook immediately gains focus, becoming the active workbook. This is the same behavior you would see if you were to add a workbook manually.

4. In Step 4 of the code, you set the DisplayAlerts method to False, effectively turning off Excel's warnings. You do this because in the next step of the code, you save the newly created workbook. You may run this macro multiple times, in which case Excel attempts to save the file multiple times.

   What happens when you try save a workbook multiple times? That's right — Excel warns you that there is already a file out there with that name and then asks if you want to overwrite the previously existing file. Because your goal is to automate the creation of the new workbook, you want to suppress that warning.

5. In Step 5, you save the file by using the SaveAs method. Note that you are entering the full path of the save location, including the final filename.

6. Because you turned application alerts off in Step 4, you need to turn them back on. If you don't, Excel continues to suppress all warnings for the life of the current session.

How to use it

To implement this macro, you can copy and paste it into a standard module:

1. **Activate the Visual Basic Editor by pressing Alt+F11 on your keyboard.**

2. **Right-click the project/workbook name in the Project window.**

3. **Choose Insert ⇨ Module.**

4. **Type or paste the code in the newly created module.**

   You will probably need to change the sheet name, the range address, and the save location.

Saving a Workbook when a Particular Cell Is Changed

Sometimes, you may be working on data that is so sensitive that you'll want to save every time a particular cell or range of cells is changed. This macro allows you to define the range of cells that, when changed, forces the workbook to save.

In the example demonstrated in Figure 4-1, you want the workbook to save when an edit is made to any of the cells in the range C5:C16.

▲	A	B	C	D
3				
4				
5		January	26,263	
6		February	25,343	
7		March	52,149	
8		April	72,579	
9		May	38,635	
10		June	60,175	
11		July	32,305	
12		August	14,288	
13		September	71,787	
14		October	48,402	
15		November	71,850	
16		December	77,798	
17				

FIGURE 4-1:
Changing any cell in range C5:C16 forces the workbook to save.

How it works

The secret to this code is the Intersect method. Because you don't want to save the worksheet when any old cell changes, you use the Intersect method to determine if the target cell (the cell that changed) intersects with the range you have specified to be the trigger range (C5:C16 in this case).

The Intersect method returns one of two things: either a Range object that defines the intersection between the two given ranges, or nothing. So in essence, you need to throw the target cell against the Intersect method to check for a value of Nothing. At that point, you can make the decision whether to save the workbook.

```
Private Sub Worksheet_Change(ByVal Target As Range)

'Step 1:  Does the changed range intersect?
    If Intersect(Target, Range("C5:C16")) Is Nothing Then

'Step 2: If there is no intersection, exit procedure
    Exit Sub

'Step 3: If there is an intersection, save the workbook
    Else
    ActiveWorkbook.Save
```

```
'Close out the If statement
    End If


End Sub
```

1. In Step 1, you are simply checking to see if the target cell (the cell that has changed) is in the range specified by the Intersect method. A value of Nothing means the target cell falls outside the range specified.

2. Step 2 forces the macro to stop and exit the procedure if there is no intersection between the target cell and the specified range.

3. If there is an intersection, Step 3 fires the Save method of the active workbook, overwriting the previous version.

4. In Step 4, you simply close out the If statement. Every time you instantiate an If. . .Then. . .Else check, you must close it out with a corresponding End If.

How to use it

To implement this macro, you need to copy and paste it into the Worksheet_ Change event code window. Placing the macro here allows it to run each time you make any change to the sheet.

1. **Activate the Visual Basic Editor by pressing Alt+F11 on your keyboard.**

2. **In the Project window, find your project/workbook name and click the plus sign next to it in order to see all the sheets.**

3. **Click in the sheet from which you want to trigger the code.**

4. **Select the Change event from the Event drop-down menu (see Figure 4-2).**

5. **Type or paste the code in the newly created module, changing the range address to suit your needs.**

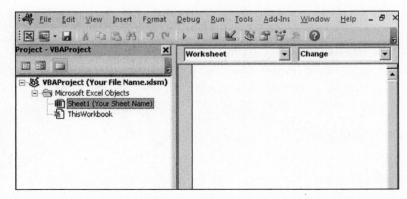

FIGURE 4-2:
Enter or paste your code in the Worksheet_ Change event code window.

Saving a Workbook before Closing

This macro is an excellent way to protect users from inadvertently closing their file before saving. When implemented, this macro ensures that Excel automatically saves before closing the workbook.

Excel normally warns users who are attempting to close an unsaved workbook, giving them an option to save before closing. However, many users may blow past the warning and inadvertently click No, telling Excel to close without saving. With this macro, you are protecting against this by automatically saving before close.

How it works

This code is triggered by the workbook's BeforeClose event. When you try to close the workbook, this event fires, running the code within. The crux of the code is simple — it asks the user whether he really wants to close the workbook (see Figure 4-3). The macro then evaluates whether the user clicked OK or Cancel.

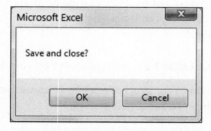

FIGURE 4-3:
A message box
activates when
you attempt to
close the
workbook.

The evaluation is done with a Select Case statement. The Select Case statement is an alternative to the If. . .Then. . .Else statement, allowing you to perform condition checks in your macros. The basic construct of a Select Case statement is simple:

```
Select Case <some expression to check>
Case Is = <some value>
     <do something>
Case Is=<some other value>
     <do something else>
Case Is=<some 3rd value>
     <do some 3rd thing>
End Select
```

With a Select Case statement, you can perform many conditional checks. In this case, you are simply checking for OK or Cancel. Take a look at the code:

```vba
Private Sub Workbook_BeforeClose(Cancel As Boolean)

'Step 1:  Activate the message box and start the check
    Select Case MsgBox("Save and close?", vbOKCancel)

'Step 2: Cancel button pressed, cancel the close
    Case Is = vbCancel
    Cancel = True

'Step 3: OK button pressed, save the workbook and close
    Case Is = vbOK
    ActiveWorkbook.Save

'Step 4: Close your Select Case statement
End Select

End Sub
```

1. In Step 1, you activate the message box as the condition check for the Select Case statement. Here, you use the vbOKCancel argument to ensure that the OK and Cancel buttons are presented as choices.

2. If the user clicked Cancel in the message box, the macro tells Excel to cancel the Workbook_Close event. This is done by passing True to the Cancel Boolean (this effectively cancels action, preventing the workbook from closing).

3. If the user clicked the OK button in the message box, Step 3 takes effect. Here, you tell Excel to save the workbook. And because you did not set the Cancel Boolean to True, Excel continues with the close.

4. In Step 4, you simply close out the Select Case statement. Every time you instantiate a Select Case, you must close it out with a corresponding End Select.

How to use it

To implement this macro, you need to copy and paste it into the Workbook_ BeforeClose event code window. Placing the macro there allows it to run each time you try to close the workbook.

1. **Activate the Visual Basic Editor by pressing Alt+F11 on your keyboard.**

2. **In the Project window, find your project/workbook name and click the plus sign next to it in order to see all the sheets.**

3. **Click ThisWorkbook.**

4. **Select the BeforeClose event in the Event drop-down list (see Figure 4-4).**

5. **Type or paste the code in the newly created module.**

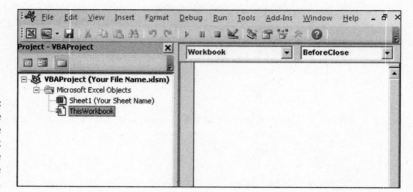

FIGURE 4-4:
Type or paste
your code in the
Workbook
BeforeClose
event code
window.

Protecting a Worksheet on Workbook Close

Sometimes you need to send your workbook out into the world with specific work-sheets protected. If you find that you're constantly protecting and unprotecting sheets before distributing your workbooks, this macro can help you.

How it works

This code is triggered by the workbook's BeforeClose event. When you try to close the workbook, this event fires, running the code within. The macro automatically protects the specified sheet with the given password, and then saves the workbook.

```vba
Private Sub Workbook_BeforeClose(Cancel As Boolean)

'Step 1: Protect the sheet with a password
    Sheets("Sheet1").Protect Password:="RED"

'Step 2: Save the workbook
    ActiveWorkbook.Save

End Sub
```

1. In Step 1, you are explicitly specifying which sheet you want to protect — Sheet1, in this case. You are also providing the password argument, Password:=RED. This defines the password needed to remove the protection.

This password argument is completely optional. If you omit this altogether, the sheet is still protected, but you won't need a password to unprotect it.

Also, be aware that Excel passwords are case-sensitive, so you'll want pay attention to the exact password and capitalization that you are using.

2. Step 2 tells Excel to save the workbook. If you don't save the workbook, the sheet protection you just applied won't be in effect the next time the workbook is opened.

How to use it

To implement this macro, you need to copy and paste it into the Workbook_ BeforeClose event code window. Placing the macro here allows it to run each time you try to close the workbook.

1. Activate the Visual Basic Editor by pressing Alt+F11 on your keyboard.

2. In the Project window, find your project/workbook name and click the plus sign next to it in order to see all the sheets.

3. Click ThisWorkbook.

4. Select the BeforeClose event in the Event drop-down list (see Figure 4-5).

5. Type or paste the code in the newly created module, modifying the sheet name (if necessary) and the password.

Note that you can protect additional sheets by adding additional statements before the Activeworkbook.Save statement.

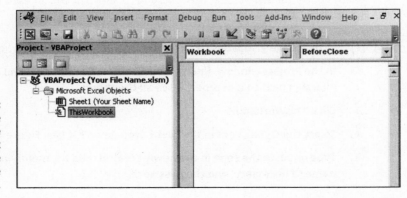

FIGURE 4-5:
Type or paste your code in the Workbook BeforeClose event code window.

Unprotecting a Worksheet on Workbook Open

If you've distributed workbooks with protected sheets, you likely get the workbooks back with the sheets still protected. Often, you need to unprotect the worksheets in a workbook before continuing your work. If you find that you are continuously unprotecting worksheets, this macro may be just the ticket.

How it works

This code is triggered by the workbook's Open event. When you open a workbook, this event triggers, running the code within. This macro automatically unprotects the specified sheet with the given password when the workbook is opened.

```
Private Sub Workbook_Open()

'Step 1: Protect the sheet with a password
    Sheets("Sheet1").Unprotect Password:="RED"

End Sub
```

The macro explicitly names the sheet you want to unprotect — Sheet1, in this case. Then it passes the password required to unprotect the sheet. Be aware that Excel passwords are case-sensitive, so pay attention to the exact password and capitalization that you are using.

How to use it

To implement this macro, you need to copy and paste it into the Workbook_Open event code window. Placing the macro here allows it to run each time the workbook opens.

1. Activate the Visual Basic Editor by pressing Alt+F11 on your keyboard.

2. In the Project window, find your project/workbook name and click the plus sign next to it in order to see all the sheets.

3. Click ThisWorkbook.

4. Select the Open event in the Event drop-down list (see Figure 4-6).

5. Type or paste the code in the newly created module, modifying the sheet name (if necessary) and the password.

Note that you can unprotect additional sheets by adding additional statements.

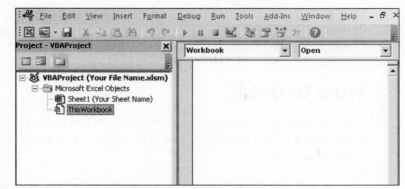

FIGURE 4-6:
Type or paste your code in the Workbook Open event code window.

Opening a Workbook to a Specific Tab

In some situations, it's imperative that your workbook be started on a specific worksheet. With this macro, if a user is working with your workbook, he or she can't go astray because the workbook starts on the exact worksheet it needs to.

In the example illustrated in Figure 4-7, you want the workbook to go immediately to the sheet called Start Here.

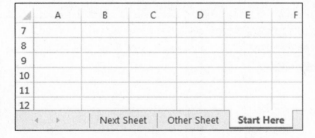

FIGURE 4-7:
You want your workbook to automatically open to the sheet called Start Here.

How it works

This macro uses the workbook's Open event to start the workbook on the specified sheet when the workbook is opened.

```
Private Sub Workbook_Open()

'Step 1: Select the specified sheet
    Sheets("Start Here").Select

End Sub
```

The macro explicitly names the sheet the workbook should jump to when it's opened.

How to use it

To implement this macro, you need to copy and paste it into the Workbook_Open event code window. Placing the macro here allows it to run each time the workbook opens.

1. **Activate the Visual Basic Editor by pressing Alt+F11 on your keyboard.**

2. **In the Project window, find your project/workbook name and click the plus sign next to it in order to see all the sheets.**

3. **Click ThisWorkbook.**

4. **Select the Open event in the Event drop-down list (see Figure 4-8).**

5. **Type or paste the code in the newly created module, changing the sheet name, if necessary.**

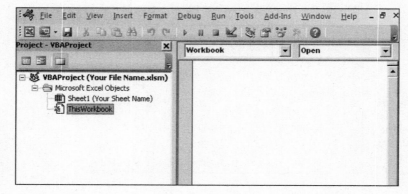

FIGURE 4-8:
Type or paste your code in the Workbook Open event code window.

Opening a Specific Workbook Defined by the User

Want to give yourself or your users a quick way to search for and open a file? This macro uses a simple technique that opens a friendly dialog box, allowing you to browse for and open the Excel file of your choosing.

How it works

This macro opens the dialog box you see in Figure 4-9, allowing the user to browse for and open an Excel file.

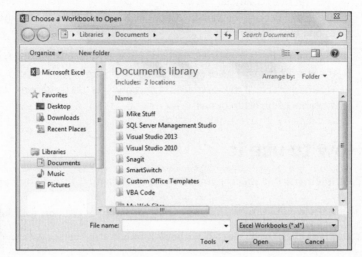

FIGURE 4-9:
The Open dialog
box activated by
your macro.

Here's how this macro works:

```
Sub Macro1()

'Step 1: Define a string variable.
    Dim FName As Variant

'Step 2: GetOpenFilename Method activates dialog box.
    FName = Application.GetOpenFilename( _
            FileFilter:="Excel Workbooks,*.xl*", _
            Title:="Choose a Workbook to Open", _
            MultiSelect:=False)

'Step 3: If a file was chosen, open it!
    If FName <> False Then
    Workbooks.Open Filename:=FName
    End If

End Sub
```

1. The first thing this macro does is to declare a variant variable that holds the filename that the user chooses. FName is the name of the variable.

2. In Step 2, you use the GetOpenFilename method to call up a dialog box that allows you to browse and select the file you need.

The GetOpenFilename method supports a few customizable parameters. The FileFilter parameter allows you to specify the type of file you are looking for. The Title parameter allows you to change the title that appears at the top of the dialog box. The MultiSelect parameter allows you to limit the selection to one file.

3. If the user selects a file from the dialog box, the FName variable is filled with the name of the file he or she has chosen. In Step 3, you check for an empty FName variable. If the variable is not empty, you use the Open method of the Workbooks object to open the file.

How to use it

To implement this macro, you can copy and paste it into a standard module:

1. Activate the Visual Basic Editor by pressing Alt+F11 on your keyboard.

2. Right-click the project/workbook name in the Project window.

3. Choose Insert ➪ Module.

4. Type or paste the code in the newly created module.

5. Optionally, you can assign the macro to a button (see Chapter 1).

Determining Whether a Workbook Is Already Open

The previous macro automatically opened a workbook based on the user's selection. As you think about automatically opening workbooks, you must consider what may happen if you attempt to open a book that is already open. In the non-VBA world, Excel attempts to open the file again, with the message shown in Figure 4-10 warning that any unsaved changes will be lost. You can protect against such an occurrence by checking if a given file is already open before trying to open it again.

FIGURE 4-10:
You can avoid
this annoying
message box
when opening a
workbook that is
already open.

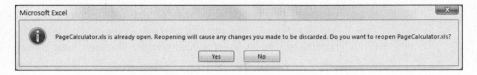

How it works

The first thing to notice about this macro is that it is a function, not a sub procedure. As you will see, making this macro a function enables you to pass any filename to it to test whether that file is already open.

The gist of this code is simple: You are testing a given filename to see if it can be assigned to an object variable. Only opened workbooks can be assigned to an object variable. When you try to assign a closed workbook to the variable, an error occurs.

So if the given workbook can be assigned, the workbook is open; if an error occurs, the workbook is closed.

```vba
Function FileIsOpenTest(TargetWorkbook As String) As Boolean

'Step 1:  Declare variables
    Dim TestBook As Workbook

'Step 2: Tell Excel to Resume on Error
    On Error Resume Next

'Step 3: Try to assign the target workbook to TestBook
    Set TestBook = Workbooks(TargetWorkbook)

'Step 4: If no error occurred then Workbook is already open
    If Err.Number = 0 Then
    FileIsOpenTest = True
    Else
    FileIsOpenTest = False
    End If

End Function
```

1. The first thing the macro does is to declare a string variable that holds the filename that the user chooses. TestBook is the name of your string variable.

2. In Step 2, you are telling Excel that there may be an error running this code. In the event of an error, resume the code. Without this line, the code would simply stop when an error occurs. Again, you are testing a given filename to see if it can be assigned to an object variable. So if the given workbook can be assigned, it's open; if an error occurs, it's closed. You need to have the code continue if an error occurs.

3. In Step 3, you are attempting to assign the given workbook to the TestBook object variable. The workbook you are trying to assign is itself a string variable called TargetWorkbook. TargetWorkbook is passed to the function in the function declarations (see the first line of the code). This structure eliminates the need to hard-code a workbook name, allowing you to pass it as a variable instead.

4. In Step 4, you simply check to see if an error occurred. If an error did not occur, the workbook is open, so you set the FileIsOpenTest to True. If an error occurred, that means the workbook is not open. In that case, you set the FileIsOpenTest to False.

TIP

Again, you can use this function to evaluate any file passed to it, via its TargetWorkbook argument. That is the beauty of putting this macro into a function.

The following macro demonstrates how to implement this function. Here, you are using the same macro you saw in the previous section, "Opening a Specific Workbook Defined by the User," but this time, you are calling the new FileIsOpenTest function to make sure the user cannot open an already opened file.

```
Sub Macro1()

'Step 1: Define a string variable.
    Dim FName As Variant
    Dim FNFileOnly As String


'Step 2: GetOpenFilename Method activates dialog box.
    FName = Application.GetOpenFilename( _
            FileFilter:="Excel Workbooks,*.xl*", _
            Title:="Choose a Workbook to Open", _
            MultiSelect:=False)

'Step 3: Open the chosen file if not already opened.
    If FName <> False Then
    FNFileOnly = StrReverse(Left(StrReverse(FName), _
                InStr(StrReverse(FName), "\") - 1))
```

```
        If FileIsOpenTest(FNFileOnly) = True Then
            MsgBox "The given file is already open"
        Else
            Workbooks.Open Filename:=FName


        End If
        End If


    End Sub
```

With this macro implemented, you get the friendlier message box shown in Figure 4-11.

FIGURE 4-11:
The final macro gives you a cleaner, more concise message.

Microsoft Excel

The given file is already open

OK

How to use it

To implement this macro, you can copy and paste both pieces of code into a standard module:

1. Activate the Visual Basic Editor by pressing Alt+F11 on your keyboard.

2. Right-click the project/workbook name in the Project window.

3. Choose Insert ⇨ Module.

4. Type or paste the code in the newly created module.

5. Optionally, you can assign the macro to a button (see Chapter 1).

Determining Whether a Workbook Exists in a Directory

You may have a process that manipulates a file somewhere on your PC. For example, you may need to open an existing workbook to add new data to it on a daily basis. In these cases, you may need to test to see whether the file you need to manipulate actually exists. This macro allows you to pass a file path to evaluate whether the file is there.

How it works

The first thing to notice about this macro is that it is a function, not a sub procedure. Making this macro a function enables you to pass any file path to it.

This macro uses the Dir function. The Dir function returns a string that represents the name of the file that matches what you pass to it. This function can be used in lots of ways, but here, you are using it to check if the file path you pass to it exists:

```
Function FileExists(FPath As String) As Boolean

'Step 1: Declare your variables.
    Dim FName As String

'Step 2: Use the Dir function to get the file name
    FName = Dir(FPath)

'Step 3:  If file exists, return True else False
    If FName <> "" Then FileExists = True _
    Else: FileExists = False

End Function
```

1. Step 1 declares a string variable that holds the filename that returns from the Dir function. FName is the name of the string variable.

2. In Step 2, you attempt to set the FName variable. You do this by passing the FPath variable to the Dir function. This FPath variable is passed via the function declarations (see the first line of the code). This structure prevents you from having to hard-code a file path, passing it as a variable instead.

3. If the FName variable can't be set, this means the path you passed does not exist. Thus the FName variable is empty. Step 3 merely translates that result to a True or False expression.

TIP

Again, you can use this function to evaluate any file path passed to it. That's the beauty of writing this macro as a function.

The following macro demonstrates how to use this function:

```
Sub Macro1()

    If FileExists("C:\Temp\MyNewBook.xlsx") = True Then
        MsgBox "File exists."
    Else
        MsgBox "File does not exist."
    End If

End Sub
```

How to use it

To implement this macro, you can copy and paste both pieces of code into a standard module:

1. **Activate the Visual Basic Editor by pressing Alt+F11 on your keyboard.**
2. **Right-click the project/workbook name in the Project window.**
3. **Choose Insert ⇨ Module.**
4. **Type or paste the code in the newly created module.**

Closing All Workbooks at Once

One of the more annoying things in Excel occurs when you try to close many workbooks at once. For each workbook you have opened, you need to activate the work, close it, and confirm save changes. There is no easy way to close them all down at one time. This little macro takes care of that annoyance.

How it works

In this macro, the Workbooks collection loops through all the opened workbooks. As the macro loops through each workbook, it saves and closes them down.

```
Sub Macro1()

'Step 1: Declare your variables
    Dim wb As Workbook
```

```
'Step 2: Loop through workbooks, save and close
    For Each wb In Workbooks
        wb.Close SaveChanges:=True
    Next wb

End Sub
```

1. Step 1 declares an object variable that represents a Workbook object. This allows you to enumerate through all the open workbooks, capturing their names as you go.

2. Step 2 simply loops through the open workbooks, saving and closing them. If you don't want to save them, change the SaveChanges argument from True to False.

How to use it

The best place to store this macro is in your Personal Macro Workbook. This way, the macro is always available to you. The Personal Macro Workbook is loaded whenever you start Excel. In the VBE Project window, it is named personal.xlsb.

1. **Activate the Visual Basic Editor by pressing Alt+F11 on your keyboard.**
2. **Right-click personal.xlb in the Project window.**
3. **Choose Insert ⇨ Module.**
4. **Type or paste the code in the newly created module.**

If you don't see personal.xlb in your project window, it doesn't exist yet. You'll have to record a macro, using Personal Macro Workbook as the destination.

TIP

To record the macro in your Personal Macro Workbook, select the Personal Macro Workbook option in the Record Macro dialog box before you start recording. This option is in the Store Macro In drop-down box. Simply record a couple of cell clicks and then stop recording. You can discard the recorded macro and replace it with this one.

Printing All Workbooks in a Directory

If you need to print from multiple workbooks in a directory, you can use this macro.

How it works

In this macro, you use the Dir function to return a string that represents the name of the file that matches what you pass to it.

In this code, you use the Dir function to enumerate through all the .xlsx files in a given directory, capturing each file's name. Then you open each file, print it, then close the file.

```
Sub Macro1()

'Step 1:Declare your variables
    Dim MyFiles As String

'Step 2: Specify a target directory
    MyFiles = Dir("C:\Temp\*.xlsx")
    Do While MyFiles <> ""

'Step 3: Open Workbooks one by one
    Workbooks.Open "C:\Temp\" & MyFiles
    ActiveWorkbook.Sheets("Sheet1").PrintOut Copies:=1
    ActiveWorkbook.Close SaveChanges:=False

'Step 4: Next File in the Directory
    MyFiles = Dir
    Loop

End Sub
```

1. Step 1 declares the MyFiles string variable that captures each filename in the enumeration.

2. Step 2 uses the Dir function to specify the directory and file type you are looking for. Note that the code here is looking for *.xlsx. This means that only xlsx files are looped through. If you are looking for .xls files, you need to specify that (along with the directory you need to search). The macro passes any filename it finds to the MyFiles string variable.

3. Step 3 opens the file and then prints out one copy of Sheet1. Needless to say, you probably want to change which sheets to print. You can also change the number of copies to print.

4. Step 4 loops back to find more files. If there are no more files, the MyFiles variable is blank. If that is the case, the loop and macro end.

How to use it

To implement this macro, you can copy and paste it into a standard module:

1. **Activate the Visual Basic Editor by pressing Alt+F11.**
2. **Right-click the project/workbook name in the Project window.**
3. **Choose Insert ⇨ Module.**
4. **Type or paste the code in the newly created module, modifying the print statement as needed.**

Preventing the Workbook from Closing Until a Cell Is Populated

There are times when you don't want a user closing out a workbook without entering a specific piece of data. In these situations, it would be useful to deny the user the ability to close the workbook until the target cell is filled in (see Figure 4-12). This is where this macro comes in.

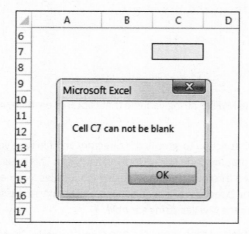

FIGURE 4-12: You can prevent your workbook from closing until a specific cell is populated.

How it works

This code is triggered by the workbook's BeforeClose event. When you try to close the workbook, this event fires, running the code within. This macro checks to see if the target cell (cell C7, in this case) is empty. If it is empty, the close process is cancelled. If C7 is not empty, the workbook saves and closes.

```
Private Sub Workbook_BeforeClose(Cancel As Boolean)

'Step 1: Check to see if Cell C7 is blank
If Sheets("Sheet1").Range("C7").Value = "" Then

'Step 2: Blank: cancel the Close and tell the user
    Cancel = True
    MsgBox "Cell C7 cannot be blank"

'Step 3: Not Blank; Save and Close
Else
    ActiveWorkbook.Close SaveChanges:=True
End If

End Sub
```

1. Step 1 checks to see whether C7 is blank.

2. If it is blank, Step 2 takes effect, cancelling the close process. This is done by passing True to the Cancel Boolean. Step 2 also activates a message box notifying the user of his stupidity (well, it's not quite that harsh, really).

3. If cell C7 is not blank, the workbook saves and closes.

How to use it

To implement this macro, you need to copy and paste it into the Workbook_BeforeClose event code window. Placing the macro here allows it to run each time you try to close the workbook.

1. Activate the Visual Basic Editor by pressing Alt+F11.

2. In the Project window, find your project/workbook name and click the plus sign next to it in order to see all the sheets.

3. Click ThisWorkbook.

4. Select the BeforeClose event in the Event drop-down list (see Figure 4-13).

5. Type or paste the code in the newly created module.

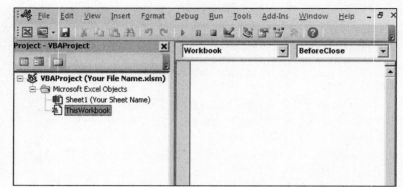

FIGURE 4-13:
Type or paste
your code in the
Workbook_
BeforeClose
event code
window.

Creating a Backup of the Current Workbook with Today's Date

We all know that making backups of your work is important. Now you can have a macro do it for you. This simple macro saves your workbook to a new file with today's date as part of the name.

How it works

The trick to this macro is piecing together the new filename. The new filename has three pieces: the path, today's date, and the original filename.

The path is captured by using the Path property of the ThisWorkbook object. Today's date is grabbed with the Date function.

You'll notice that you are formatting the date (Format(Date, "mm-dd-yy")). This is because by default, the Date function returns mm/dd/yyyy. You use hyphens rather than forward slashes because the forward slashes would cause the file save to fail. (Windows does not allow forward slashes in filenames.)

The last piece of new filename is the original filename. You use the Name property of the ThisWorkbook object to capture that:

```
Sub Macro1()

'Step 1: Save workbook with new filename
    ThisWorkbook.SaveCopyAs _
    Filename:=ThisWorkbook.Path & "\" & _
```

```
        Format(Date, "mm-dd-yy") & " " & _
    ThisWorkbook.Name

End Sub
```

In the one and only step, the macro builds a new filename and uses the Save-CopyAs method to save the file.

How to use it

To implement this macro, you can copy and paste it into a standard module:

1. Activate the Visual Basic Editor by pressing Alt+F11.
2. Right-click the project/workbook name in the Project window.
3. Choose Insert ⇨ Module.
4. Type or paste the code in the newly created module.

Chapter **5**

Working with Worksheets

Excel analysts often need to automate tasks related to worksheets. Whether it is unhiding all sheets in a workbook, or printing all sheets at the same time, many tasks can be automated to save time and gain efficiencies. This chapter covers some of the more useful macros related to worksheets.

Adding and Naming a New Worksheet

We start off this chapter with one of the simplest worksheet-related automations you can apply with a macro — adding and naming a new worksheet.

How it works

If you read through the lines of the code, you'll see this macro is relatively intuitive.

```
Sub Macro1()

'Step 1: Tell Excel what to do if Error
    On Error GoTo MyError


'Step 2:  Add a sheet and name it
    Sheets.Add
    ActiveSheet.Name = _
    WorksheetFunction.Text(Now(), "m-d-yyyy h_mm_ss am/pm")
    Exit Sub


'Step 3: If here, an error happened; tell the user
    MyError:
    MsgBox "There is already a sheet called that."

End Sub
```

1. You must anticipate that if you give the new sheet a name that already exists, an error occurs. So in Step 1, the macro tells Excel to immediately skip to the line that says MyError (in Step 3) if there is an error.

2. Step 2 uses the Add method to add a new sheet. By default, the sheet is called Sheet*xx*, where *xx* represents the number of the sheet. You give the sheet a new name by changing the Name property of the ActiveSheet object. In this case, you are naming the worksheet with the current date and time.

   As with workbooks, each time you add a new sheet via VBA, it automatically becomes the active sheet. Finally, in Step 2, notice that the macro exits the procedure. It has to do this so that it doesn't accidentally go into Step 3 (which should come into play only if an error occurs).

3. Step 3 notifies the user that the sheet name already exists. Again, this Step should only be activated if an error occurs.

How to use it

To implement this macro, you can copy and paste it into a standard module:

1. **Activate the Visual Basic Editor by pressing Alt+F11.**
2. **Right-click the project/workbook name in the Project window.**
3. **Choose Insert ⇨ Module.**
4. **Type or paste the code in the newly created module.**

Deleting All but the Active Worksheet

At times, you may want to delete all but the active worksheet. In these situations, you can use this macro.

How it works

This macro loops the worksheets and matches each worksheet name to the active sheet's name. Each time the macro loops, it deletes any unmatched worksheet. Note the use of the DisplayAlerts method in Step 4. This effectively turns off Excel's warnings so you don't have to confirm each delete.

```
Sub Macro1()

'Step 1:  Declare your variables
    Dim ws As Worksheet

'Step 2: Start looping through all worksheets
    For Each ws In ThisWorkbook.Worksheets

'Step 3: Check each worksheet name
    If ws.Name <> ThisWorkbook.ActiveSheet.Name Then

'Step 4: Turn off warnings and delete
    Application.DisplayAlerts = False
    ws.Delete
    Application.DisplayAlerts = True
    End If

'Step 5:  Loop to next worksheet
    Next ws

End Sub
```

1. The macro first declares an object called ws. This creates a memory container for each worksheet it loops through.

2. In Step 2, the macro begins to loop, telling Excel it will evaluate all worksheets in this workbook. There is a difference between ThisWorkbook and ActiveWorkbook. The ThisWorkBook object refers to the workbook that the code is contained in. The ActiveWorkBook object refers to the currently active workbook. They often return the same object, but if the workbook running the code is not the active workbook, they return different objects. In this case, you don't want to risk deleting sheets in other workbooks, so you use ThisWorkBook.

3. In this step, the macro simply compares the active sheet name to the sheet that is currently being looped.

4. If the sheet names are different, the macro deletes the sheet. As mentioned before, you use DisplayAlerts to suppress any confirmation checks from Excel. If you want to be warned before deleting the sheets, you can omit the Application.DisplayAlerts = False. This ensures you get the message in Figure 5-1, allowing you to back out of the decision to delete worksheets.

5. In Step 5, the macro loops back to get the next sheet. After all sheets are evaluated, the macro ends.

FIGURE 5-1:
Omit the
Application.
DisplayAlerts =
False line in
the macro to
ensure you get
the opportunity
to cancel the
deletion.

How to use it

To implement this macro, you can copy and paste it into a standard module:

1. **Activate the Visual Basic Editor by pressing Alt+F11 on your keyboard.**

2. **Right-click the project/workbook name in the Project window.**

3. **Choose Insert ⇨ Module.**

4. **Type or paste the code in the newly created module.**

REMEMBER

Note that when you use ThisWorkbook in a macro rather than ActiveWorkbook, you can't run the macro from the Personal Macro Workbook. This is because ThisWorkbook refers to the Personal Macro Workbook, not the workbook to which the macro should apply.

Hiding All but the Active Worksheet

You may not want to delete all but the active sheet as you did in the last macro. Instead, a more gentle option is to simply hide the sheets. Excel doesn't let you hide all sheets in a workbook; at least one has to be showing. However, you can hide all but the active sheet.

How it works

This macro loops the worksheets and matches each worksheet name to the active sheet's name. Each time the macro loops, it hides any unmatched worksheet.

```
Sub Macro1()

'Step 1:  Declare your variables
    Dim ws As Worksheet
'Step 2: Start looping through all worksheets
    For Each ws In ThisWorkbook.Worksheets

'Step 3: Check each worksheet name
    If ws.Name <> ThisWorkbook.ActiveSheet.Name Then

'Step 4: Hide the sheet
    ws.Visible = xlSheetHidden
    End If

'Step 5:  Loop to next worksheet
    Next ws

End Sub
```

1. Step 1 declares an object called ws. This creates a memory container for each worksheet the macro loops through.

2. Step 2 begins the looping, telling Excel to evaluate all worksheets in this workbook. There is a difference between ThisWorkbook and ActiveWorkbook. The ThisWorkBook object refers to the workbook that the code is contained in. The ActiveWorkBook object refers to the currently active workbook. They often return the same object, but if the workbook running the code is not the active workbook, they return different objects. In this case, you don't want to risk hiding sheets in other workbooks, so you use ThisWorkBook.

3. In this step, the macro simply compares the active sheet name to the sheet currently being looped.

4. If the sheet names are different, the macro hides the sheet.

5. In Step 5, you loop back to get the next sheet. After all the sheets are evaluated, the macro ends.

TIP

You'll notice the use of xlsheetHidden in the macro. This applies the default hide state you would normally get when you right-click a sheet and select Hide. In this default hide state, a user can right-click on any tab and choose Unhide. This shows all the hidden sheets. But there is another, more clandestine hide state than the default. If you use xlSheetVeryHidden to hide your sheets, users will not be able to see them at all — not even if they right-click on any tab and choose Unhide. The only way to unhide a sheet hidden in this manner is to use VBA.

How to use it

To implement this macro, you can copy and paste it into a standard module:

1. **Activate the Visual Basic Editor by pressing Alt+F11.**
2. **Right-click the project/workbook name in the Project window.**
3. **Choose Insert ➪ Module.**
4. **Type or paste the code in the newly created module.**

Unhiding All Worksheets in a Workbook

If you've ever had to unhide multiple sheets in Excel, you know what a pain it is. You are forced to use the Unhide dialog box shown in Figure 5-2 to unhide one sheet at a time.

FIGURE 5-2:
Without a macro, you're stuck using Excel's Unhide dialog box to unhide one worksheet at a time.

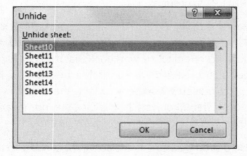

Although that may not sound like a big deal, try to unhide 10 or more sheets; it gets to be a pain fast. This macro makes easy work of that task.

How it works

This macro loops the worksheets and changes the visible state.

```
Sub Macro1()

'Step 1:  Declare your variables
    Dim ws As Worksheet

'Step 2: Start looping through all worksheets
    For Each ws In ActiveWorkbook.Worksheets

'Step 3:  Loop to next worksheet
    ws.Visible = xlSheetVisible
    Next ws

End Sub
```

1. Step 1 declares an object called ws. This creates a memory container for each worksheet the macro loops through.

2. In Step 2, the macro starts the looping, telling Excel to enumerate through all worksheets in this workbook.

3. Step 3 changes the visible state to xlSheetVisible. Then it loops back to get the next worksheet.

How to use it

The best place to store this macro is in your Personal Macro Workbook. That way, the macro is always available to you. The Personal Macro Workbook is loaded whenever you start Excel. In the VBE Project window, it is named personal.xlsb.

1. **Activate the Visual Basic Editor by pressing Alt+F11.**

2. **Right-click personal.xlb in the Project window.**

3. **Choose Insert ⇨ Module.**

4. **Type or paste the code in the newly created module.**

If you don't see personal.xlb in your Project window, it means it doesn't exist yet. You'll have to record a macro using Personal Macro Workbook as the destination.

To record the macro in your Personal Macro Workbook, select the Personal Macro Workbook option in the Record Macro dialog box before you start recording. This option is in the Store Macro In drop-down box. Simply record a couple of cell clicks and then stop recording. You can discard the recorded macro and replace it with this one.

Moving Worksheets Around

We've all had to rearrange our spreadsheet so that some sheets came before or after other sheets. If you find that you often have to do this, here is a macro that can help.

How it works

When you want to rearrange sheets, you use the Move method of either the Sheets object or the ActiveSheet object. When using the Move method, you need to specify where to move the sheet to. You can do this using the After argument, the Before argument, or both.

```vba
Sub Macro1()

'Move the active sheet to the end
    ActiveSheet.Move After:=Worksheets(Worksheets.Count)

'Move the active sheet to the beginning
    ActiveSheet.Move Before:=Worksheets(1)

'Move Sheet 1 before Sheet 12
    Sheets("Sheet1").Move Before:=Sheets("Sheet12")

End Sub
```

This macro demonstrates how to move the active worksheet to three locations.

>> **Move the active sheet to the end:** When you need to move a worksheet to the end of the workbook, you essentially want to tell Excel to move the sheet After the last sheet. There is no code in VBA that lets you point to "the last sheet." But you *can* find the maximum count of worksheets, and then use that number as an index for the Worksheets object. This means that you can enter something like Worksheets(1) to point to the first sheet in a workbook. You can enter Worksheet(3) to point to the third sheet in the workbook. To point to the last sheet in the workbook, you can replace the index number with the Worksheets.Count property. Worksheets.Count gives you the total number of worksheets, which so happens to be the same number as the index for the last sheet. Thus Worksheet(Worksheets.Count) points to the last sheet.

>> **Move the active sheet to the beginning:** Moving a sheet to the beginning of the workbook is simple. You use Worksheets(1) to point to the first sheet in the workbook, and then move the active sheet Before that one.

>> **Move Sheet 1 before Sheet *X*:** You can also move a sheet before or after another sheet simply by calling that other sheet out by name. In the example demonstrated in the previous macro, you are moving Sheet1 before Sheet12.

How to use it

The best place to store this kind of macro is in your Personal Macro Workbook. This way, the macro is always available to you. The Personal Macro Workbook is loaded whenever you start Excel. In the VBE Project window, it is named personal.xlsb.

1. **Activate the Visual Basic Editor by pressing Alt+F11 on your keyboard.**

2. **Right-click personal.xlb in the Project window.**

3. **Choose Insert ⇨ Module.**

4. **Type or paste the code in the newly created module.**

If you don't see personal.xlb in your Project window, it means it doesn't exist yet. You'll have to record a macro, using Personal Macro Workbook as the destination.

To record the macro in your Personal Macro Workbook, select the Personal Macro Workbook option in the Record Macro dialog box before you start recording. This option is in the Store Macro In drop-down list. Simply record a couple of cell clicks and then stop recording. You can discard the recorded macro and replace it with this one.

Sorting Worksheets by Name

You may often need to sort worksheets alphabetically by name (see Figure 5-3). You would think Excel would have a native function to do this, but alas, it does not. If you don't want to manually sort your spreadsheets anymore, you can use this macro to do it for you.

How it works

This macro looks more complicated than it is. The activity in this macro is actually fairly simple. It simply iterates through the sheets in the workbook, comparing the current sheet to the previous one. If the name of previous sheet is greater than the current sheet (alphabetically), the macro moves the current sheet before it. By the time all the iterations are done, you've got a sorted workbook!

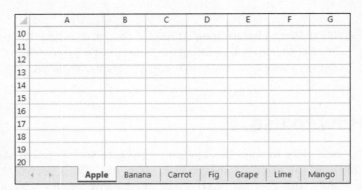

FIGURE 5-3:
It's often useful
to have your
worksheets
sorted in
alphabetical
order.

```
Sub Macro1()

'Step 1: Declare your Variables
    Dim CurrentSheetIndex As Integer
    Dim PrevSheetIndex As Integer

'Step 2: Set the starting counts and start looping
    For CurrentSheetIndex = 1 To Sheets.Count
    For PrevSheetIndex = 1 To CurrentSheetIndex - 1

'Step 3: Check Current Sheet against Previous Sheet
    If UCase(Sheets(PrevSheetIndex).Name) > _
        UCase(Sheets(CurrentSheetIndex).Name) Then

'Step 4: If Move Current sheet Before Previous
    Sheets(CurrentSheetIndex).Move _
    Before:=Sheets(PrevSheetIndex)
    End If

'Step 5 Loop back around to iterate again
    Next PrevSheetIndex
    Next CurrentSheetIndex

End Sub
```

Note this technique is doing a text-based sorting. So you may not get the results you were expecting when working with number-based sheet names. For example, Sheet10 will come before Sheet2 because textually, 1 comes before 2. Excel does not do the numbers-based sorting that says 2 comes before 10.

REMEMBER

1. Step 1 declares two integer variables. The CurrentSheetIndex holds the index number for the current sheet iteration, and the PrevSheetIndex variable holds the index number for the previous sheet iteration.

2. In Step 2, the macro starts iteration counts for both variables. Note that the count for the PrevSheetIndex is one number behind the CurrentSheetIndex. After the counts are set, it starts looping.

3. In Step 3, you check to see whether the name of the previous sheet is greater than that of the current sheet.

In this step, note the use of the UCase function. You use this to get both names in the same uppercase state. This prevents sorting errors due to differing case states.

4. Step 4 is reached only if the previous sheet name is greater than the current sheet name. In this step, you use the Move method to move the current sheet before the previous sheet.

5. In Step 5, you go back around to the start of the loop. Every iteration of the loop increments both variables up one number until the last worksheet is touched. After all iterations have been spent, the macro ends.

How to use it

The best place to store this macro is in your Personal Macro Workbook. This way, the macro is always available to you. The Personal Macro Workbook is loaded whenever you start Excel. In the VBE Project window, it is named personal.xlsb.

1. Activate the Visual Basic Editor by pressing Alt+F11 on your keyboard.

2. Right-click personal.xlb in the Project window.

3. Choose Insert ⇨ Module.

4. Type or paste the code in the newly created module.

If you don't see personal.xlb in your Project window, it means it doesn't exist yet. You'll have to record a macro, using Personal Macro Workbook as the destination.

To record the macro in your Personal Macro Workbook, select the Personal Macro Workbook option in the Record Macro dialog box before you start recording. This option is in the Store Macro In drop-down list. Simply record a couple of cell clicks and then stop recording. You can discard the recorded macro and replace it with this one.

Grouping Worksheets by Color

Many of us assign colors to our worksheet tabs. You can right-click any tab and select the Tab Color option (shown in Figure 5-4) to choose a color for your tab.

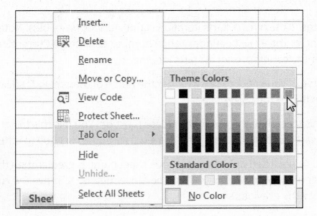

FIGURE 5-4:
You can right-click
on any worksheet
to choose a
tab color for
the sheet.

This allows for the visual confirmation that the data in a certain tab is somehow related to another tab because both have the same color. When you have many colored sheets, it's often useful to group tabs of similar color together for ease of navigation.

This macro groups worksheets based on their tab colors.

How it works

You may think it's impossible to sort or group by color, but Excel offers a way. Excel assigns an index number to every color. A light yellow color may have an index number of 36, whereas a maroon color has the index number 42.

This macro iterates through the sheets in the workbook, comparing the tab color index of the current sheet to that of the previous one. If the previous sheet has the same color index number as the current sheet, the macro moves the current sheet before it. By the time all the iterations are done, all the sheets are grouped together based on their tab colors.

```
Sub Macro1()

'Step 1: Declare your Variables
    Dim CurrentSheetIndex As Integer
    Dim PrevSheetIndex As Integer

'Step 2: Set the starting counts and start looping
    For CurrentSheetIndex = 1 To Sheets.Count
    For PrevSheetIndex = 1 To CurrentSheetIndex - 1
```

```
'Step 3: Check Current Sheet against Previous Sheet
    If Sheets(PrevSheetIndex).Tab.ColorIndex = _
    Sheets(CurrentSheetIndex).Tab.ColorIndex Then

'Step 4: If Move Current sheet Before Previous
    Sheets(PrevSheetIndex).Move _
    Before:=Sheets(CurrentSheetIndex)
    End If

'Step 5 Loop back around to iterate again
    Next PrevSheetIndex
    Next CurrentSheetIndex

End Sub
```

1. Step 1 declares two integer variables. The CurrentSheetIndex holds the index number for the current sheet iteration, and the PrevSheetIndex variable holds the index number for the previous sheet iteration.

2. Step 2 starts iteration counts for both variables. Note that the count for the PrevSheetIndex is one number behind the CurrentSheetIndex. After the counts are set, the macro starts looping.

3. In Step 3, the macro checks to see whether the color index of the previous sheet is the same as that of the current sheet. Note the use of the Tab. ColorIndex property.

4. Step 4 is reached only if the color index of previous sheet is equal to the color index of the current sheet. In this step, the macro uses the Move method to move the current sheet before the previous sheet.

5. In Step 5, the macro goes back around to the start of the loop. Every iteration of the loop increments both variables up one number until the last worksheet is touched. After all of the iterations have run, the macro ends.

How to use it

The best place to store this macro is in your Personal Macro Workbook. This way, the macro is always available to you. The Personal Macro Workbook is loaded whenever you start Excel. In the VBE Project window, it is named personal.xlsb.

1. **Activate the Visual Basic Editor by pressing Alt+F11 on your keyboard.**

2. **Right-click personal.xlb in the Project window.**

3. **Choose Insert ⇨ Module.**

4. **Type or paste the code in the newly created module.**

If you don't see personal.xlb in your project window, it doesn't exist yet. You'll have to record a macro, using Personal Macro Workbook as the destination.

To record the macro in your Personal Macro Workbook, select the Personal Macro Workbook option in the Record Macro dialog box before you start recording. This option is in the Store Macro In drop-down list. Simply record a couple of cell clicks and then stop recording. You can discard the recorded macro and replace it with this one.

Copying a Worksheet to a New Workbook

In Excel, you can manually copy an entire sheet to a new workbook by right-clicking the target sheet and selecting the Move or Copy option. Unfortunately, if you try to record a macro while you do this, the macro recorder fails to accurately write the code to reflect the task. So if you need to programmatically copy an entire sheet to a brand new workbook, this macro delivers.

How it works

In this macro, the active sheet is first being copied. Then you use the Before parameter to send the copy to a new workbook that is created on the fly. The copied sheet is positioned as the first sheet in the new workbook.

The use of the ThisWorkbook object is important here. This ensures that the active sheet being copied is from the workbook that the code is in, not the newly created workbook.

```
Sub Macro1()

'Copy sheet, and send to new workbook
    ThisWorkbook.ActiveSheet.Copy _
    Before:=Workbooks.Add.Worksheets(1)

End Sub
```

How to use it

To implement this macro, you can copy and paste it into a standard module:

1. Activate the Visual Basic Editor by pressing Alt+F11 on your keyboard.

2. Right-click the project/workbook name in the Project window.

3. **Choose Insert ⇨ Module.**

4. **Type or paste the code in the newly created module.**

Creating a New Workbook for Each Worksheet

Many Excel analysts need to parse their workbooks into separate books per worksheet tab. In other words, they need to create a new workbook for each of the worksheets in their existing workbook. You can imagine what an ordeal this would be if you were to do it manually. The following macro helps automate that task.

How it works

In this macro, you are looping the worksheets, copying each sheet, and then sending the copy to a new workbook that is created on the fly. The thing to note here is that the newly created workbooks are being saved in the same directory as your original workbook, with the same filename as the copied sheet (wb.SaveAs ThisWorkbook.Path & "\" & ws.Name).

```
Sub Macro1()

'Step 1:  Declare all the variables.
    Dim ws As Worksheet
    Dim wb As Workbook

'Step 2:  Start the looping through sheets
    For Each ws In ThisWorkbook.Worksheets

'Step 3:  Create new workbook and save it.
    Set wb = Workbooks.Add
    wb.SaveAs ThisWorkbook.Path & "\" & ws.Name

'Step 4:  Copy the target sheet to the new workbook
    ws.Copy Before:=wb.Worksheets(1)
    wb.Close SaveChanges:=True

'Step 5:  Loop back around to the next worksheet
    Next ws

End Sub
```

REMEMBER

Not all valid worksheet names translate to valid filenames.

Windows has specific rules that prevent you from naming files with certain characters. You cannot use these characters when naming a file: back slash (\), forward slash (/), colon (:), asterisk (*), question mark (?), pipe (|), double quote ("), greater than (>), and less than (<).

The twist is that you can use a few of these restricted characters in your sheet names; specifically, double quote, pipe (|), greater than (>), and less than (<).

So as you're running this macro, naming the newly created files to match the sheet name may cause an error. For example, the macro throws an error when creating a new file from a sheet called "May| Revenue" (because of the pipe character).

Long story short, avoid naming your worksheets with the restricted characters just mentioned.

1. Step 1 declares two object variables. The ws variable creates a memory container for each worksheet the macro loops through. The wb variable creates the container for the new workbooks you create.

2. In Step 2, the macro starts looping through the sheets. The use of the ThisWorkbook object ensures that the active sheet being copied is from the workbook the code is in, not the newly created workbook.

3. In Step 3, you create the new workbook and save it. You save this new book in the same path as the original workbook (ThisWorkbook). The filename is set to be the same name as the currently active sheet.

4. Step 4 copies the currently active sheet, using the Before parameter to send it to the new book as the first tab. Step 4 then saves and closes the newly created workbook.

5. Step 5 loops back to get the next sheet. After all of the sheets are evaluated, the macro ends.

How to use it

To implement this macro, you can copy and paste it into a standard module:

1. **Activate the Visual Basic Editor by pressing Alt+F11 on your keyboard.**

2. **Right-click the project/workbook name in the Project window.**

3. **Choose Insert ➪ Module.**

4. **Type or paste the code in the newly created module.**

Printing Specified Worksheets

If you want to print specific sheets manually in Excel, you need to hold down the Ctrl key on the keyboard, select the sheets you want to print, and then click Print. If you do this often enough, you may consider using this very simple macro.

How it works

This one is easy. All you have to do is pass the sheets you want printed in an array as seen here in this macro, then use the PrintOut method to trigger the print job. All the sheets you have entered are printed in one go.

```
Sub Macro1()

'Print Certain Sheets
    ActiveWorkbook.Sheets( _
    Array("Sheet1", "Sheet3", "Sheet5")).PrintOut Copies:=1

End Sub
```

Want to print all worksheets in a workbook? This one is even easier.

```
Sub Macro1()

'Print All Sheets
    ActiveWorkbook.Worksheets.PrintOut Copies:=1

End Sub
```

How to use it

The best place to store this macro is in your Personal Macro Workbook. This way, the macro is always available to you. The Personal Macro Workbook is loaded whenever you start Excel. In the VBE Project window, it is named personal.xlsb.

1. **Activate the Visual Basic Editor by pressing Alt+F11 on your keyboard.**

2. **Right-click personal.xlb in the Project window.**

3. **Choose Insert ⇨ Module.**

4. **Type or paste the code in the newly created module.**

If you don't see personal.xlb in your Project window, it means it doesn't exist yet. You'll have to record a macro using Personal Macro Workbook as the destination.

To record the macro in your Personal Macro Workbook, select the Personal Macro Workbook option in the Record Macro dialog box before you start recording. This option is in the Store Macro In drop-down list. Simply record a couple of cell clicks and then stop recording. You can discard the recorded macro and replace it with this one.

Protecting All Worksheets

Before you distribute your workbook, you may want to apply sheet protection to all the sheets. However, as you can see in Figure 5-5, Excel disables the Protect Sheet command if you try to protect multiple sheets at one time. You are forced to protect one sheet at a time.

FIGURE 5-5:
The Protect Sheet command is disabled if you try to protect more than one sheet at a time.

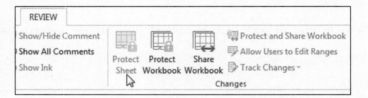

You can use this macro to save you from protecting each sheet manually.

How it works

In this macro, you are looping the worksheets and simply applying protection with a password. The Password argument defines the password needed to remove the protection. The Password argument is completely optional. If you omit it altogether, the sheet is still protected; you just won't need to enter a password to unprotect it. Also, be aware that Excel passwords are case-sensitive, so you'll want pay attention to the exact capitalization you are using.

```
Sub Macro1()

'Step 1:  Declare your variables
    Dim ws As Worksheet

'Step 2: Start looping through all worksheets
    For Each ws In ActiveWorkbook.Worksheets

'Step 3:  Protect and loop to next worksheet
    ws.Protect Password:="RED"
    Next ws

End Sub
```

1. Step 1 declares an object called ws. This creates a memory container for each worksheet you loop through.

2. Step 2 starts the looping, telling Excel you want to enumerate through all worksheets in this workbook.

3. In Step 3, the macro applies protection with the given password, and then loops back to get the worksheet.

How to use it

The best place to store this macro is in your Personal Macro Workbook. This way, the macro is always available to you. The Personal Macro Workbook is loaded whenever you start Excel. In the VBE Project window, it is named personal.xlsb.

1. **Activate the Visual Basic Editor by pressing Alt+F11 on your keyboard.**

2. **Right-click personal.xlb in the Project window.**

3. **Choose Insert ⇨ Module.**

4. **Type or paste the code in the newly created module.**

If you don't see personal.xlb in your Project window, it doesn't exist yet. You'll have to record a macro using Personal Macro Workbook as the destination.

To record the macro in your Personal Macro Workbook, select the Personal Macro Workbook option in the Record Macro dialog box before you start recording. This option is in the Store Macro In drop-down list. Simply record a couple of cell clicks and then stop recording. You can discard the recorded macro and replace it with this one.

Unprotecting All Worksheets

You may find yourself constantly having to unprotect multiple worksheets manually. However, as you can see in Figure 5-6, Excel disables the Unprotect Sheet command if you try to unprotect multiple sheets at one time. You are forced to unprotect one sheet at a time.

FIGURE 5-6:
The Unprotect
Sheet command
is disabled if you
try to unprotect
more than one
sheet at a time.

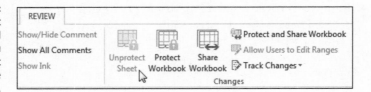

You can use this macro to save you from unprotecting each sheet manually.

How it works

This macro loops the worksheets and uses the Password argument to unprotect each sheet.

```
Sub Macro1()

'Step 1:  Declare your variables
    Dim ws As Worksheet

'Step 2: Start looping through all worksheets
    For Each ws In ActiveWorkbook.Worksheets

'Step 3:  Loop to next worksheet
    ws.UnProtect Password:="RED"
    Next ws

End Sub
```

1. Step 1 declares an object called ws. This creates a memory container for each worksheet you loop through.

2. Step 2 starts the looping, telling Excel to enumerate through all worksheets in this workbook.

3. Step 3 unprotects the active sheet, providing the password as needed, and then loops back to get the worksheet.

Obviously, the assumption is that all the worksheets that need to be unprotected have the same password. If this is not the case, you need to explicitly unprotect each sheet with its corresponding password.

```
Sub Macro1()

Sheets("Sheet1").UnProtect Password:="RED"
Sheets("Sheet2").UnProtect Password:="BLUE"
Sheets("Sheet3").UnProtect Password:="YELLOW"
Sheets("Sheet4").UnProtect Password:="GREEN"

End Sub
```

How to use it

The best place to store this kind of a macro is in your Personal Macro Workbook. This way, the macro is always available to you. The Personal Macro Workbook is loaded whenever you start Excel. In the VBE Project window, it will be named personal.xlsb.

1. Activate the Visual Basic Editor by pressing Alt+F11 on your keyboard.

2. Right-click personal.xlb in the Project window.

3. Choose Insert ⇨ Module.

4. Type or paste the code in the newly created module.

If you don't see personal.xlb in your Project window, it means it doesn't exist yet. You'll have to record a macro, using Personal Macro Workbook as the destination.

To record the macro in your Personal Macro Workbook, select the Personal Macro Workbook option in the Record Macro dialog box before you start recording. This option is in the Store Macro In drop-down list. Simply record a couple of cell clicks and then stop recording. You can discard the recorded macro and replace it with this one.

Creating a Table of Contents for Your Worksheets

Outside of sorting worksheets, creating a table of contents for the worksheets in a workbook is the most commonly requested Excel macro. The reason is probably not lost on you. We often have to work with files that have more worksheet tabs than can easily be seen or navigated. A table of contents like the one shown in Figure 5-7 definitely helps.

	A	B
1	Table Of Contents	
2	Sheet1	
3	Sheet2	
4	Sheet3	
5	Sheet10	
6	Sheet11	
7	Sheet13	
8		
9		
10		

FIGURE 5-7: A table of contents can help you more easily navigate your workbook.

The following macro not only creates a list of worksheet names in the workbook, but it also adds hyperlinks so that you can easily jump to a sheet with a simple click.

How it works

It's easy to get intimidated when looking at this macro. There is a lot going on here. However, if you step back and consider the few simple actions it does, it becomes a little less scary:

>> It removes any previous Table of Contents sheet.

>> It creates a new Table of Contents sheet.

>> It grabs the name of each worksheet and pastes it on the Table of Contents.

>> It adds a hyperlink to each entry in the Table of Contents.

That doesn't sound so bad. Now look at the code:

```
Sub Macro1()

'Step 1: Declare Variables
    Dim i As Long

'Step 2:  Delete Previous TOC if Exists
    On Error Resume Next
    Application.DisplayAlerts = False
    Sheets("Table Of Contents").Delete
    Application.DisplayAlerts = True
    On Error GoTo 0

'Step 3:  Add a new TOC sheet as the first sheet
    ThisWorkbook.Sheets.Add _
    Before:=ThisWorkbook.Worksheets(1)
    ActiveSheet.Name = "Table Of Contents"

'Step 4: Start the i Counter
    For i = 1 To Sheets.Count

'Step 5: Select Next available row
    ActiveSheet.Cells(i, 1).Select

'Step 6:  Add Sheet Name and Hyperlink
    ActiveSheet.Hyperlinks.Add _
    Anchor:=ActiveSheet.Cells(i, 1), _
    Address:="", _
    SubAddress:="'" & Sheets(i).Name & "'!A1", _
    TextToDisplay:=Sheets(i).Name

'Step 7: Loop back increment i
    Next i

End Sub
```

1. Step 1 declares an integer variable called i to serve as the counter as the macro iterates through the sheets.

   Note that this macro is not looping through the sheets the way previous macros in this chapter did. In previous macros, you looped through the worksheets collection and selected each worksheet there. In this procedure, you are using a counter (your i variable). The main reason is because you not only have to keep track of the sheets, but you also have to manage to enter each sheet name on a new row into a table of contents. The idea is that as the counter progresses through the sheets, it also serves to move the cursor down in the Table of Contents so each new entry goes on a new row.

2. Step 2 essentially attempts to delete any previous sheet called Table of Contents. Because there may not be any Table of Contents sheet to delete, you have to start Step 2 with the On Error Resume Next error handler. This tells Excel to continue the macro if an error is encountered here. You then delete the Table of Contents sheet using the DisplayAlerts method, which effectively turns off Excel's warnings so you don't have to confirm the deletion. Finally, you reset the error handler to trap all errors again by entering On Error GoTo 0.

3. In Step 3, you add a new sheet to the workbook using the Before argument to position the new sheet as first sheet. You then name the sheet Table of Contents. As mentioned previously in this chapter, when you add a new worksheet, it automatically becomes the active sheet. Because this new sheet has the focus throughout the procedure, any references to ActiveSheet in this code refer to the Table of Contents sheet.

4. Step 4 starts the i counter at 1 and ends it at the maximum count of all sheets in the workbook. Again, instead of looping through the Worksheets collection like you've done in previous macros, you are simply using the i counter as an index number that you can pass to the Sheets object. When the maximum number is reached, the macro ends.

5. Step 5 selects the corresponding row in the Table of Contents sheet. That is to say, if the i counter is on 1, it selects the first row in the Table of Contents sheet. If the i counter is at 2, it selects the second row, and so on.

You are able to do this using the Cells item. The Cells item provides an extremely handy way of selecting ranges through code. It requires only relative row and column positions as parameters. So Cells(1,1) translates to row 1, column 1 (or cell A1). Cells(5, 3) translates to row 5, column 3 (or cell C5). The numeric parameters in the Cells item are particularly handy when you want to loop through a series of rows or columns using an incrementing index number.

6. Step 6 uses the Hyperlinks.Add method to add the sheet name and hyperlinks to the selected cell. This step feeds the Hyperlinks.Add method the parameters it needs to build out the hyperlinks.

7. The last step in the macro loops back to increment the i counter to the next count. When the i counter reaches a number that equals the count of work-sheets in the workbook, the macro ends.

How to use it

To implement this macro, you can copy and paste it into a standard module:

1. **Activate the Visual Basic Editor by pressing Alt+F11.**
2. **Right-click the project/workbook name in the Project window.**
3. **Choose Insert ⇨ Module.**
4. **Type or paste the code in the newly created module.**

Zooming In and Out of a Worksheet with Double-Click

Some spreadsheets are huge. Sometimes, you are forced to shrink the font size down so that you can see a decent portion of the spreadsheet on the screen. If you find that you are constantly zooming in and out of a spreadsheet, alternating between scanning large sections of data and reading specific cells, here is a handy macro that auto-zooms on double-click.

How it works

With this macro in place, you can double-click on a cell in the spreadsheet to zoom in 200 percent. Double-click again and Excel zooms back to 100 percent. Obviously, you can change the values and complexity in the code to fit your needs.

```
Private Sub Worksheet_BeforeDoubleClick(ByVal Target As Range,
    Cancel As Boolean)

'Check current Zoom state
'Zoom to 100% if to at 100
'Zoom 200% if currently at 100
    If ActiveWindow.Zoom <> 100 Then
    ActiveWindow.Zoom = 100
    Else
    ActiveWindow.Zoom = 200
    End If

End Sub
```

TIP

Note that the side effect of double-clicking a cell is that it goes into edit mode. You can exit edit mode by pressing the escape key (Esc) on your keyboard. If you find it annoying to keep pressing Esc when triggering this macro, you can add this statement to the end of the procedure:

```
Application.SendKeys ("{ESC}")
```

This statement mimics you pressing the escape key on your keyboard.

How to use it

To implement this macro, you need to copy and paste it into the Worksheet_ BeforeDoubleClick event code window. Placing the macro there allows it to run each time you double-click on the sheet.

1. Activate the Visual Basic Editor by pressing Alt+F11 on your keyboard.

2. In the Project window, find your project/workbook name and click the plus sign next to it in order to see all the sheets.

3. Click on the sheet from which you want to trigger the code.

4. Select the BeforeDoubleClick event from the Event drop-down list (see Figure 5-8).

5. Type or paste the code in the newly created module.

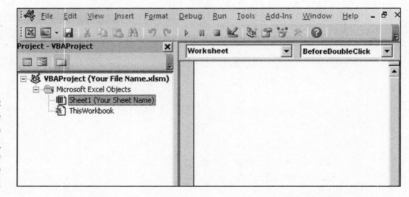

FIGURE 5-8: Type or paste your code into the Worksheet_ BeforeDouble Click event code window.

Highlighting the Active Row and Column

When looking at a table of numbers, it would be nice if Excel automatically high-lighted the row and column you're on (as demonstrated in Figure 5-9). This effect gives your eyes a lead line up and down the column as well as left and right across the row.

The following macro enables the effect you see in Figure 5-9 with just a simple double-click. When the macro is in place, Excel highlights the row and column for the active cell, greatly improving your ability to view and edit a large grid.

	A	B	C	D	E	F	
1							
2		Jan	Feb	Mar	Apr	May	Jun
3	Product 1	$74,084	$41,353	$37,032	$77,941	$35,221	$55
4	Product 2	$70,049	$42,425	$51,966	$25,159	$35,929	$16
5	Product 3	$13,513	$98,468	$18,818	$27,001	$11,373	$2
6	Product 4	$72,705	$25,553	$68,709	$86,278	$58,278	$47
7	Product 5	$35,637	$81,467	$83,445	$51,797	$58,971	$52
8	Product 6	$61,118	$71,932	$42,153	$20,370	$44,917	$25
9	Product 7	$42,303	$19,757	$78,250	$32,396	$1,863	$30
10	Product 8	$74,735	$53,599	$52,357	$55,778	$89,745	$43
11	Product 9	$29,764	$31,476	$92,661	$76,510	$93,957	$90
12	Product 10	$37,577	$68,726	$42,900	$60,592	$7,627	$17
13	Product 11	$98,304	$19,809	$56,834	$62,311	$54,039	$55
14	Product 12	$64,827	$85,195	$16,953	$47,824	$26,565	$52
15							

FIGURE 5-9: A highlighted row and column makes it easy to track data horizontally and vertically.

How it works

Take a look at how this macro works:

```
Private Sub Worksheet_BeforeDoubleClick(ByVal Target As Range, _
    Cancel As Boolean)

'Step 1:  Declare Variables
    Dim strRange As String

'Step2:  Build the range string
    strRange = Target.Cells.Address & "," & _
               Target.Cells.EntireColumn.Address & "," & _
               Target.Cells.EntireRow.Address

'Step 3: Pass the range string to a Range
    Range(strRange).Select

End Sub
```

1. You first declare an object called strRange. This creates a memory container you can use to build a range string.

2. A range string is nothing more than the address for a range. "A1" is a range string that points to cell A1. "A1:G5" is also a range string; this points to a range of cells encompassing cells A1 to G5. In Step 2, you are building a range string that encompasses the double-clicked cell (called Target in this macro), the entire active row, and the entire active column. The Address property for these three ranges is captured and pieced together into the strRange variable.

3. In Step 3, you feed the strRange variable as the address for a Range.Select statement. This is the line of the code that finally highlights the double-clicked selection.

How to use it

To implement this macro, you need to copy and paste it into the Worksheet_ BeforeDoubleClick event code window. Placing the macro there allows it to run each time you double-click on the sheet.

1. Activate the Visual Basic Editor by pressing Alt+F11 on your keyboard.

2. In the Project window, find your project/workbook name and click the plus sign next to it in order to see all the sheets.

3. Click on the sheet from which you want to trigger the code.

4. Select the BeforeDoubleClick event from the Event drop-down list (see Figure 5-10).

5. Type or paste the code in the newly created module.

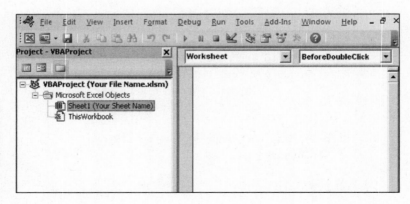

FIGURE 5-10:
Type or paste your code into the Worksheet_ BeforeDouble Click event code window.

3
One-Touch Data Manipulation

Go beyond basic macros and look at some advanced techniques for navigating ranges through VBA.

See how macros can automate the selection and manipulation of specific cells.

Explore how you can use macros to clean and transform the data in your workbooks.

Uncover techniques that can help you automate the export of your Excel data.

Chapter **6**

Feeling at Home on the Range

O ne of the most important things you do in Excel is navigate the worksheet. When you work with Excel manually, you are constantly navigating to appropriate ranges, finding the last row, moving to the last column, hiding and unhiding ranges, and so on. This all comes instinctively as part of doing work in Excel.

When you attempt to automate your work through VBA, you'll find that navigating your spreadsheet remains an important part of the automation process. In many cases, you need to dynamically navigate and manipulate Excel ranges, just as you would manually — only through VBA code. This chapter provides some of the most commonly used macros in terms of navigating and working with ranges.

Selecting and Formatting a Range

One of the basic things you need to do in VBA is select a specific range to do something with it. This simple macro selects the range D5:D16.

How it works

In this macro, you explicitly define the range to select by using the Range object.

```
Sub Macro1()

Range("D5:D16").Select

End Sub
```

After the range of cells is selected, you can use any of the Range properties to manipulate the cells. Alter this macro so that the range is colored yellow, converted to number formatting, and bold.

```
Sub Macro1()

    Range("D5:D16").Select
    Selection.NumberFormat = "#,##0"
    Selection.Font.Bold = True
    Selection.Interior.ColorIndex = 36

End Sub
```

TIP

You don't have to memorize all the properties of the cell object in order to manipulate them. You can simply record a macro, do your formatting, and then look at the code that Excel has written. After you've seen what the correct syntax is, you can apply it as needed. Many Excel programmers start learning VBA this way!

You'll notice that Selection is referred to many times in the previous sample code. To write more efficient code, you can simply refer to the range, using the With...End With statement. This statement tells Excel that any action you perform applies to the object to which you've pointed. Note that this macro doesn't actually select the range at all. This is a key point. In a macro, you can work with a range without selecting it first.

```
Sub Macro1()

    With Range("D5:D16")
        .NumberFormat = "#,##0"
```

```
            .Font.Bold = True
            .Interior.ColorIndex = 36
        End With

    End Sub
```

Another way you can select a range is by using the Cells item of the Range object.

The Cells item gives you an extremely handy way of selecting ranges through code. It requires only relative row and column positions as parameters. Cells(5,4) translates to row 5, column 4 (or Cell D5). Cells(16, 4) translates to row 16, column 4 (or cell D16).

If you want to select a range of cells, simply pass two items into the Range object. This macro performs the same selection of range D5:D16:

```
Sub Macro1()

Range(Cells(5, 4), Cells(16, 4)).Select

End Sub
```

Here is the full formatting code using the Cells item. Again, note that this macro doesn't actually select the range you are altering at all. You can work with a range without selecting it first.

```
Sub Macro1()

    With Range(Cells(5, 4), Cells(16, 4))
        .NumberFormat = "#,##0"
        .Font.Bold = True
        .Interior.ColorIndex = 36
    End With

End Sub
```

How to use it

To implement this kind of a macro, you can copy and paste it into a standard module:

1. **Activate the Visual Basic Editor by pressing Alt+F11 on your keyboard.**

2. **Right-click the project/workbook name in the Project window.**

3. **Choose Insert ⇨ Module.**

4. **Type or paste the code into the code window.**

Creating and Selecting Named Ranges

One of the more useful features in Excel is the ability to name your range (that is, to give your range a user-friendly name, so that you can more easily identify and refer to it via VBA).

Here are the steps you would perform to create a named range manually:

1. **Select the range you want to name.**

2. **Go to the Formulas tab in the Ribbon and choose the Define Name command (see Figure 6-1).**

3. **Give the chosen range a user-friendly name in the New Name dialog box, as shown in Figure 6-2.**

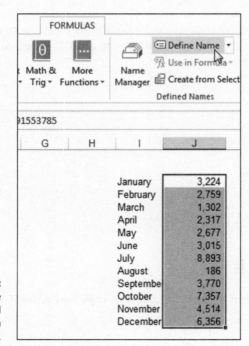

FIGURE 6-1:
Click the Define Name command to name a chosen range.

When you click OK, your range is named. To confirm this, you can go to the Formula tab and select the Name Manager command. This activates the Name Manager dialog box (see Figure 6-3), where you can see all the applied named ranges.

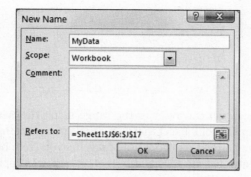

FIGURE 6-2:
Give your
range a name.

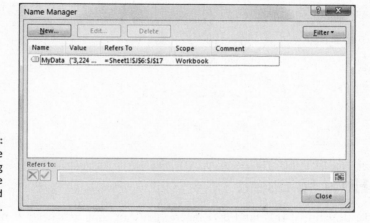

FIGURE 6-3:
The Name
Manager dialog
box lists all the
applied named
ranges.

Creating a named range via VBA is much less involved. You can directly define the Name property of the Range object:

```
Sub Macro1()

Range("J6:J17").Name = "MyData"

End Sub
```

Admittedly, you'd be hard pressed to find a situation where you would need to automate the creation of named ranges. The real efficiency comes in manipulating them via VBA.

How it works

You simply pass the name of the range through the Range object. This allows you to select the range:

```
Sub Macro1()

Range("MyData").Select

End Sub
```

As with normal ranges, you can refer to the range using the With. . .End With statement. This statement tells Excel that any action you perform applies to the object to which you've pointed. This not only prevents you from having to repeat syntax, but it also allows for the easy addition of actions by simply adding them between the With and End With statements.

```
Sub Macro1()

    With Range("MyData")
        .NumberFormat = "#,##0"
        .Font.Bold = True
        .Interior.ColorIndex = 36
    End With

End Sub
```

How to use it

To implement this kind of a macro, you can copy and paste it into a standard module:

1. **Activate the Visual Basic Editor by pressing Alt+F11.**

2. **Right-click the project/workbook name in the Project window.**

3. **Choose Insert ➪ Module.**

4. **Type or paste the code.**

Enumerating Through a Range of Cells

One must-have VBA skill is the ability to enumerate (or loop) through a range. If you do any serious macro work in Excel, you will soon encounter the need to go through a range of cells one by one and perform some action.

This basic macro shows you a simple way to enumerate through a range.

How it works

In this macro, you are essentially using two Range object variables. One of the variables captures the scope of data you are working with, whereas the other is used to hold each individual cell as you go through the range. Then you use the For Each statement to activate or bring each cell in the target range into focus:

```
Sub Macro1()

'Step 1:  Declare your variables.
    Dim MyRange As Range
    Dim MyCell As Range

'Step 2:  Define the target Range.
    Set MyRange = Range("D6:D17")

'Step 3:  Start looping through the range.
    For Each MyCell In MyRange

'Step 4:  Do something with each cell.

    If MyCell.Value > 3000 Then
        MyCell.Font.Bold = True
    End If

'Step 5: Get the next cell in the range
    Next MyCell

End Sub
```

1. The macro first declares two Range object variables. One, called MyRange, holds the entire target range. The other, called MyCell, holds each cell in the range as the macro enumerates through them one by one.

2. In Step 2, you fill the MyRange variable with the target range. In this example, you are using Range("D6:D17"). If your target range is a named range, you could simply enter its name — Range("MyNamedRange").

3. In this step, the macro starts looping through each cell in the target range, activating each cell as it goes through.

4. After a cell is activated, you would do something with it. That "something" really depends on the task at hand. You may want to delete rows when the active cell has a certain value, or you may want to insert a row between each active cell. In this example, the macro is changing the font to Bold for any cell that has a value greater than 3,000.

5. In Step 5, the macro loops back to get the next cell. After all cells in the target range are activated, the macro ends.

How to use it

To implement this macro, you can copy and paste it into a standard module:

1. **Activate the Visual Basic Editor by pressing Alt+F11 on your keyboard.**

2. **Right-click the project/workbook name in the Project window.**

3. **Choose Insert ⇨ Module.**

4. **Type or paste the code.**

Inserting Blank Rows in a Range

Occasionally, you may need to dynamically insert rows into your dataset. Although blank rows are generally bothersome, in some situations, the final formatted version of your report requires them to separate data. The macro in this section adds blank rows into a range.

How it works

This macro performs a reverse loop through the chosen range using a counter. It starts at the last row of the range by inserting two blank rows, and then moves to the previous row in the range. It keeps doing that same insert for every loop, each time incrementing the counter to the previous row.

```
Sub Macro1()

'Step1:  Declare your variables.
    Dim MyRange As Range
    Dim iCounter As Long
```

```
'Step 2:  Define the target Range.
    Set MyRange = Range("C6:D17")

'Step 3:  Start reverse looping through the range.
    For iCounter = MyRange.Rows.Count To 2 Step -1

'Step 4: Insert two blank rows.
    MyRange.Rows(iCounter).EntireRow.Insert
    MyRange.Rows(iCounter).EntireRow.Insert

'Step 5: Increment the counter down
    Next iCounter

End Sub
```

1. You first declare two variables. The first variable is an object variable called MyRange. This is an object variable that defines the target range. The other variable is a Long Integer variable called iCounter. This variable serves as an incremental counter.

2. In Step 2, the macro fills the MyRange variable with the target range. In this example, you are using Range("C6:D17"). If your target range is a named range, you could simply enter its name — Range("MyNamedRange").

3. In this step, the macro sets the parameters for the incremental counter to start at the max count for the range (MyRange.Rows.Count) and end at 2 (the second row of the chosen range). Note that you are using the Step-1 qualifier. Because you specify Step -1, Excel knows you are going to increment the counter backward, moving back one increment on each iteration. In all, Step 3 tells Excel to start at the last row of the chosen range, moving backward until it gets to the second row of the range.

4. When working with a range, you can explicitly call out a specific row in the range by passing a row index number to the Rows collection of the range. For example, Range("D6:D17").Rows(5) points to the fifth row in the range D6:D17.

   In Step 4, the macro uses the iCounter variable as an index number for the Rows collection of MyRange. This helps pinpoint which exact row the macro is working with in the current loop. The macro then uses the EntireRow.Insert method to insert a new blank row. Because you want two blank rows, you do this twice.

5. In Step 5, the macro loops back to increment the counter down.

How to use it

To implement this macro, you can copy and paste it into a standard module:

1. **Activate the Visual Basic Editor by pressing Alt+F11.**
2. **Right-click the project/workbook name in the Project window.**
3. **Choose Insert ⇨ Module.**
4. **Type or paste the code.**

Unhiding All Rows and Columns

When you are auditing a spreadsheet that you did not create, you often want to ensure you're getting a full view of what is exactly in the spreadsheet. To do so, you need to ensure that no columns and rows are hidden. This simple macro automatically unhides all rows and columns for you.

How it works

In this macro, you call on the Columns collection and the Rows collection of the worksheet. Each collection has properties that dictate where its objects are hidden or visible. Running this macro unhides every column in the Columns collection and every row in the Rows collection.

```
Sub Macro1()

Columns.EntireColumn.Hidden = False
Rows.EntireRow.Hidden = False

End Sub
```

How to use it

The best place to store this macro is in your Personal Macro Workbook. This way, the macro is always available to you. The Personal Macro Workbook is loaded whenever you start Excel. In the VBE Project window, it is named personal.xlsb.

1. **Activate the Visual Basic Editor by pressing Alt+F11.**
2. **Right-click personal.xlb in the Project window.**

3. **Choose Insert ⇨ Module.**

4. **Type or paste the code.**

If you don't see personal.xlb in your Project window, it means it doesn't exist yet. You'll have to record a macro, using Personal Macro Workbook as the destination.

To record the macro in your Personal Macro Workbook, select the Personal Macro Workbook option in the Record Macro dialog box before you start recording. This option is in the Store Macro In drop-down list. Simply record a couple of cell clicks and then stop recording. You can discard the recorded macro and replace it with this one.

Deleting Blank Rows

Work with Excel long enough, and you'll find out that blank rows can often cause havoc on many levels. They can cause problems with formulas, introduce risk when copying and pasting, and sometimes cause strange behaviors in PivotTables. If you find that you are manually searching out and deleting blank rows in your data sets, this macro can help automate that task.

How it works

In this macro, you are using the UsedRange property of the Activesheet object to define the range you are working with. The UsedRange property gives you a range that encompasses the cells that have been used to enter data. You then establish a counter that starts at the last row of the used range to check if the entire row is empty. If the entire row is indeed empty, you remove the row. You keep doing that same delete for every loop, each time incrementing the counter to the previous row.

```
Sub Macro1()

'Step 1:  Declare your variables.
    Dim MyRange As Range
    Dim iCounter As Long

'Step 2:  Define the target Range.
    Set MyRange = ActiveSheet.UsedRange

'Step 3:  Start reverse looping through the range.
    For iCounter = MyRange.Rows.Count To 1 Step -1
```

```
'Step 4: If entire row is empty then delete it.
      If Application.CountA(Rows(iCounter).EntireRow) = 0 Then
      Rows(iCounter).Delete
      End If

'Step 5: Increment the counter down
    Next iCounter

End Sub
```

1. The macro first declares two variables. The first variable is an Object variable called MyRange. This is an object variable that defines your target range. The other variable is a Long Integer variable called iCounter. This variable serves as an incremental counter.

2. In Step 2, the macro fills the MyRange variable with the UsedRange property of the ActiveSheet object. The UsedRange property gives you a range that encompasses the cells that have been used to enter data. Note that if you wanted to specify an actual range or a named range, you could simply enter its name — Range("MyNamedRange").

3. In this step, the macro sets the parameters for the incremental counter to start at the max count for the range (MyRange.Rows.Count) and end at 1 (the first row of the chosen range). Note that you are using the Step-1 qualifier. Because you specify Step -1, Excel knows you are going to increment the counter backward, moving back one increment on each iteration. In all, Step 3 tells Excel to start at the last row of the chosen range, moving backward until it gets to the first row of the range.

4. When working with a range, you can explicitly call out a specific row in the range by passing a row index number to the Rows collection of the range. For example, Range("D6:D17").Rows(5) points to the fifth row in the range D6:D17.

   In Step 4, the macro uses the iCounter variable as an index number for the Rows collection of MyRange. This helps pinpoint which exact row you are working with in the current loop. The macro checks to see whether the cells in that row are empty. If they are, the macro deletes the entire row.

5. In Step 5, the macro loops back to increment the counter down.

How to use it

The best place to store this macro is in your Personal Macro Workbook. This way, the macro is always available to you. The Personal Macro Workbook is loaded whenever you start Excel. In the VBE Project window, it is named personal.xlsb.

1. **Activate the Visual Basic Editor by pressing Alt+F11.**
2. **Right-click personal.xlb in the Project window.**
3. **Choose Insert ⇨ Module.**
4. **Type or paste the code.**

If you don't see personal.xlb in your Project window, it means it doesn't exist yet. You'll have to record a macro, using Personal Macro Workbook as the destination.

To record the macro in your Personal Macro Workbook, select the Personal Macro Workbook option in the Record Macro dialog box before you start recording. This option is in the Store Macro In drop-down list. Simply record a couple of cell clicks and then stop recording. You can discard the recorded macro and replace it with this one.

Deleting Blank Columns

Just as with blank rows, blank columns also have the potential of causing unforeseen errors. If you find that you are manually searching out and deleting blank columns in your data sets, this macro can automate that task.

How it works

In this macro, you are using the UsedRange property of the ActiveSheet object to define the range to work with. The UsedRange property gives you a range that encompasses the cells that have been used to enter data. You then establish a counter that starts at the last column of the used range, checking if the entire column is empty. If the entire column is indeed empty, you remove the column. You keep doing that same delete for every loop, each time incrementing the counter to the previous column.

```
Sub Macro1()

'Step 1:  Declare your variables.
    Dim MyRange As Range
    Dim iCounter As Long
```

```
'Step 2:  Define the target Range.
    Set MyRange = ActiveSheet.UsedRange

'Step 3:  Start reverse looping through the range.
    For iCounter = MyRange.Columns.Count To 1 Step –1

'Step 4: If entire column is empty then delete it.
    If Application.CountA(Columns(iCounter).EntireColumn) = 0
  Then
        Columns(iCounter).Delete
    End If

'Step 5: Increment the counter down
    Next iCounter

End Sub
```

1. You first declare two variables. The first variable is an object variable called MyRange. This is an Object variable that defines your target range. The other variable is a Long Integer variable called iCounter. This variable serves as your incremental counter.

2. In Step 2, you fill the MyRange variable with the UsedRange property of the ActiveSheet object. The UsedRange property gives you a range that encompasses the cells that have been used to enter data. Note that if you wanted to specify an actual range or a named range, you could simply enter its name — Range("MyNamedRange").

3. In this step, you set the parameters for your incremental counter to start at the max count for the range (MyRange.Columns.Count) and end at 1 (the first row of the chosen range). Note that you are using the Step-1 qualifier. Because you specify Step -1, Excel knows you are going to increment the counter backward; moving back one increment on each iteration. In all, Step 3 tells Excel that you want to start at the last column of the chosen range, moving backward until you get to the first column of the range.

4. When working with a range, you can explicitly call out a specific column in the range by passing a column index number to the Columns collection of the range. For example, Range("A1:D17").Columns(2) points to the second column in the range (column B).

In Step 4, the macro uses the iCounter variable as an index number for the Columns collection of MyRange. This helps pinpoint exactly which column you are working with in the current loop. The macro checks to see whether all the cells in that column are empty. If they are, the macro deletes the entire column.

5. In Step 5, the macro loops back to increment the counter down.

How to use it

The best place to store this macro is in your Personal Macro Workbook. This way, the macro is always available to you. The Personal Macro Workbook is loaded whenever you start Excel. In the VBE Project window, it is named personal.xlsb.

1. **Activate the Visual Basic Editor by pressing Alt+F11.**
2. **Right-click personal.xlb in the Project window.**
3. **Choose Insert ⇨ Module.**
4. **Type or paste the code.**

If you don't see personal.xlb in your Project window, it doesn't exist yet. You'll have to record a macro, using Personal Macro Workbook as the destination.

To record the macro in your Personal Macro Workbook, select the Personal Macro Workbook option in the Record Macro dialog box before you start recording. This option is in the Store Macro In drop-down box. Simply record a couple of cell clicks and then stop recording. You can discard the recorded macro and replace it with this one.

Limiting Range Movement to a Particular Area

Excel gives you the ability to limit the range of cells that a user can scroll through. The macro demonstrated here is something you can easily implement today.

How it works

Excel's ScrollArea property allows you to set the scroll area for a particular worksheet. For example, this statement sets the scroll area on Sheet1 so the user cannot activate any cells outside of A1:M17.

```
Sheets("Sheet1").ScrollArea = "A1:M17"
```

Because this setting is not saved with a workbook, you'll have to reset it each time the workbook is opened. You can accomplish this by implementing this statement in the Workbook_Open event:

```
Private Sub Worksheet_Open()

Sheets("Sheet1").ScrollArea = "A1:M17"

End Sub
```

If for some reason you need to clear the scroll area limits, you can remove the restriction with this statement:

```
ActiveSheet.ScrollArea = ""
```

How to use it

To implement this macro, you will need to copy and paste it into the Workbook_Open event code window. Placing the macro here allows it to run each time the workbook opens.

1. Activate the Visual Basic Editor by pressing Alt+F11 on your keyboard.

2. In the Project window, find your project/workbook name and click the plus sign next to it in order to see all the sheets.

3. Click ThisWorkbook.

4. Select the Open event in the Event dropdown (see Figure 6-4).

5. Type or paste the code.

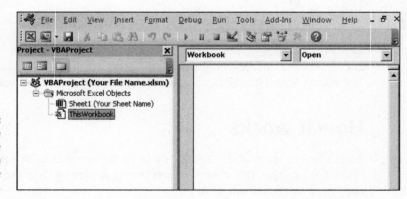

FIGURE 6-4:
Type or paste your code in the Workbook Open event code window.

Selecting and Formatting All Formulas in a Workbook

When auditing an Excel workbook, it's paramount to have a firm grasp of all the formulas in each sheet. This means finding all the formulas, which can be an arduous task if done manually.

However, Excel provides a slick way of finding and tagging all the formulas on a worksheet. The macro in this section exploits this functionality to dynamically find all cells that contain formulas.

How it works

Excel has a set of predefined "special cells" that you can select by using the Go To Special dialog box. To select special cells manually, go to the Home tab on the Ribbon, click the Find & Select dropdown, and then select Go To Special. This opens the Go To Special dialog box shown in Figure 6-5. Alternatively, you can press the F5 key on your keyboard to activate the Go To Special dialog box.

Here, you can select a set of cells based on a few defining attributes. One of those defining attributes is formulas. Selecting the Formulas option effectively selects all cells that contain formulas (see Figure 6-6). At this point, you can color the cells to indicate they contain a formula.

FIGURE 6-5:
The Go To Special dialog box.

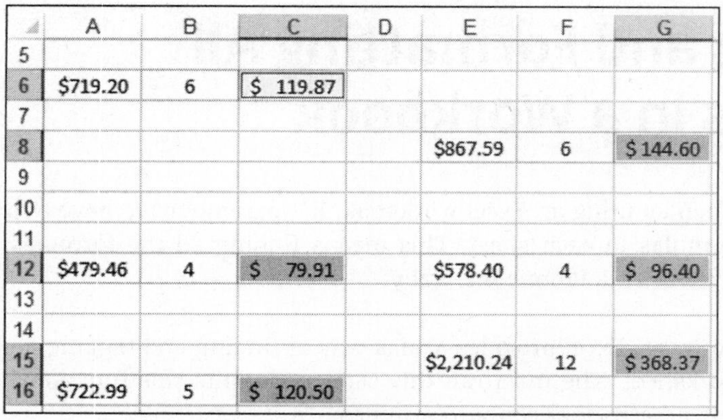

	A	B	C	D	E	F	G
5							
6	$719.20	6	$ 119.87				
7							
8					$867.59	6	$ 144.60
9							
10							
11							
12	$479.46	4	$ 79.91		$578.40	4	$ 96.40
13							
14							
15					$2,210.24	12	$ 368.37
16	$722.99	5	$ 120.50				

FIGURE 6-6: Choosing Formulas in the Go To Special dialog box tells Excel to select all cells containing a formula.

This macro programmatically does the same thing for the entire workbook at the same time. Here, you are using the SpecialCells method of the Cells collection. The SpecialCells method requires a Type parameter that represents the type of special cell. In this case, you use xlCellTypeFormulas.

In short, you are referring to a special range that consists only of cells that contain formulas. You refer to this special range using the With. . .End With statement. This statement tells Excel that any action you perform applies only to the range to which you've pointed. Here, you are coloring the interior of the cells in the chosen range.

```
Sub Macro1()

'Step 1:  Declare your Variables
    Dim ws As Worksheet

'Step 2: Avoid Error if no formulas are found
    On Error Resume Next

'Step 3:  Start looping through worksheets
    For Each ws In ActiveWorkbook.Worksheets

'Step 4:  Select cells and highlight them
    With ws.Cells.SpecialCells(xlCellTypeFormulas)
    .Interior.ColorIndex = 36
    End With

'Step 5: Get next worksheet
    Next ws

End Sub
```

1. Step 1 declares an object called ws. This creates a memory container for each worksheet the macro loops through.

2. If there are no formulas in the spreadsheet, Excel throws an error. To avoid the error, you tell Excel to continue with the macro if an error is triggered.

3. Step 3 begins the looping, telling Excel to evaluate all worksheets in the active workbook.

4. In this step, the macro selects all cells containing formulas, then formats them.

5. In Step 5, you loop back to get the next sheet. After all of the sheets are evaluated, the macro ends.

How to use it

The best place to store this macro is in your Personal Macro Workbook. This way, the macro is always available. The Personal Macro Workbook is loaded whenever you start Excel. In the VBE Project window, it's named personal.xlsb.

1. **Activate the Visual Basic Editor by pressing Alt+F11.**

2. **Right-click personal.xlb in the Project window.**

3. **Choose Insert ⇨ Module.**

4. **Type or paste the code.**

If you don't see personal.xlb in your Project window, it doesn't exist yet. You'll have to record a macro, using Personal Macro Workbook as the destination.

To record the macro in your Personal Macro Workbook, select the Personal Macro Workbook option in the Record Macro dialog box before you start recording. This option is in the Store Macro In drop-down list. Simply record a couple of cell clicks and then stop recording. You can discard the recorded macro and replace it with this one.

Finding and Selecting the First Blank Row or Column

You may often run across scenarios where you have to append rows or columns to an existing data set. When you need to append rows, you will need to be able to find the last used row and then move down to the next empty cell (illustrated in Figure 6-7). Likewise, in situations where you need to append columns, you need to be able to find the last used column and then move over to the next empty cell.

The macros in this section allow you to dynamically find and select the first blank row or column.

	A	B	C	D	E	F	G
5		January	February	March	April	May	June
6	Product 1	72,542	70,916	49,289	3,538	87,442	61,69
7	Product 2	28,187	18,175	71,645	99,211	10,516	91,07
8	Product 3	75,043	8,280	24,234	40,255	77,472	85,50
9	Product 4	4,984	31,805	47,905	45,292	89,648	94,80
10	Product 5	42,680	47,574	35,982	18,860	56,353	91,80
11	Product 6	16,140	3,676	76,712	27,619	68,199	36,28
12	Product 7	97,001	56,895	40,052	79,893	78,703	40,25
13	Product 8	21,227	28,168	97,923	16,585	1,843	98,59
14	Product 9	56,692	17,489	82,649	28,960	68,233	21,50
15	Product 10	64,906	54,698	93,271	29,388	29,712	54,32
16	Product 11	68,672	29,475	58,379	16,282	2,953	69,43
17	Product 12	38,676	1,457	3,833	98,225	99,695	2,71
18							

FIGURE 6-7: You can use a macro to tell Excel to dynamically find the first available cell in a row or column.

How it works

These macros both use the Cells item and the Offset property as key navigation tools.

The Cells item belongs to the Range object. It provides an extremely handy way of selecting ranges through code. It requires only relative row and column positions as parameters. Cells(5,4) translates to row 5, column 4 (or Cell D5). Cells(16, 4) translates to row 16, column 4 (or cell D16).

In addition to passing hard numbers to the Cells item, you can also pass expressions.

Cells(Rows.Count, 1) is the same as selecting the last row in the spreadsheet and the first column in the spreadsheet. In Excel 2007 and later, that essentially translates to cell A1048576.

Cells(1, Columns.Count) is the same as selecting the first row in the spreadsheet and the last column in the spreadsheet. In Excel 2007 and later, that translates to cell XFD1.

Combining the Cells statement with the End property allows you to jump to the last used row or column. This statement is equivalent to going to cell A1048576 and pressing Ctrl+Shift+Up Arrow on the keyboard. When you run this statement, Excel automatically jumps to the last used row in column A:

```
Cells(Rows.Count, 1).End(xlUp).Select
```

Running this statement is equivalent to going to cell XFD1 and pressing Ctrl+Shift+Left Arrow on the keyboard. This gets you to the last used column in row 1:

```
Cells(1, Columns.Count).End(xlToLeft).Select
```

When you get to the last used row or column, you can use the Offset property to move down or over to the next blank row or column.

The Offset property uses a row and column index to specify a changing base point.

For example, this statement selects cell A2 because the row index in the offset is moving the row base point by one:

```
Range("A1").Offset(1, 0).Select
```

This statement selects cell C4 because the row and column indexes move the base point by three rows and two columns:

```
Range("A1").Offset(3, 2).Select
```

Pulling all these concepts together, you can create a macro that selects the first blank row or column.

This macro selects the first blank row:

```
Sub Macro1()

'Step 1:  Declare Your Variables.
    Dim LastRow As Long

'Step 2:  Capture the last used row number.
    LastRow = Cells(Rows.Count, 1).End(xlUp).Row

'Step 3:  Select the next row down
    Cells(LastRow, 1).Offset(1, 0).Select

End Sub
```

1. You first declare a Long Integer variable called LastRow to hold the row number of the last used row.

2. In Step 2, you capture the last used row by starting at the very last row in the worksheet and using the End property to jump up to the first non-empty cell (the equivalent of going to cell A1048576 and pressing Ctrl+Shift+Up Arrow on the keyboard).

3. In this step, you use the Offset property to move down one row and select the first blank cell in column A.

This macro selects the first blank column:

```
Sub Macro1()

'Step 1:  Declare Your Variables.
    Dim LastColumn As Long

'Step 2:  Capture the last used column number.
    LastColumn = Cells(5, Columns.Count).End(xlToLeft).Column

'Step 3:  Select the next column over
    Cells(5, LastColumn).Offset(0, 1).Select

End Sub
```

1. You first declare a Long Integer variable called LastColumn to hold the column number of the last used column.

2. In Step 2, you capture the last used column by starting at the very last column in the worksheet and using the End property to jump up to the first non-empty column (the equivalent of going to cell XFD5 and pressing Ctrl+Shift+Left Arrow on the keyboard).

3. In this step, you use the Offset property to move over one column and select the first blank column in row 5.

How to use it

You can implement these macros by pasting them into a standard module:

1. Activate the Visual Basic Editor by pressing Alt+F11.

2. Right-click the project/workbook name in the Project window.

3. Choose Insert ⇨ Module.

4. Type or paste the code.

Chapter **7**

Manipulating Data with Macros

When working with information in Excel, you often have to transform the data in some way. Transforming it generally means cleaning, standardizing, or shaping data in ways that are appropriate for your work. This can mean anything from cleaning out extra spaces, to padding numbers with zeros, to filtering data for certain criteria.

This chapter shows you some of the more useful macros you can use to dynamically transform the data in your workbooks. If you want, you can combine these macros into one, running each piece of code in a sequence that essentially automates the scrubbing and shaping of your data.

Copying and Pasting a Range

One of the basic data manipulation skills you'll need to learn is copying and pasting a range of data. It's fairly easy to do this manually. Luckily, it's just as easy to copy and paste via VBA.

How it works

In this macro, you use the Copy method of the Range object to copy data from D6:D17 and paste to L6:L17. Note the use of the Destination argument. This argument tells Excel where to paste the data.

```
Sub Macro1()

Sheets("Sheet1").Range("D6:D17").Copy _
Destination:=Sheets("Sheet1").Range("L6:L17")

End Sub
```

When working with your spreadsheet, you likely often have to copy formulas and paste them as values. To do this in a macro, you can use the PasteSpecial method. In this example, you copy the formulas in F6:F17 to M6:M17. Notice that you are not only pasting as values using xlPasteValues, but you are also using xlPasteFormats to apply the formatting from the copied range.

```
Sub Macro1()

Sheets("Sheet1").Range("F6:F17").Copy
Sheets("Sheet1").Range("M6:M17").PasteSpecial xlPasteValues
Sheets("Sheet1").Range("M6:M17").PasteSpecial xlPasteFormats

End Sub
```

REMEMBER

Keep in mind that the ranges specified here are for demonstration purposes. Alter the ranges to suit the data in your worksheet.

How to use it

To implement this macro, you can copy and paste it into a standard module:

1. **Activate the Visual Basic Editor by pressing Alt+F11 on your keyboard.**
2. **Right-click the project/workbook name in the Project window.**
3. **Choose Insert ⇨ Module.**
4. **Type or paste the code.**

Converting All Formulas in a Range to Values

In some situations, you may want to apply formulas in a certain workbook, but you don't necessarily want to keep or distribute the formulas with your workbook. In these situations, you may want to convert all the formulas in a given range to values.

How it works

In this macro, you essentially use two Range object variables. One of the variables captures the scope of data you are working with, whereas the other is used to hold each individual cell as you go through the range. Then you use the For Each statement to activate or bring each cell in the target range into focus. Every time a cell is activated, you check to see whether the cell contains a formula. If it does, you replace the formula with the value shown in the cell.

```
Sub Macro1()

'Step 1: Declare your variables
    Dim MyRange As Range
    Dim MyCell As Range


'Step 2: Save the Workbook before changing cells?
    Select Case MsgBox("Can't Undo this action. " & _
        "Save Workbook First?", vbYesNoCancel)
    Case Is = vbYes
    ThisWorkbook.Save
```

```
      Case Is = vbCancel
      Exit Sub
   End Select


   'Step 3: Define the target Range.
   Set MyRange = Selection


   'Step 4: Start looping through the range.
   For Each MyCell In MyRange


   'Step 5: If cell has formula, set to the value shown.
     If MyCell.HasFormula Then
     MyCell.Formula = MyCell.Value
     End If



   'Step 6: Get the next cell in the range
     Next MyCell


End Sub
```

1. Step 1 declares two Range object variables, one called MyRange to hold the entire target range, and the other called MyCell to hold each cell in the range as you enumerate through the cells one by one.

2. When you run a macro, it destroys the undo stack. This means you can't undo the changes a macro makes. Because you are actually changing data, you need to give yourself the option of saving the workbook before running the macro. This is what Step 2 does.

Here, you call up a message box that asks if you want to save the workbook first. It then gives you three choices: Yes, No, and Cancel. Clicking Yes saves the workbook and continues with the macro. Clicking Cancel exits the procedure without running the macro. Clicking No runs the macro without saving the workbook.

3. Step 3 fills the MyRange variable with the target range. In this example, you use the selected range — the range that was selected on the spreadsheet. You can easily set the MyRange variable to a specific range such as Range("A1:Z100"). Also, if your target range is a named range, you could simply enter its name: Range("MyNamedRange").

4. This step starts looping through each cell in the target range, activating each cell as it goes through.

5. After a cell is activated, the macro uses the HasFormula property to check whether the cell contains a formula. If it does, you set the cell to equal the value shown in the cell. This effectively replaces the formula with a hard-coded value.

6. Step 6 loops back to get the next cell. After all cells in the target range are activated, the macro ends.

How to use it

To implement this macro, you can copy and paste it into a standard module:

1. **Activate the Visual Basic Editor by pressing Alt+F11 on your keyboard.**

2. **Right-click the project/workbook name in the Project window.**

3. **Choose Insert ⇨ Module.**

Text to Columns on All Columns

When you import data from other sources, you may sometimes wind up with cells where the number values are formatted as text. You typically recognize this problem because no matter what you do, you can't format the numbers in these cells to numeric, currency, or percentage formats. You may also see a smart tag on the cells (see Figure 7-1) that tells you the cell is formatted as text.

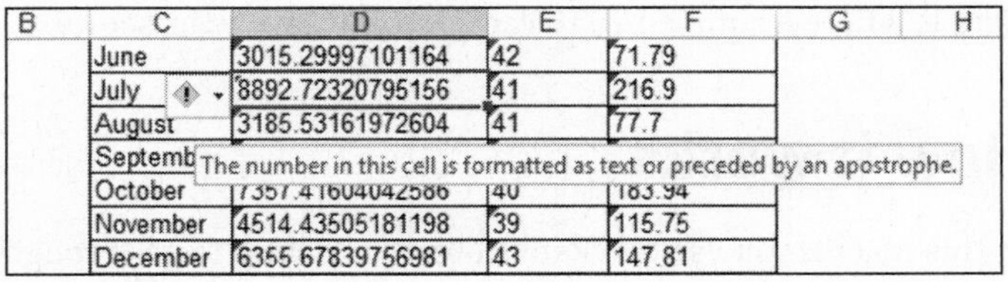

FIGURE 7-1:
Imported
numbers are
sometimes
formatted as text.

B	C	D	E	F	G	H
	June	3015.29997101164	42	71.79		
	July	8892.72320795156	41	216.9		
	August	3185.53161972604	41	77.7		
	Septemb	The number in this cell is formatted as text or preceded by an apostrophe.				
	October	7357.41604042586	40	183.94		
	November	4514.43505181198	39	115.75		
	December	6355.67839756981	43	147.81		

It's easy enough to fix this manually by clicking on the Text to Columns command on the Data tab (Figure 7-2). This opens the Text to Columns dialog box shown in Figure 7-3. There is no need to go through all the steps in this Wizard; simply click the Finish button to apply the fix.

FIGURE 7-2:
Click on the Text
to Columns
command.

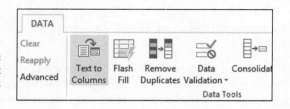

DATA

Clear

Reapply

Advanced

Text to Columns

Flash Fill

Remove Duplicates

Data Validation

Consolidat

Data Tools

FIGURE 7-3:
Clicking Finish in
the Text to
Columns dialog
box corrects
incorrectly
formatted
numbers.

Convert Text to Columns Wizard - Step 1 of 3

The Text Wizard has determined that your data is Delimited.

If this is correct, choose Next, or choose the data type that best describes your data.

Original data type

Choose the file type that best describes your data:

⦿ Delimited   - Characters such as commas or tabs separate each field.

○ Fixed width - Fields are aligned in columns with spaces between each field.

Preview of selected data:

```
5 Revenue
6 3224.1791553785
7 2758.83834214959
8 1301.70489760339
9 2316.69407974405
```

Cancel   < Back   Next >   Finish

Again, this is a fairly simple action. The problem, however, is that Excel doesn't let you perform the Text to Columns fix on multiple columns. You have to apply this fix one column at a time. This can be a real nuisance if you've got this issue in many columns.

Here is where a simple macro can help you save your sanity.

How it works

In this macro, you use two Range object variables to go through your target range, leveraging the For Each statement to activate each cell in the target range. Every time a cell is activated, you simply reset the value of the cell. This in effect does the same thing as the Text to Columns command.

```
Sub Macro1()

'Step 1: Declare your variables
    Dim MyRange As Range
    Dim MyCell As Range
```

```
'Step 2: Save the Workbook before changing cells?
  Select Case MsgBox("Can't Undo this action. " & _
          "Save Workbook First?", vbYesNoCancel)

    Case Is = vbYes
    ThisWorkbook.Save

    Case Is = vbCancel
    Exit Sub
  End Select


'Step 3: Define the target Range.
  Set MyRange = Selection


'Step 4: Start looping through the range.
  For Each MyCell In MyRange


'Step 5: Reset the cell value.
  If Not IsEmpty(MyCell) Then
  MyCell.Value = MyCell.Value
  End If


'Step 6: Get the next cell in the range
  Next MyCell

End Sub
```

1. Step 1 declares two Range object variables, one called MyRange to hold the entire target range, and the other called MyCell to hold each cell in the range as the macro enumerates through the cells one by one.

2. When you run a macro, it destroys the undo stack. This means you can't undo the changes a macro makes. Because the macro is actually changing data, you need to give yourself the option of saving the workbook before running the macro. This is what Step 2 does. Here, you call up a message box that asks if you want to save the workbook first. It gives you three choices: Yes, No, and Cancel. Clicking Yes saves the workbook and continues with the macro. Clicking Cancel exits the procedure without running the macro. Clicking No runs the macro without saving the workbook.

3. Step 3 fills the MyRange variable with the target range. In this example, you are using the selected range — the range that was selected on the spreadsheet. You can easily set the MyRange variable to a specific range such as Range("A1:Z100"). Also, if your target range is a named range, you could simply enter its name: Range("MyNamedRange").

4. Step 4 starts looping through each cell in the target range, activating each cell as it goes through.

5. After a cell is activated, the macro uses the IsEmpty function to make sure the cell is not empty. You do this to save a little on performance by skipping the cell if there is nothing in it. You then simply reset the cell to its own value. This removes any formatting mismatch.

6. Step 6 loops back to get the next cell. After all cells in the target range are activated, the macro ends.

How to use it

To implement this macro, you can copy and paste it into a standard module:

1. Activate the Visual Basic Editor by pressing Alt+F11 on your keyboard.

2. Right-click the project/workbook name in the Project window.

3. Choose Insert ➪ Module.

4. Type or paste the code.

Converting Trailing Minus Signs

Legacy and mainframe systems are notorious for outputting trailing minus signs. In other words, instead of a number such as –142, some systems output 142–. This obviously wreaks havoc on your spreadsheet — especially if you need to perform mathematic operations on the data. This nifty macro goes through a target range and fixes all the negative minus signs so that they show up in front of the number rather than the end.

How it works

In this macro, you use two Range object variables to go through your target range, leveraging the For Each statement to activate each cell in the target range. Every time a cell is activated, you convert the value of the cell into a Double numeric data type by using the Cdbl function. The Double data type forces any negative signs to show at the front of the number.

```
Sub Macro1()

'Step 1: Declare your variables
  Dim MyRange As Range
  Dim MyCell As Range


'Step 2: Save the Workbook before changing cells?
  Select Case MsgBox("Can't Undo this action. " & _
          "Save Workbook First?", vbYesNoCancel)
    Case Is = vbYes
    ThisWorkbook.Save

    Case Is = vbCancel
    Exit Sub
  End Select


'Step 3: Define the target Range.
  Set MyRange = Selection


'Step 4: Start looping through the range.
  For Each MyCell In MyRange


'Step 5: Convert the value to a Double.
  If IsNumeric(MyCell) Then
    MyCell = CDbl(MyCell)
  End If


'Step 6: Get the next cell in the range
  Next MyCell

End Sub
```

1. Step 1 declares two Range object variables, one called MyRange to hold the entire target range, and the other called MyCell to hold each cell in the range as you enumerate through the cells one by one.

2. When you run a macro, it destroys the undo stack. This means you can't undo the changes a macro makes. Because you are actually changing data, you need to give yourself the option of saving the workbook before running the macro. This is what Step 2 does. Here, you call up a message box that asks if you want to save the workbook first. It then gives you three choices: Yes, No, and Cancel. Clicking Yes saves the workbook and continues with the macro. Clicking Cancel exits the procedure without running the macro. Clicking No runs the macro without saving the workbook.

3. Step 3 fills the MyRange variable with the target range. In this example, you use the selected range — the range that was selected on the spreadsheet. You can easily set the MyRange variable to a specific range such as Range("A1:Z100"). Also, if your target range is a named range, you could simply enter its name — Range("MyNamedRange").

4. Step 4 starts looping through each cell in the target range, activating each cell as it goes through.

5. After a cell is activated, Step 5 uses the IsNumeric function to check to see if the value can be evaluated as a number. This is to ensure you don't affect textual fields. You then pass the cell's value through the Cdbl function. This effectively converts the value to the Double numeric data type, forcing the minus sign to the front.

6. Step 6 loops back to get the next cell. After all cells in the target range are activated, the macro ends.

TIP

Because you define the target range as the current selection, you want to be sure to select the area where your data exists before running this code. In other words, you wouldn't want to select the entire worksheet. Otherwise, every empty cell in the spreadsheet would be filled with a zero. Of course, you can ensure this is never a problem by explicitly defining the target range, such as Set MyRange = Range("A1:Z100").

How to use it

To implement this macro, you can copy and paste it into a standard module:

1. **Activate the Visual Basic Editor by pressing Alt+F11 on your keyboard.**

2. **Right-click the project/workbook name in the Project window.**

3. **Choose Insert ⇨ Module.**

4. **Type or paste the code.**

Trimming Spaces from All Cells in a Range

A frequent problem when you import dates from other sources is leading or trailing spaces. That is, the imported values have spaces at the beginning or end of the cell. This obviously makes it difficult to do things like VLOOKUP or sorting. Here is a macro that makes it easy to search for and remove extra spaces in your cells.

How it works

In this macro, you enumerate through a target range, passing each cell in that range through the Trim function.

```
Sub Macro1()

'Step 1: Declare your variables
  Dim MyRange As Range
  Dim MyCell As Range


'Step 2: Save the Workbook before changing cells?
  Select Case MsgBox("Can't Undo this action. " & _
          "Save Workbook First?", vbYesNoCancel)
    Case Is = vbYes
    ThisWorkbook.Save

    Case Is = vbCancel
    Exit Sub
  End Select


'Step 3: Define the target Range.
  Set MyRange = Selection


'Step 4: Start looping through the range.
  For Each MyCell In MyRange


'Step 5: Trim the Spaces.
  If Not IsEmpty(MyCell) Then
  MyCell = Trim(MyCell)
  End If
```

```
'Step 6: Get the next cell in the range
  Next MyCell

End Sub
```

1. Step 1 declares two Range object variables, one called MyRange to hold the entire target range, and the other called MyCell to hold each cell in the range as the macro enumerates through the cells one by one.

2. When you run a macro, it destroys the undo stack. You can't undo the changes a macro makes. Because you are actually changing data, you need to give yourself the option of saving the workbook before running the macro. Step 2 does this. Here, you call up a message box that asks if you want to save the workbook first. It then gives you three choices: Yes, No, and Cancel. Clicking Yes saves the workbook and continues with the macro. Clicking Cancel exits the procedure without running the macro. Clicking No runs the macro without saving the workbook.

3. Step 3 fills the MyRange variable with the target range. In this example, you use the selected range — the range that was selected on the spreadsheet. You can easily set the MyRange variable to a specific range such as Range("A1:Z100"). Also, if your target range is a named range, you could simply enter its name — Range("MyNamedRange").

4. Step 4 starts looping through each cell in the target range, activating each cell as it goes through.

5. After a cell is activated, the macro uses the IsEmpty function to make sure the cell is not empty. You do this to save a little on performance by skipping the cell if there is nothing in it. You then pass the value of that cell to the Trim function. The Trim function is a native Excel function that removes leading and trailing spaces.

6. Step 6 loops back to get the next cell. After all cells in the target range are activated, the macro ends.

How to use it

To implement this macro, you can copy and paste it into a standard module:

1. **Activate the Visual Basic Editor by pressing Alt+F11 on your keyboard.**

2. **Right-click the project/workbook name in the Project window.**

3. **Choose Insert ⇨ Module.**

4. **Type or paste the code.**

Truncating ZIP Codes to the Left Five

U.S. ZIP codes come in either five or ten digits. Some systems output a 10-digit ZIP code, which, for the purposes of a lot of Excel analysis, is too many. A common data standardization task is to truncate ZIP codes to the left five digits. Many of us use formulas to do this, but if you are constantly cleaning up your ZIP codes, the macro outlined in this section can help automate that task.

It's important to note that although this macro solves a specific problem, the concept of truncating data remains useful for many other types of data cleanup activities.

How it works

This macro uses the Left function to extract the left five characters of each ZIP code in the given range.

```
Sub Macro1()

'Step 1: Declare your variables
    Dim MyRange As Range
    Dim MyCell As Range


'Step 2: Save the Workbook before changing cells?
    Select Case MsgBox("Can't Undo this action. " & _
            "Save Workbook First?", vbYesNoCancel)
    Case Is = vbYes
    ThisWorkbook.Save

    Case Is = vbCancel
    Exit Sub
    End Select


'Step 3: Define the target Range.
    Set MyRange = Selection


'Step 4: Start looping through the range.
    For Each MyCell In MyRange
```

```
'Step 5: Extract out the left 5 characters.
  If Not IsEmpty(MyCell) Then
  MyCell = Left(MyCell, 5)
  End If



'Step 6: Get the next cell in the range
  Next MyCell

End Sub
```

1. Step 1 declares two Range object variables, one called MyRange to hold the entire target range, and the other called MyCell to hold each cell in the range as the macro enumerates through the cells one by one.

2. When you run a macro, it destroys the undo stack. This means you can't undo the changes a macro makes. Because you are actually changing data, you need to give yourself the option of saving the workbook before running the macro. This is what Step 2 does. Here, you call up a message box that asks if you want to save the workbook first. It gives you three choices: Yes, No, and Cancel. Clicking Yes saves the workbook and continues with the macro. Clicking Cancel exits the procedure without running the macro. Clicking No runs the macro without saving the workbook.

3. Step 3 fills the MyRange variable with the target range. In this example, you use the selected range — the range that was selected on the spreadsheet. You can easily set the MyRange variable to a specific range such as Range("A1:Z100"). Also, if your target range is a named range, you could simply enter its name: Range("MyNamedRange").

4. Step 4 starts looping through each cell in the target range, activating each cell.

5. After a cell is activated, Step 5 uses the IsEmpty function to make sure the cell is not empty. You do this to save a little on performance by skipping the cell if there is nothing in it. You then pass the cell's value through Left function. The Left function allows you to extract out the *n*th leftmost characters in a string. In this scenario, you need the left five characters in order to truncate the ZIP code to five digits.

6. Step 6 loops back to get the next cell. After all of the cells in the target range are activated, the macro ends.

TIP

As you may have guessed, you can also use the Right function to extract out the *n*th rightmost characters in a string. As an example, it's not uncommon to work with product numbers where the first few characters hold a particular attribute or meaning, whereas the last few characters point to the actual product (as in 100-4567). You can extract out the actual product by using Right(Product_Number, 4).

REMEMBER

Because the target range is defined as the current selection, you need to select the area where your data exists before running this code. In other words, you wouldn't want to select cells that don't conform to the logic you placed in this macro. Otherwise, every cell you select is truncated, whether you mean it to be or not. Of course, you can ensure this is never a problem by explicitly defining the target range, such as Set MyRange = Range("A1:Z100").

How to use it

To implement this macro, you can copy and paste it into a standard module:

1. **Activate the Visual Basic Editor by pressing Alt+F11 on your keyboard.**
2. **Right-click the project/workbook name in the Project window.**
3. **Choose Insert ⇨ Module.**
4. **Type or paste the code.**

Padding Cells with Zeros

Many systems require unique identifiers (such as customer number, order number, or product number) to have a fixed character length. For example, you frequently see customer numbers that look like this: 00000045478. This concept of taking a unique identifier and forcing it to have a fixed length is typically referred to as *padding*. The number is padded with zeros to achieve the prerequisite character length.

It's a pain to do this manually in Excel. However, with a macro, padding numbers with zeros is a breeze.

TIP

Some Excel gurus are quick to point out that you can apply a custom number format to pad numbers with zeros by going to the Format Cells dialog box, selecting Custom on the Number tab, and entering "0000000000" as the custom format.

The problem with this solution is that the padding you get is cosmetic only. A quick glance at the formula bar reveals that the data actually remains numeric without the padding (it does not become textual). So if you copy and paste the data into another platform or non–Excel table, you lose the cosmetic padding.

How it works

Say that all of your customer numbers need to be ten characters long. So for each customer number, you need to pad the number with enough zeros to get it to ten characters. This macro does just that.

As you review this macro, keep in mind that you need to change the padding logic in Step 5 to match your situation.

```vba
Sub Macro1()

'Step 1: Declare your variables
   Dim MyRange As Range
   Dim MyCell As Range


'Step 2: Save the Workbook before changing cells?
   Select Case MsgBox("Can't Undo this action. " & _
            "Save Workbook First?", vbYesNoCancel)

      Case Is = vbYes
      ThisWorkbook.Save

      Case Is = vbCancel
      Exit Sub
   End Select


'Step 3: Define the target Range.
   Set MyRange = Selection


'Step 4: Start looping through the range.
   For Each MyCell In MyRange


'Step 5: Pad with ten zeros then take the right 10
   If Not IsEmpty(MyCell) Then

      MyCell.NumberFormat = "@"
      MyCell = "0000000000" & MyCell
      MyCell = Right(MyCell, 10)

   End If
```

```
'Step 6: Get the next cell in the range
  Next MyCell

End Sub
```

1. Step 1 declares two Range object variables, one called MyRange to hold the entire target range, and the other called MyCell to hold each cell in the range as the macro enumerates through the cells one by one.

2. When you run a macro, it destroys the undo stack, meaning that you can't undo the changes a macro makes. Because you are actually changing data, you need to give yourself the option of saving the workbook before running the macro. This is what Step 2 does. Here, you call up a message box that asks if you want to save the workbook first. It then gives you three choices: Yes, No, and Cancel. Clicking Yes saves the workbook and continues with the macro. Clicking Cancel exits the procedure without running the macro. Clicking No runs the macro without saving the workbook.

3. Step 3 fills the MyRange variable with the target range. In this example, you use the selected range — the range that was selected on the spreadsheet. You can easily set the MyRange variable to a specific range such as Range("A1:Z100"). Also, if your target range is a named range, you could simply enter its name: Range("MyNamedRange").

4. Step 4 starts looping through each cell in the target range, activating each cell.

5. After a cell is activated, Step 5 uses the IsEmpty function to make sure the cell is not empty. You do this to save a little on performance by skipping the cell if there is nothing in it.

   The macro then ensures that the cell is formatted as text. This is because a cell formatted as a number cannot have leading zeros — Excel would automatically remove them. On the next line, you use the NumberFormat property to specify that the format is @. This symbol indicates text formatting.

   Next, the macro concatenates the cell value with ten zeros. You do this simply by explicitly entering ten zeros in the code, and then using the ampersand (&) to combine them with the cell value.

   Finally, Step 5 uses the Right function to extract out the ten rightmost characters. This effectively gives us the cell value, padded with enough zeros to make ten characters.

6. Step 6 loops back to get the next cell. After all of the cells in the target range are activated, the macro ends.

How to use it

To implement this macro, you can copy and paste it into a standard module:

1. **Activate the Visual Basic Editor by pressing Alt+F11 on your keyboard.**
2. **Right-click the project/workbook name in the Project window.**
3. **Choose Insert ➪ Module.**
4. **Type or paste the code.**

Replacing Blanks Cells with a Value

In some analyses, blank cells can cause all kinds of trouble. They can cause sorting issues, they can prevent proper auto filling, they can cause your PivotTables to apply the Count function rather than the Sum function, and so on.

Blanks aren't always bad, but if they are causing you trouble, you can use this macro to quickly replace the blanks in a given range with a value that indicates a blank cell.

How it works

This macro enumerates through the cells in the given range and then uses the Len function to check the length of the value in the active cell. Blank cells have a character length of 0. If the length is indeed 0, the macro enters a 0 in the cell, effectively replacing the blanks.

```
Sub Macro1()

'Step 1: Declare your variables
  Dim MyRange As Range
  Dim MyCell As Range


'Step 2: Save the Workbook before changing cells?
  Select Case MsgBox("Can't Undo this action. " & _
           "Save Workbook First?", vbYesNoCancel)
    Case Is = vbYes
    ThisWorkbook.Save
```

```
      Case Is = vbCancel
        Exit Sub
    End Select



 'Step 3: Define the target Range.
    Set MyRange = Selection



 'Step 4: Start looping through the range.
    For Each MyCell In MyRange



 'Step 5: Ensure the cell has Text formatting.
    If IsEmpty(MyCell.Value) Or Len(MyCell.Value) = 0 Then
    MyCell = 0
    End If



 'Step 6: Get the next cell in the range
    Next MyCell

End Sub
```

1. You first declare two Range object variables, one called MyRange to hold the entire target range, and the other called MyCell to hold each cell in the range as the macro enumerates through the cells one by one.

2. When you run a macro, it destroys the undo stack. This means you can't undo the changes a macro makes. Because you are actually changing data, you need to give yourself the option of saving the workbook before running the macro. This is what Step 2 does. Here, you call up a message box that asks if you want to save the workbook first. It then gives you three choices: Yes, No, and Cancel. Clicking Yes saves the workbook and continues with the macro. Clicking Cancel exits the procedure without running the macro. Clicking No runs the macro without saving the workbook.

3. Step 3 fills the MyRange variable with the target range. This example uses the selected range — the range that was selected on the spreadsheet. You can easily set the MyRange variable to a specific range such as Range("A1:Z100"). Also, if your target range is a named range, you could simply enter its name: Range("MyNamedRange").

4. Step 4 starts looping through each cell in the target range, activating each cell.

5. After a cell is activated, you use the IsEmpty function to make sure the cell is not empty. You do this to save a little on performance by skipping the cell if nothing is in it. You then use the Len function, which is a standard Excel function that returns a number corresponding to the length of the string being evaluated. If the cell is blank, the length will be 0, at which point, the macro replaces the blank with a 0. You could obviously replace the blank with any value you want (N/A, TBD, No Data, and so on).

6. Step 6 loops back to get the next cell. After all of the cells in the target range are activated, the macro ends.

REMEMBER

Because the target range is defined as the current selection, you want to be sure to select the area where your data exists before running this code. That is to say, you wouldn't want to select the entire worksheet. Otherwise, every empty cell in the spreadsheet would be filled with a zero. Of course, you can ensure this is never a problem by explicitly defining a range, such as Set MyRange = Range("A1:Z100").

How to use it

To implement this macro, you can copy and paste it into a standard module:

1. **Activate the Visual Basic Editor by pressing Alt+F11 on your keyboard.**

2. **Right-click the project/workbook name in the Project window.**

3. **Choose Insert ⇨ Module.**

4. **Type or paste the code.**

Appending Text to the Left or Right of Your Cells

Every so often, you come upon a situation where you need to attach data to the beginning or end of the cells in a range. For example, you may need to add an area code to a set of phone numbers. The macro demonstrates how you can automate the data standardization tasks that require appending data to values.

How it works

This macro uses two Range object variables to go through the target range, leveraging the For Each statement to activate each cell in the target range. Every time a cell is activated, the macro attaches an area code to the beginning of the cell value.

```vba
Sub Macro1()

'Step 1: Declare your variables
    Dim MyRange As Range
    Dim MyCell As Range


'Step 2: Save the Workbook before changing cells?
    Select Case MsgBox("Can't Undo this action. " & _
            "Save Workbook First?", vbYesNoCancel)
      Case Is = vbYes
      ThisWorkbook.Save

      Case Is = vbCancel
      Exit Sub
    End Select


'Step 3: Define the target Range.
    Set MyRange = Selection


'Step 4: Start looping through the range.
    For Each MyCell In MyRange


'Step 5: Ensure the cell has Text formatting.
    If Not IsEmpty(MyCell) Then
    MyCell = "(972) " & MyCell
    End If


'Step 6: Get the next cell in the range
    Next MyCell

End Sub
```

1. Step 1 declares two Range object variables, one called MyRange to hold the entire target range, and the other called MyCell to hold each cell in the range as you enumerate through the cells one by one.

2. When you run a macro, it destroys the undo stack. This means you can't undo the changes a macro makes. Because you are actually changing data, you need to give yourself the option of saving the workbook before running the macro. This is what Step 2 does. Here, you call up a message box that asks if you want to save the workbook first. It then gives you three choices: Yes, No, and Cancel. Clicking Yes saves the workbook and continues with the macro. Clicking Cancel exits the procedure without running the macro. Clicking No runs the macro without saving the workbook.

3. Step 3 fills the MyRange variable with the target range. This example uses the selected range — the range that was selected on the spreadsheet. You can easily set the MyRange variable to a specific range such as Range("A1:Z100"). Also, if your target range is a named range, you could simply enter its name: Range("MyNamedRange").

4. Step 4 starts looping through each cell in the target range, activating each cell as it goes through.

5. After a cell is activated, you use the ampersand (&) to combine an area code with the cell value. If you need to append text to the end of the cell value, you would simply place the ampersand and the text at the end. For example, MyCell = MyCell & "Added Text".

6. Step 6 loops back to get the next cell. After all of the cells in the target range are activated, the macro ends.

How to use it

To implement this macro, you can copy and paste it into a standard module:

1. Activate the Visual Basic Editor by pressing Alt+F11 on your keyboard.

2. Right-click the project/workbook name in the Project window.

3. Choose Insert ⇨ Module.

4. Type or paste the code.

Cleaning Up Non-Printing Characters

Sometimes you have non-printing characters in your data such as line feeds, carriage returns, and non-breaking spaces. These characters often need to be removed before you can use the data for serious analysis.

Now, anyone who has worked with Excel for more than a month knows about the Find and Replace functionality. You may have even recorded a macro while performing a Find and Replace (a recorded macro is an excellent way to automate your find and replace procedures). So your initial reaction may be to simply find and replace these characters. The problem is that these non-printing characters are for the most part invisible and thus difficult to clean up with the normal Find and Replace routines. The easiest way to clean them up is through VBA.

If you find yourself struggling with those pesky invisible characters, use this general-purpose macro to find and remove all the non-printing characters.

How it works

This macro is a relatively simple Find and Replace routine. You are using the Replace method, telling Excel what to find and what to replace it with. This is similar to the syntax you would see when recording a macro while manually performing a Find and Replace.

The difference is that instead of hard-coding the text to find, this macro uses character codes to specify your search text.

Every character has an underlying ASCII code, similar to a serial number. For example, the lowercase letter *a* has an ASCII code of 97. The lowercase letter *c* has an ASCII code of 99. Likewise, invisible characters also have a code:

>> The line feed character code is 10.

>> The carriage return character code is 13.

>> The non-breaking space character code is 160.

This macro utilizes the Replace method, passing each character's ASCII code as the search item. Each character code is then replaced with an empty string:

```
Sub Macro1()

'Step 1: Remove Line Feeds
    ActiveSheet.UsedRange.Replace What:=Chr(10), Replacement:=""

'Step 2: Remove Carriage Returns
    ActiveSheet.UsedRange.Replace What:=Chr(13), Replacement:=""
```

```
'Step 3: Remove Non-Breaking Spaces
  ActiveSheet.UsedRange.Replace What:=Chr(160), Replacement:=""

End Sub
```

1. Step 1 looks for and removes the Line Feed character. The code for this character is 10. You can identify the code 10 character by passing id through the Chr function. After Chr(10) is identified as the search item, this step then passes an empty string to the Replacement argument.

   Note the use of ActiveSheet.UsedRange. This essentially tells Excel to look in all the cells that have had data entered into them. You can replace the UsedRange object with an actual range if needed.

2. Step 2 finds and removes the carriage return character.

3. Step 3 finds and removes the non-breaking spaces character.

TIP

The characters covered in this macro are only a few of many non-printing characters. However, these are the ones you most commonly run into. If you work with others, you can simply add a new line of code, specifying the appropriate character code. You can enter "ASCII Code Listing" in any search engine to see a list of the codes for various characters.

How to use it

To implement this macro, you can copy and paste it into a standard module:

1. **Activate the Visual Basic Editor by pressing Alt+F11 on your keyboard.**

2. **Right-click the project/workbook name in the Project window.**

3. **Choose Insert ⇨ Module.**

4. **Type or paste the code.**

Highlighting Duplicates in a Range of Data

Ever wanted to expose the duplicate values in a range? The macro in this section does just that. There are many manual ways to find and highlight duplicates — ways involving formulas, conditional formatting, sorting, and so on. However, all these manual methods take setup and some level of maintenance as the data changes.

This macro simplifies the task, allowing you find and highlight duplicates in your data with a click of the mouse (see Figure 7-4).

FIGURE 7-4:
This Macro
dynamically
finds and
highlights the
duplicate values
in a selected
range.

Customers	Product Number
0000011112	C5567
0000046047	P8844
0000046047	R7609
0000047329	P8895
0000056510	P8867
0000058682	M2244
0000058682	C3322
0000058682	R7786
0000086362	M7765
0000086362	C8874
0000089129	M3345
0000090210	C5521

How it works

This macro enumerates through the cells in the target range, leveraging the For Each statement to activate each cell one at a time. It then uses the CountIf function to count the number of times the value in the active cell occurs in the range selected. If that number is greater than 1, it formats the cell yellow.

```
Sub Macro1()

'Step 1: Declare your variables
   Dim MyRange As Range
   Dim MyCell As Range


'Step 2: Define the target Range.
   Set MyRange = Selection

'Step 3: Start looping through the range.
   For Each MyCell In MyRange


'Step 4: Ensure the cell has Text formatting.
   If WorksheetFunction.CountIf(MyRange, MyCell.Value) > 1 Then
   MyCell.Interior.ColorIndex = 36
   End If


'Step 5: Get the next cell in the range
   Next MyCell

End Sub
```

1. Step 1 declares two Range object variables, one called MyRange to hold the entire target range, and the other called MyCell to hold each cell in the range as the macro enumerates through the cells one by one.

2. Step 2 fills the MyRange variable with the target range. This example uses the selected range — the range that was selected on the spreadsheet. You can easily set the MyRange variable to a specific range such as Range("A1:Z100"). Also, if your target range is a named range, you could simply enter its name: Range("MyNamedRange").

3. Step 3 starts looping through the cells in the target range, activating each cell.

4. The WorksheetFunction object provides a way to run many of Excel's spreadsheet functions in VBA. Step 4 uses the WorksheetFunction object to run a CountIf function in VBA.

   In this case, you are counting the number of times the active cell value (MyCell. Value) is found in the given range (MyRange). If the CountIf expression evaluates to greater than 1, the macro changes the interior color of the cell.

5. Step 5 loops back to get the next cell. After all of the cells in the target range are activated, the macro ends.

How to use it

To implement this macro, you can copy and paste it into a standard module:

1. **Activate the Visual Basic Editor by pressing Alt+F11 on your keyboard.**

2. **Right-click the project/workbook name in the Project window.**

3. **Choose Insert ⇨ Module.**

4. **Type or paste the code.**

Hiding All but Rows Containing Duplicate Data

With the previous macro, you can quickly find and highlight duplicates in your data. This in itself can be quite useful. But if you have many records in your range, you may want to take the extra step of hiding all the non-duplicate rows.

Take the example in Figure 7-5. Note that only the rows that contain duplicate values are visible. This more readily exposes the duplicate values because they are the only rows showing.

How it works

This macro enumerates through the cells in the target range, leveraging the For Each statement to activate each cell one at a time. It then uses the CountIf function to count the number of times the value in the active cell occurs in the range selected. If that number is one, it hides the row in which the active cell resides. If that number is greater than one, it formats the cell yellow and leaves the row visible.

```
Sub Macro1()

'Step 1: Declare your variables
  Dim MyRange As Range
  Dim MyCell As Range


'Step 2: Define the target Range.
  Set MyRange = Selection


'Step 3: Start looping through the range.
  For Each MyCell In MyRange


'Step 4: Ensure the cell has Text formatting.
  If Not IsEmpty(MyCell) Then

    If WorksheetFunction.CountIf(MyRange, MyCell) > 1 Then
      MyCell.Interior.ColorIndex = 36
      MyCell.EntireRow.Hidden = False
    Else
      MyCell.EntireRow.Hidden = True
    End If
```

```
    End If

'Step 5: Get the next cell in the range
    Next MyCell

End Sub
```

1. Step 1 declares two Range object variables, one called MyRange to hold the entire target range, and the other called MyCell to hold each cell in the range as you enumerate through the cells one by one.

2. Step 2 fills the MyRange variable with the target range. In this example, you use the selected range — the range selected on the spreadsheet. You can easily set the MyRange variable to a specific range such as Range("A1:Z100"). Also, if your target range is a named range, you could simply enter its name: Range("MyNamedRange").

3. Step 3 loops through cells in the target range, activating each cell as you go through.

4. You first use the IsEmpty function to make sure the cell is not empty. You do this so the macro won't automatically hide rows with no data in the target range.

   You then use the WorksheetFunction object to run a CountIf function in VBA. In this particular scenario, you are counting the number of times the active cell value (MyCell.Value) is found in the given range (MyRange).

   If the CountIf expression evaluates to greater than 1, you change the interior color of the cell and set the EntireRow property to Hidden=False. This ensures the row is visible.

   If the CountIf expression does not evaluate to greater than 1, the macro jumps to the Else argument. Here you set the EntireRow property to Hidden=True. This ensures the row is not visible.

5. Step 5 loops back to get the next cell. After all cells in the target range are activated, the macro ends.

TIP

Because the target range is defined as the current selection, you want to be sure to select the area where your data exists before running this code. You wouldn't want to select an entire column or the entire worksheet. Otherwise, any cell that contains data that is unique (not duplicated) triggers the hiding of the row. Alternatively, you can explicitly define the target range to ensure this is never a problem — such as Set MyRange = Range("A1:Z100").

How to use it

To implement this macro, you can copy and paste it into a standard module:

1. **Activate the Visual Basic Editor by pressing Alt+F11 on your keyboard.**
2. **Right-click the project/workbook name in the Project window.**
3. **Choose Insert ⇨ Module.**
4. **Type or paste the code.**

Selectively Hiding AutoFilter Drop-down Arrows

It goes without saying that the AutoFilter function in Excel is one of the most useful. Nothing else allows for faster on-the-spot filtering and analysis. The only problem is that the standard AutoFilter functionality applies drop-down arrows to every column in the chosen dataset (see Figure 7-6). This is all right in most situations, but what if you want to prevent your users from using the AutoFilter drop-down arrows on some of the columns in your data?

The good news is that with a little VBA, you can selectively hide AutoFilter drop-down arrows, as shown in Figure 7-7.

FIGURE 7-6:
The standard AutoFilter functionality adds drop-down arrows to all the columns in your data.

Region	Q1	Q2	Q3	Q4	Product Number
East	771	930	0	376	M2244
East	392	9	657	39	M3345
East	0	190	557	0	M7765
East	240	499	827	135	P8895
North	908	553	924	421	P8867
North	90	201	0	645	P8844
North	565	0	596	13	C3322
South	982	885	660	437	C5521
South	87	0	478	502	C5567
South	236	800	687	0	C8874
West	0	0	172	96	R7786
West	104	886	421	56	R7609

How it works

In VBA, you can use the AutoFilter object to turn on AutoFilters for a specific range. For example:

```
Range("B5:G5").AutoFilter
```

FIGURE 7-7:
With a little VBA,
you can choose
to hide certain
AutoFilter
drop-down
arrows.

Region	Q1	Q2	Q3	Q4	Product Number
East	771	930	0	376	M2244
East	392	9	657	39	M3345
East	0	190	557	0	M7765
East	240	499	827	135	P8895
North	908	553	924	421	P8867
North	90	201	0	645	P8844
North	565	0	596	13	C3322
South	982	885	660	437	C5521
South	87	0	478	502	C5567
South	236	800	687	0	C8874
West	0	0	172	96	R7786
West	104	886	421	56	R7609

After an AutoFilter is applied, you can manipulate each of the columns in the AutoFilter by pointing to it. For example, you can perform some action on the third column in the AutoFilter, like this:

```
Range("B5:G5").AutoFilter Field:3
```

You can perform many actions on an AutoFilter field. In this scenario, you are interested in making the drop-down arrow on field 3 invisible. For this, you can use the VisibleDropDown parameter. Setting this parameter to False makes the drop-down arrow invisible:

```
Range("B5:G5").AutoFilter Field:3, VisibleDropDown:=False
```

Here is an example of a macro where you turn on AutoFilters, and then make only the first and last drop-down arrows visible:

```
Sub Macro1()

With Range("B5:G5")
.AutoFilter
.AutoFilter Field:=1, VisibleDropDown:=True
.AutoFilter Field:=2, VisibleDropDown:=False
.AutoFilter Field:=3, VisibleDropDown:=False
.AutoFilter Field:=4, VisibleDropDown:=False
.AutoFilter Field:=5, VisibleDropDown:=False
.AutoFilter Field:=6, VisibleDropDown:=True
End With

End Sub
```

REMEMBER

Not only are you pointing to a specific range, but you are also explicitly pointing to each field. When implementing this type of macro in your environment, alter the code to suit your particular data set.

How to use it

To implement this macro, you can copy and paste it into a standard module:

1. **Activate the Visual Basic Editor by pressing Alt+F11 on your keyboard.**
2. **Right-click the project/workbook name in the Project window.**
3. **Choose Insert ⇨ Module.**
4. **Type or paste the code.**

Copying Filtered Rows to a New Workbook

Often, when you're working with an AutoFiltered set of data, you want to extract the filtered rows to a new workbook. Of course, you can manually copy the filtered rows, open a new workbook, paste the rows, and then format the newly pasted data so that all the columns fit. But if you are doing this frequently enough, you may want to have a macro to speed up the process.

How it works

This macro captures the AutoFilter range, opens a new workbook, and then pastes the data.

```
Sub Macro1()

'Step 1: Check for AutoFilter- Exit if none exists
    If ActiveSheet.AutoFilterMode = False Then
    Exit Sub
    End If


'Step 2: Copy the AutoFiltered Range to new workbook
    ActiveSheet.AutoFilter.Range.Copy
    Workbooks.Add.Worksheets(1).Paste


'Step 3: Size the columns to fit
    Cells.EntireColumn.AutoFit

End Sub
```

1. Step 1 uses the AutoFilterMode property to check whether the sheet even has AutoFilters applied. If not, you exit the procedure.

2. Each AutoFilter object has a Range property. This Range property obligingly returns the rows to which the AutoFilter applies, meaning it returns only the rows shown in the filtered data set. In Step 2, you use the Copy method to capture those rows, and then paste the rows to a new workbook. Note that you use Workbooks.Add.Worksheets(1). This tells Excel to paste the data into the first sheet of the newly created workbook.

3. Step 3 simply tells Excel to size the column widths to autofit the data you just pasted.

How to use it

To implement this macro, you can copy and paste it into a standard module:

1. **Activate the Visual Basic Editor by pressing Alt+F11 on your keyboard.**
2. **Right-click the project/workbook name in the Project window.**
3. **Choose Insert ⇨ Module.**
4. **Type or paste the code.**

Showing Filtered Columns in the Status Bar

When you have a large table with many AutoFiltered columns, it is sometimes hard to tell which columns are filtered and which aren't. Of course, you could scroll through the columns, peering at each AutoFilter drop-down list for the tell-tale icon indicating the column is filtered, but that can get old quickly.

This macro helps by specifically listing all the filtered columns in the status bar. The status bar is the bar (shown in Figure 7-8) that runs across the bottom of the Excel window.

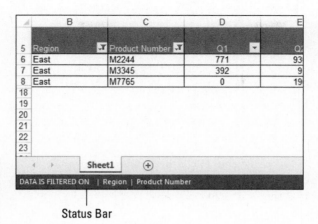

FIGURE 7-8:
This macro lists
all filtered
columns in the
status bar.

Status Bar

How it works

This macro loops through the fields in your AutoFiltered data set. As it loops, you check to see if each field is actually filtered. If so, you capture the field name in a text string. After looping through all the fields, you pass the final string to the StatusBar property.

```
Sub Macro1()


'Step 1: Declare your Variables
  Dim AF As AutoFilter
  Dim TargetField As String
  Dim strOutput As String
  Dim i As Integer


'Step 2: Check if AutoFilter exists- If not Exit
  If ActiveSheet.AutoFilterMode = False Then
    Application.StatusBar = False
    Exit Sub
  End If


'Step 3: Set AutoFilter and start looping
  Set AF = ActiveSheet.AutoFilter
  For i = 1 To AF.Filters.Count
```

```
'Step 4: Capture filtered field names
If AF.Filters(i).On Then
  TargetField = AF.Range.Cells(1, i).Value
strOutput = strOutput & " | " & TargetField
End If
Next


'Step 5: Display the filters if there are any
  If strOutput = "" Then
  Application.StatusBar = False
  Else
  Application.StatusBar = "DATA IS FILTERED ON " & strOutput
  End If

End Sub
```

1. Step 1 declares four variables. AF is an AutoFilter variable used to manipulate the AutoFilter object. TargetField is a string variable you use to hold the field names of any field that is actually filtered. strOutput is the string variable used to build out the final text that goes into the status bar. Finally, the i variable serves as a simple counter, allowing you to iterate through the fields in your AutoFilter.

2. Step 2 checks the AutoFilterMode property to see if a sheet even has AutoFilters applied. If not, you set the StatusBar property to False. This has the effect of clearing the status bar, releasing control back to Excel. You then exit the procedure.

3. Step 3 sets the AF variable to the AutoFilter on the active sheet. You then set your counter to count from 1 to the maximum number of columns in the AutoFiltered range. The AutoFilter object keeps track of its columns with index numbers. Column 1 is index 1, column 2 is index 2, and so on. The idea is that you can loop through each column in the AutoFilter by using the i variable as the index number.

4. Step 4 checks the status of the AF.Filters object for each (i), i being the index number of the column you are evaluating. If the AutoFilter for that column is filtered in any way, the status for that column is On.

   If the filter for the column is indeed on, you capture the name of the field in the TargetField variable. You actually get the name of the field by referencing the Range of your AF AutoFilter object. With this range, you can use the Cells item to pinpoint the field name. Cells(1,1) captures the value in row 1, column 1. Cells(1,2) captures the value in row 1, column 2, and so on.

As you can see in Step 4, you have hard-coded the row to 1 and used the i variable to indicate the column index. This means that as the macro iterates through the columns, it always captures the value in the first row of the auto-filtered table as the TargetField name (the first row is where the field name is likely to be).

After you have the TargetField name, you can pass that information to a simple string container (strOutput in this case). strOutput simply keeps all the target field names you find and concatenates them into a readable text string.

5. Step 5 first checks to make sure that there is something in the strOutput string. If strOutput is empty, it means the macro found no columns in your AutoFilter that were filtered. In this case, Step 5 simply sets the StatusBar property to False, releasing control back to Excel.

   If strOutput is not empty, Step 5 sets the StatusBar property to equal some helper text along with your strOutput string.

How to use it

You ideally want this macro to run each time a field is filtered. However, Excel does not have an OnAutoFilter event. The closest thing to that is the Worksheet_ Calculate event. That being said, AutoFilters in themselves don't actually calculate anything, so you need to enter a "volatile" function on the sheet that contains your AutoFiltered data. A volatile function is one that forces a recalculation when any change is made on the worksheet.

In the sample files that come with this book, notice that the =Now() function is used. The Now function is a volatile function that returns a date and time. With this on the sheet, the worksheet is sure to recalculate each time the AutoFilter is changed.

REMEMBER

To access the sample files for this chapter, visit the web site: www.dummies.com/ go/excelmacros.

Place the Now function anywhere on your sheet (by typing =**Now()** in any cell). Then copy and paste the macro into the Worksheet_Calculate event code window:

1. **Activate the Visual Basic Editor by pressing Alt+F11 on your keyboard.**

2. **In the Project window, find your project/workbook name and click the plus sign next to it in order to see all the sheets.**

3. **Click on the sheet from which you want to trigger the code.**

4. **Select the Calculate event from the Event drop-down list (see Figure 7-9).**

5. **Type or paste the code.**

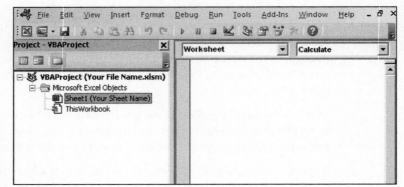

FIGURE 7-9:
Type or paste
your code in the
Worksheet_
Calculate event
code window.

In order to make the code run as smoothly as possible, consider adding these two pieces of code under the Worksheet_Calculate event:

```
Private Sub Worksheet_Deactivate()

Application.StatusBar = False

End Sub

Private Sub Worksheet_Activate()

Call Worksheet_Calculate

End Sub
```

Also, add this piece of code in the workbook BeforeClose event:

```
Private Sub Workbook_BeforeClose(Cancel As Boolean)

Application.StatusBar = False

End Sub
```

The Worksheet_Deactivate event clears the status bar when you move to another sheet or workbook. This avoids confusion as you move between sheets.

The Worksheet_Activate event fires the macro in Worksheet_Calculate. This brings back the status bar indicators when you navigate back to the filtered sheet.

The Workbook_BeforeClose event clears the status bar when you close the workbook. This avoids confusion as you move between workbooks.

4
Macro-Charging Reports and Emails

Gain an understanding of how macros can be leveraged to automate your reporting processes.

Discover how to automate the more mundane aspects of building PivotTables.

See how macros can help work with the charts in your reports and dashboards.

Explore some of the techniques you can leverage to send emails from Excel.

Discover techniques to wrangle data from external databases and data files.

IN THIS CHAPTER

» **Refreshing all PivotTables**

» **Creating a PivotTable inventory summary or a set of disconnected charts**

» **Adjusting all pivot data field titles**

» **Setting all data items to sums**

» **Setting the number format or custom sort for all data items**

» **Sorting all fields in alphabetical order**

» **Applying PivotTable and pivot field restrictions**

» **Automatically deleting PivotTable drilldown sheets**

» **Printing PivotTable for each report filter item or for all charts**

» **Creating new workbook for each report filter item**

» **Resizing or aligning charts**

Chapter **8**

Automating Common Reporting Tasks

For those of us tasked with building dashboards and reports, PivotTables and charts are a daily part of our work life. Few of us have had the inclination to automate any aspect of these reporting tools with macros. But some aspects of our work lend themselves to a bit of automation. This chapter explores a handful of macros that can help you save time and gain efficiencies when working with PivotTables and charts.

Refreshing All PivotTables in a Workbook

It's not uncommon to have multiple PivotTables in the same workbook. Many times, these PivotTables link to data that changes, requiring a refresh of the PivotTables. If you find that you need to refresh your PivotTables en mass, you can use this macro to refresh all PivotTables on demand.

How it works

It's important to know that each PivotTable object is a child of the worksheet it sits in. The macro has to loop through the worksheets in a workbook first, and then loop through the PivotTables in each worksheet. This macro does just that — loops through the worksheets, and then loops through the PivotTables. On each loop, the macro refreshes the PivotTable.

```
Sub Macro1()

'Step 1: Declare you Variables
    Dim ws As Worksheet
    Dim pt As PivotTable


'Step 2: Loop through each sheet in workbook
    For Each ws In ThisWorkbook.Worksheets


'Step 3: Loop through each PivotTable
        For Each pt In ws.PivotTables
            pt.RefreshTable
        Next pt
    Next ws

End Sub
```

1. Step 1 first declares an object called ws. This creates a memory container for each worksheet you loop through. It also declares an object called pt, which holds each PivotTable the macro loops through.

2. Step 2 starts the looping, telling Excel you want to evaluate all worksheets in this workbook. Notice the use of ThisWorkbook rather than ActiveWorkbook. The ThisWorkbook object refers to the workbook that the code is contained in.

The ActiveWorkbook object refers to the workbook that is currently active. They often return the same object, but if the workbook running the code is not the active workbook, they return different objects. In this case, you don't want to risk refreshing PivotTables in other workbooks, so use ThisWorkbook.

3. Step 3 loops through all the PivotTables in each worksheet, and then triggers the RefreshTable method. After all PivotTables have been refreshed, you move to the next sheet. After all sheets have been evaluated, the macro ends.

TIP

As an alternative method for refreshing all PivotTables in the workbook, you can use ThisWorkbook.RefreshAll. This refreshes all the PivotTables in the workbook. However, it also refreshes all query tables also. So if you have data tables connected to an external source or the web, these will be affected by the RefreshAll method. If this is not a concern, you can simply enter ThisWorkbook. RefreshAll into a standard module.

How to use it

To implement this macro, you can copy and paste it into a standard module:

1. **Activate the Visual Basic Editor by pressing Alt+F11.**
2. **Right-click the project/workbook name in the Project window.**
3. **Choose Insert ⇨ Module.**
4. **Type or paste the code.**

Creating a PivotTable Inventory Summary

When your workbook contains multiple PivotTables, it's often helpful to have an inventory summary (similar to the one shown in Figure 8-1) that outlines basic details about the PivotTables. With this type of summary, you can quickly see important information such as the location of each PivotTable, the location of each PivotTable's source data, and the pivot cache index each PivotTable is using.

The following macro outputs such a summary.

	A	B	C	D	E	F
1	Pivot Name	Worksheet	Location	Cache Index	Source Data Location	Row Count
2	PivotTable10	Product Categories	$A$3:$I$11	2	Raw Data'!$A$3:$N$59469	59466
3	PivotTable9	Internet Sales	$A$3:$D$11	3	Raw Data'!$A$3:$N$59468	59465
4	PivotTable11	Units Sold	$A$3:$I$11	1	Raw Data'!$A$3:$N$59470	59467
5	PivotTable12	Sales by Year	$A$3:$I$45	2	Raw Data'!$A$3:$N$59469	59466
6						

FIGURE 8-1:
A PivotTable inventory summary.

How it works

When you create a PivotTable object variable, you expose all of a PivotTable's properties — properties like its name, location, cache index, and so on. In this macro, you loop through each PivotTable in the workbook and extract specific properties into a new worksheet.

Because each PivotTable object is a child of the worksheet it sits in, you have to loop through the worksheets in a workbook first, and then loop through the Pivot-Tables in each worksheet.

Take a moment to walk through the steps of this macro in detail.

```
Sub Macro1()

'Step 1:  Declare you Variables
    Dim ws As Worksheet
    Dim pt As PivotTable
    Dim MyCell As Range


'Step 2: Add a new sheet with column headers
    Worksheets.Add
    Range("A1:F1") = Array("Pivot Name", "Worksheet", _
                           "Location", "Cache Index", _
                           "Source Data Location", _
                           "Row Count")


'Step 3:  Start Cursor at Cell A2 setting the anchor here
    Set MyCell = ActiveSheet.Range("A2")


'Step 4: Loop through each sheet in workbook
    For Each ws In Worksheets


'Step 5: Loop through each PivotTable
        For Each pt In ws.PivotTables
        MyCell.Offset(0, 0) = pt.Name
        MyCell.Offset(0, 1) = pt.Parent.Name
        MyRange.Offset(0, 2) = pt.TableRange2.Address
        MyRange.Offset(0, 3) = pt.CacheIndex
        MyRange.Offset(0, 4) = Application.ConvertFormula _
        (pt.PivotCache.SourceData, xlR1C1, xlA1)
         MyRange.Offset(0, 5) = pt.PivotCache.RecordCount
```

```
'Step 6:  Move Cursor down one row and set a new anchor
          Set MyRange = MyRange.Offset(1, 0)


'Step 7:  Work through all PivotTables and worksheets
      Next pt
   Next ws


'Step 8: Size columns to fit
    ActiveSheet.Cells.EntireColumn.AutoFit

End Sub
```

1. Step 1 declares an object called ws. This creates a memory container for each worksheet you loop through. You then declare an object called pt, which holds each PivotTable you loop through. Finally, you create a range variable called MyCell. This variable acts as your cursor as you fill in the inventory summary.

2. Step 2 creates a new worksheet and adds column headings that range from A1 to F1. Note that you can add column headings using a simple array that contains your header labels. This new worksheet remains your active sheet from here on out.

3. Just as you would manually place your cursor into a cell if you were to start typing data, Step 3 places the MyCell cursor in cell A2 of the active sheet. This is your anchor point, allowing you to navigate from here.

   Throughout the macro, you see the use of the Offset property. The Offset property allows you to move a cursor x number of rows and x number of columns from an anchor point. For example, Range(A2).Offset(0,1) would move the cursor one column to the right. If you wanted to move the cursor one row down, you would enter Range(A2).Offset(1, 0).

   In the macro, you navigate by using Offset on MyCell. For example, MyCell.Offset(0,4) would move the cursor four columns to the right of the anchor cell. After the cursor is in place, you can enter data.

4. Step 4 starts the looping, telling Excel you want to evaluate all worksheets in this workbook.

5. Step 5 loops through all the PivotTables in each worksheet. For each PivotTable it finds, it extracts out the appropriate property and fills in the table based on the cursor position (see Step 3).

   You are using six PivotTable properties: Name, Parent.Range, TableRange2. Address, CacheIndex, PivotCache.SourceData, and PivotCache.Recordcount.

- The Name property returns the name of the PivotTable.

- The Parent.Range property gives the sheet where the PivotTable resides.

- The TableRange2.Address property returns the range that the PivotTable object sits in.

- The CacheIndex property returns the index number of the pivot cache for the PivotTable. A pivot cache is a memory container that stores all the data for a PivotTable. When you create a new PivotTable, Excel takes a snapshot of the source data and creates a pivot cache. Each time you refresh a PivotTable, Excel goes back to the source data and takes another snapshot, thereby refreshing the pivot cache. Each pivot cache has a SourceData property that identifies the location of the data used to create the pivot cache.

- The PivotCache.SourceData property tells you which range is called upon when you refresh the PivotTable. By default, the PivotCache.SourceData property returns range addresses in the R1C1 reference style — for example: 'Raw Data'!R1C1:R5000C14. Unfortunately, range objects cannot use the R1C1 style, so you need to convert the address to the A1 reference style — 'Raw Data'!$A$1:$N$5000. This is a simple enough fix. You simply pass the SourceData property through the Application.ConvertFormula function. This handy function converts ranges to and from the R1C1 reference style.

- The PivotCache.Recordcount property outputs the count of records found in the pivot cache.

6. Each time the macro encounters a new PivotTable, it moves the MyCell cursor down a row, effectively starting a new row for each PivotTable.

7. Step 7 tells Excel to loop back around to iterate through all PivotTables and all worksheets. After all PivotTables have been evaluated, you move to the next sheet. After all sheets have been evaluated, the macro moves to the last step.

8. Step 8 finishes off with a little formatting, sizing the columns to fit the data.

How to use it

To implement this macro, you can copy and paste it into a standard module:

1. **Activate the Visual Basic Editor by pressing Alt+F11.**

2. **Right-click the project/workbook name in the Project window.**

3. **Choose Insert ▷ Module.**

4. **Type or paste the code.**

Adjusting All Pivot Data Field Titles

When you create a PivotTable, Excel tries to help you out by prefacing each data field header with Sum of, Count of, or whichever operation you use. Often, this is not conducive to your reporting needs. You want clean titles that match your data source as closely as possible. Although it's true that you can manually adjust the titles for you data fields (one at a time), this macro fixes them all in one go.

How it works

Ideally, the name of the each data item matches the field name from your source data set (the original source data used to create the PivotTable). Unfortunately, PivotTables won't allow you to name a data field the exact name as the source data field. The workaround for this is to add a space to the end of the field name. Excel considers the field name (with a space) to be different from the source data field name, so it allows it. Cosmetically, the readers of your spreadsheet don't notice the space after the name.

This macro utilizes this workaround to rename your data fields. It loops through each data field in the PivotTable, and then resets each header to match its respective field in the source data plus a space character.

```
Sub Macro1()

'Step 1: Declare your Variables
    Dim pt As PivotTable
    Dim pf As PivotField


'Step 2: Point to the PivotTable in the active cell
    On Error Resume Next
    Set pt = ActiveSheet.PivotTables(ActiveCell.PivotTable.Name)


'Step 3:  Exit if active cell is not in a PivotTable
    If pt Is Nothing Then
    MsgBox "You must place your cursor inside of a PivotTable."
    Exit Sub
    End If
```

```
'Step 4:  Loop through all pivot fields adjust titles
    For Each pf In pt.DataFields
        pf.Caption = pf.SourceName & Chr(160)
    Next pf

End Sub
```

1. Step 1 declares two object variables. It uses pt as the memory container for your PivotTable and pf as a memory container for the data fields. This allows the macro to loop through all the data fields in the PivotTable.

2. This macro is designed so that you infer the active PivotTable based on the active cell. In other words, the active cell must be inside a PivotTable for this macro to run. You assume that when the cursor is inside a particular PivotTable, you want to perform the macro action on that pivot.

   Step 2 sets the pt variable to the name of the PivotTable on which the active cell is found. You do this by using the ActiveCell.PivotTable.Name property to get the name of the target pivot.

   If the active cell is not inside of a PivotTable, an error is thrown. This is why you use the On Error Resume Next statement. This tells Excel to continue with the macro if there is an error.

3. In Step 3, you check to see if the pt variable is filled with a PivotTable object. If the pt variable is set to Nothing, the active cell was not on a PivotTable, thus no PivotTable could be assigned to the variable. If this is the case, you tell the user in a message box and then exit the procedure.

4. If the macro reaches Step 4, it has successfully pointed to a PivotTable. The macro uses a For Each statement to iterate through each data field. Each time a new pivot field is selected, the macro changes the field name by setting the Caption property to match the field's SourceName. The SourceName property returns the name of the matching field in the original source data.

To that name, the macro concatenates a nonbreaking space character: Chr(160).

Every character has an underlying ASCII code, similar to a serial number. For example, the lowercase letter *a* has an ASCII code of 97. The lowercase letter *c* has an ASCII code of 99. Likewise, invisible characters such as the space have a code. You can use invisible characters in your macro by passing their code through the CHR function.

After the name has been changed, the macro moves to the next data field. After all the data fields have been evaluated, the macro ends.

How to use it

To implement this macro, you can copy and paste it into a standard module:

1. **Activate the Visual Basic Editor by pressing Alt+F11.**
2. **Right-click the project/workbook name in the Project window.**
3. **Choose Insert ⇨ Module.**
4. **Type or paste the code.**

Setting All Data Items to Sum

When creating a PivotTable, Excel, by default, summarizes your data by either counting or summing the items. The logic Excel uses to decide whether to sum or count the fields you add to your PivotTable is fairly simple. If all the cells in a column contain numeric data, Excel chooses to Sum. If the field you are adding contains a blank or text, Excel chooses Count.

Although this seems to make sense, in many instances, a pivot field that should be summed legitimately contains blanks. In these cases, you are forced to manually go in after Excel and change the calculation type from Count back to Sum. That's if you're paying attention! It's not uncommon to miss the fact that a pivot field is being counted rather than summed up.

The macro in this section aims to help by automatically setting each data item's calculation type to Sum.

How it works

This macro loops through each data field in the PivotTable and changes the Function property to xlSum. You can alter this macro to use any one of the calculation choices: xlCount, xlAverage, xlMin, xlMax, and so on. When you go into the code window and type **pf.Function** =, you see a drop-down list showing you all your choices (see Figure 8-2).

```
Sub Macro1()

'Step 1: Declare your Variables
    Dim pt As PivotTable
    Dim pf As PivotField
```

```
'Step 2: Point to the PivotTable in the active cell
    On Error Resume Next
    Set pt = ActiveSheet.PivotTables(ActiveCell.PivotTable.Name)


'Step 3:  Exit if active cell is not in a PivotTable
    If pt Is Nothing Then
    MsgBox "You must place your cursor inside of a PivotTable."
    Exit Sub
    End If


'Step 4:  Loop through all pivot fields apply SUM
    For Each pf In pt.DataFields
        pf.Function = xlSum
    Next pf

End Sub
```

1. Step 1 declares two object variables. It uses pt as the memory container for the PivotTable and pf as a memory container for the data fields. This allows you to loop through all the data fields in the PivotTable.

2. This macro is designed so that you infer the active PivotTable based on the active cell. The active cell must be inside a PivotTable for this macro to run. The assumption is that when the cursor is inside a particular PivotTable, you want to perform the macro action on that pivot.

   Step 2 sets the pt variable to the name of the PivotTable on which the active cell is found. You do this by using the ActiveCell.PivotTable.Name property to get the name of the target pivot.

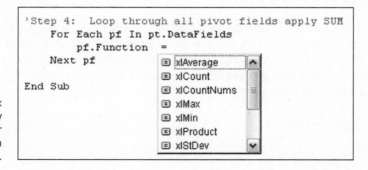

FIGURE 8-2:
Excel helps out by showing you your enumeration choices.

If the active cell is not inside of a PivotTable, an error is thrown. This is why you use the On Error Resume Next statement. This tells Excel to continue with the macro if it encounters an error.

3. Step 3 checks to see if the pt variable is filled with a PivotTable object. If the pt variable is set to Nothing, the active cell was not on a PivotTable, thus no PivotTable could be assigned to the variable. If this is the case, you tell the user in a message box and then exit the procedure.

4. If the macro has reached Step 4, it has successfully pointed to a PivotTable. It uses a For Each statement to iterate through each data field. Each time a new pivot field is selected, it alters the Function property to set the calculation used by the field. In this case, you are setting all the data fields in the PivotTable to Sum.

After the name has been changed, you move to the next data field. After all the data fields have been evaluated, the macro ends.

How to use it

To implement this macro, you can copy and paste it into a standard module:

1. Activate the Visual Basic Editor by pressing Alt+F11.

2. Right-click the project/workbook name in the Project window.

3. Choose Insert ▷ Module.

4. Type or paste the code.

Applying Number Formatting for All Data Items

A PivotTable does not inherently store number formatting in its pivot cache. Formatting takes up memory; so in order to be as lean as possible, the pivot cache contains only data. Unfortunately, this results in the need to apply number formatting to every field you add to a PivotTable. This takes from eight to ten clicks of the mouse for every data field you add. When you have PivotTables that contain five or more data fields, you're talking about more than 40 clicks of the mouse!

Ideally, a PivotTable should be able to look back at its source data and adopt the number formatting from the fields there. The macro outlined in this section is designed to do just that. It recognizes the number formatting in the PivotTable's source data and applies the appropriate formatting to each field automatically.

How it works

Before running this code, you want to make sure that

>> The source data for your PivotTable is accessible. The macro needs to see it in order to capture the correct number formatting.

>> The source data is appropriately formatted. Money fields are formatted as currency, value fields are formatted as numbers, and so on.

This macro uses the PivotTable SourceData property to find the location of the source data. It then loops through each column in the source, capturing the header name and the number format of the first value under each column. After it has that information, the macro determines whether any of the data fields match the evaluated column. If it finds a match, the number formatting is applied to that data field.

```
Sub Macro1()


'Step 1: Declare your Variables
    Dim pt As PivotTable
    Dim pf As PivotField
    Dim SrcRange As Range
    Dim strFormat As String
    Dim strLabel As String
    Dim i As Integer

'Step 2: Point to the PivotTable in the activecell
    On Error Resume Next
    Set pt = ActiveSheet.PivotTables(ActiveCell.PivotTable.Name)


'Step 3:  Exit if active cell is not in a PivotTable
    If pt Is Nothing Then
    MsgBox "You must place your cursor inside of a PivotTable."
    Exit Sub
    End If
```

```
'Step 4: Capture the source range
    Set SrcRange = _
    Range(Application.ConvertFormula(pt.SourceData, xlR1C1,
 xlA1))


'Step 5: Start looping through the columns in source range
    For i = 1 To SrcRange.Columns.Count


'Step 6: Trap the source column name and number format
        strLabel = SrcRange.Cells(1, i).Value
        strFormat = SrcRange.Cells(2, i).NumberFormat


'Step 7: Loop through the fields PivotTable data area
        For Each pf In pt.DataFields


'Step 8: Check for match on SourceName then apply format
            If pf.SourceName = strLabel Then
            pf.NumberFormat = strFormat
            End If
        Next pf
    Next i

End Sub
```

1. Step 1 declares six variables. It uses pt as the memory container for the PivotTable and pf as a memory container for the data fields. The SrcRange variable holds the data range for the source data. The strFormat and strLabel variables are both text string variables used to hold the source column label and number formatting respectively. The i variable serves as a counter, helping you enumerate through the columns of the source data range.

2. The active cell must be inside a PivotTable for this macro to run. The assumption is that when the cursor is inside a particular PivotTable, you want to perform the macro action on that pivot.

   Step 2 sets the pt variable to the name of the PivotTable on which the active cell is found. You do this by using the ActiveCell.PivotTable.Name property to get the name of the target pivot.

   If the active cell is not inside a PivotTable, an error is thrown. This is why the macro uses the On Error Resume Next statement. This tells Excel to continue with the macro if it encounters an error.

3. Step 3 checks to see whether the pt variable is filled with a PivotTable object. If the pt variable is set to Nothing, the active cell was not on a PivotTable, thus no PivotTable could be assigned to the variable. If this is the case, you tell the user in a message box and then exit the procedure.

4. If the macro reaches Step 4, it has successfully pointed to a PivotTable. You immediately fill your SrcRange object variable with the PivotTable's source data range.

   All PivotTables have a SourceData property that points to the address of its source. Unfortunately, the address is stored in the R1C1 reference style — like this: 'Raw Data'!R3C1:R59470C14. Range objects cannot use the R1C1 style, so you need the address to be converted to 'Raw Data'!$A$3:$N$59470.

   This is a simple enough fix. You simply pass the SourceData property through the Application.ConvertFormula function. This handy function converts ranges to and from the R1C1 reference style.

5. After the range is captured, the macro starts looping through the columns in the source range. In this case, you manage the looping by using the i integer as an index number for the columns in the source range. You start the index number at 1 and end it at the maximum number of rows in the source range.

6. As the macro loops through the columns in the source range, you capture the column header label and the column format.

   You do this with the aid of the Cells item. The Cells item gives you an extremely handy way of selecting ranges through code. It requires only relative row and column positions as parameters. Cells(1,1) translates to row 1, column 1 (or the header row of the first column). Cells(2, 1) translates to row 2, column 1 (or the first value in the first column).

   strLabel is filled by the header label taken from row 1 of the selected column. strFormat is filled with the number formatting from row 2 of the selected column.

7. At this point, the macro has connected with the PivotTable's source data and captured the first column name and number formatting for that column. Now it starts looping through the data fields in the PivotTable.

8. Step 8 simply compares each data field to see if its source matches the name in strLabel. If it does, that means the number formatting captured in strFormat belongs to that data field.

9. After all data fields have been evaluated, the macro increments i to the next column in the source range. After all columns have been evaluated, the macro ends.

How to use it

To implement this macro, you can copy and paste it into a standard module:

1. **Activate the Visual Basic Editor by pressing Alt+F11.**
2. **Right-click the project/workbook name in the Project window.**
3. **Choose Insert ➪ Module.**
4. **Type or paste the code.**

Sorting All Fields in Alphabetical Order

If you frequently add data to your PivotTables, you may notice that new data doesn't automatically fall into the sort order of the existing pivot data. Instead, it gets tacked to the bottom of the existing data. This means that your drop-down lists show all new data at the very bottom, whereas existing data is sorted alphabetically.

How it works

This macro works to reset the sorting on all data fields, ensuring that any new data snaps into place. The idea is to run it each time you refresh your PivotTable. In the code, you enumerate through each data field in the PivotTable, sorting each one as you go.

```
Sub Macro1()

'Step 1: Declare your Variables
    Dim pt As PivotTable
    Dim pf As PivotField


'Step 2: Point to the PivotTable in the activecell
    On Error Resume Next
    Set pt = ActiveSheet.PivotTables(ActiveCell.PivotTable.Name)


'Step 3:  Exit if active cell is not in a PivotTable
    If pt Is Nothing Then
    MsgBox "You must place your cursor inside of a PivotTable."
```

```
        Exit Sub
      End If


'Step 4:  Loop through all pivot fields and sort
      For Each pf In pt.PivotFields
          pf.AutoSort xlAscending, pf.Name
      Next pf

End Sub
```

1. Step 1 declares two object variables, using pt as the memory container for the PivotTable and using pf as a memory container for the data fields. This allows the macro to loop through all the data fields in the PivotTable.

2. The active cell must be inside a PivotTable for this macro to run. The assumption is that when the cursor is inside a particular PivotTable, you want to perform the macro action on that pivot.

   In Step 2, you set the pt variable to the name of the PivotTable on which the active cell is found. You do this by using the ActiveCell.PivotTable.Name property to get the name of the target pivot.

   If the active cell is not inside of a PivotTable, an error is thrown. This is why you use the On Error Resume Next statement. This tells Excel to continue with the macro if it encounters an error.

3. Step 3 checks to see whether the pt variable is filled with a PivotTable object. If the pt variable is set to Nothing, the active cell was not on a PivotTable, thus no PivotTable could be assigned to the variable. If this is the case, the macro puts up a message box to notify the user, and then exits the procedure.

4. Finally, you use a For Each statement to iterate through each pivot field. Each time a new pivot field is selected, you use the AutoSort method to reset the automatic sorting rules for the field. In this case, you are sorting all fields ascending order. After all the data fields have been evaluated, the macro ends.

How to use it

To implement this macro, you can copy and paste it into a standard module:

1. **Activate the Visual Basic Editor by pressing Alt+F11.**
2. **Right-click the project/workbook name in the Project window.**

3. **Choose Insert ⇨ Module.**

4. **Type or paste the code.**

Applying a Custom Sort to Data Items

On occasion, you may need to apply a custom sort to the data items in your Pivot-Table. For example, if you work for a company in California, your organization may want the West region to come before the North and South. In these types of situations, neither the standard ascending nor descending sort order will work.

How it works

You can automate the custom sorting of your fields by using the Position property of the PivotItems object. With the Position property, you can assign a position number that specifies the order in which you want to see each pivot item.

In this example code, you first point to the Region pivot field in the Pvt1 Pivot-Table. Then you list each item along with the position number indicating the customer sort order you need.

```
Sub Macro1()

With Sheets("Sheet1").PivotTables("Pvt1").PivotFields _
    ("Region ")
    .PivotItems("West").Position = 1
    .PivotItems("North").Position = 2
    .PivotItems("South").Position = 3

End With

End Sub
```

TIP

The other solution is to set up a custom sort list. Custom sort lists are defined lists stored in your instance of Excel. To create a custom sort list, go to the Excel Options Dialog and choose Edit Custom Lists. Here, you can type West, North, and South in the List Entries box and click the Add button. After setting up a custom list, you can select a data item in the target field (in this case, Region) and then click Data ⇨ Sort & Filter ⇨ Custom Sort on the Excel Ribbon. This will activate the Sort dialog box. Here, you can click the Order dropdown and select a Custom List as the sort order.

As brilliant as this option is, custom lists do not travel with your workbook. So a macro helps in cases where it's impractical to expect your audience to set up their own custom lists.

How to use it

You can implement this kind of macro in a standard module:

1. **Activate the Visual Basic Editor by pressing Alt+F11.**
2. **Right-click the project/workbook name in the Project window.**
3. **Choose Insert ⇨ Module.**
4. **Type or paste the code.**

Applying PivotTable Restrictions

We often send PivotTables to clients, co-workers, managers, and other groups of people. In some cases, we'd like to restrict the types of actions our users can take on the PivotTable reports we send them. The macro outlined in this section demonstrates some of the protection settings available via VBA.

How it works

The PivotTable object exposes several properties that allow you (the developer) to restrict different features and components of a PivotTable:

>> EnableWizard: Setting this property to False disables the PivotTable Tools context menu that normally activates when clicking inside of a PivotTable. In Excel 2003, this setting disables the PivotTable and Pivot Chart Wizard.

>> EnableDrilldown: Setting this property to False prevents users from getting to detailed data by double-clicking a data field.

>> EnableFieldList: Setting this property to False prevents users from activating the field list or moving pivot fields around.

>> EnableFieldDialog: Setting this property to False disables the users' ability to alter the pivot field via the Value Field Settings dialog box.

>> PivotCache.EnableRefresh: Setting this property to False disables the ability to refresh the PivotTable.

You can set any or all of these properties independently to either True or False. In this macro, you apply all the restrictions to the target PivotTable.

```
Sub Macro1()

'Step 1: Declare your Variables
    Dim pt As PivotTable


'Step 2: Point to the PivotTable in the activecell
    On Error Resume Next
    Set pt = ActiveSheet.PivotTables(ActiveCell.PivotTable.Name)


'Step 3:  Exit if active cell is not in a PivotTable
    If pt Is Nothing Then
    MsgBox "You must place your cursor inside of a PivotTable."
    Exit Sub
    End If


'Step 4:  Apply Pivot Table Restrictions
    With pt
      .EnableWizard = False
      .EnableDrilldown = False
      .EnableFieldList = False
      .EnableFieldDialog = False
      .PivotCache.EnableRefresh = False
    End With

End Sub
```

1. Step 1 declares the pt PivotTable object variable that serves as the memory container for your PivotTable.

2. Step 2 sets the pt variable to the name of the PivotTable on which the active cell is found. You do this by using the ActiveCell.PivotTable.Name property to get the name of the target pivot.

3. Step 3 checks to see if the pt variable is filled with a PivotTable object. If the pt variable is set to Nothing, the active cell was not on a PivotTable, thus no PivotTable could be assigned to the variable. If this is the case, you tell the user in a message box and then exit the procedure.

4. In the last step of the macro, you are applying all PivotTable restrictions.

How to use it

You can implement this kind of macro in a standard module:

1. **Activate the Visual Basic Editor by pressing Alt+F11.**
2. **Right-click the project/workbook name in the Project window.**
3. **Choose Insert ➪ Module.**
4. **Type or paste the code.**

Applying Pivot Field Restrictions

Like PivotTable restrictions, pivot field restrictions enable you to restrict the types of actions users can take on the pivot fields in a PivotTable. The macro outlined in this section demonstrates some of the protection settings available via VBA.

How it works

The PivotField object exposes several properties that allow you (the developer) to restrict different features and components of a PivotTable:

» DragToPage: Setting this property to False prevents the users from dragging any pivot field into the Report Filter area of the PivotTable.

» DragToRow: Setting this property to False prevents the users from dragging any pivot field into the Row area of the PivotTable.

» DragToColumn: Setting this property to False prevents the users from dragging any pivot field into the Column area of the PivotTable.

» DragToData: Setting this property to False prevents the users from dragging any pivot field into the Data area of the PivotTable.

» DragToHide: Setting this property to False prevents the users from dragging pivot fields off the PivotTable. It also prevents the use of the right-click menu to hide or remove pivot fields.

» EnableItemSelection: Setting this property to False disables the drop-down lists on each pivot field.

You can set any or all of these properties independently to either True or False. In this macro, you apply all the restrictions to the target PivotTable.

```
Sub Macro1()

'Step 1: Declare your Variables
    Dim pt As PivotTable
    Dim pf As PivotField


'Step 2: Point to the PivotTable in the activecell
    On Error Resume Next
    Set pt = ActiveSheet.PivotTables(ActiveCell.PivotTable.Name)


'Step 3:  Exit if active cell is not in a PivotTable
    If pt Is Nothing Then
    MsgBox "You must place your cursor inside of a PivotTable."
    Exit Sub
    End If


'Step 4:  Apply Pivot Field Restrictions
    For Each pf In pt.PivotFields
        pf.EnableItemSelection = False
        pf.DragToPage = False
        pf.DragToRow = False
        pf.DragToColumn = False
        pf.DragToData = False
        pf.DragToHide = False
    Next pf

End Sub
```

1. Step 1 declares two object variables, using pt as the memory container for the PivotTable and pf as a memory container for the pivot fields. This allows you to loop through all the pivot fields in the PivotTable.

2. Set the pt variable to the name of the PivotTable on which the active cell is found. You do this by using the ActiveCell.PivotTable.Name property to get the name of the target pivot.

3. Step 3 checks to see whether the pt variable is filled with a PivotTable object. If the pt variable is set to Nothing, the active cell was not on a PivotTable, thus no PivotTable could be assigned to the variable. If this is the case, the macro notifies the user via a message box and then exits the procedure.

4. Step 4 of the macro uses a For Each statement to iterate through each pivot field. Each time a new pivot field is selected, you apply all of your pivot field restrictions.

How to use it

You can implement this kind of macro in a standard module:

1. **Activate the Visual Basic Editor by pressing Alt+F11.**
2. **Right-click the project/workbook name in the Project window.**
3. **Choose Insert ➪ Module.**
4. **Type or paste the code.**

Automatically Deleting PivotTable Drill-Down Sheets

One of the coolest features of a PivotTable is that it gives you the ability to double-click on a number and drill into the details. The details are output to a new sheet that you can review. In most cases, you don't want to keep these sheets. In fact, they often become a nuisance, forcing you to take the time to clean them up by deleting them.

This is especially a problem when you distribute PivotTable reports to users who frequently drill into details. There is no guarantee they will remember to clean up the drill-down sheets. Although these sheets probably won't cause issues, they can clutter up the workbook.

Here is a technique you can implement to have your workbook automatically remove these drill-down sheets.

How it works

The basic premise of this macro is actually very simple. When the user clicks for details, outputting a drill-down sheet, the macro simply renames the output sheet so that the first ten characters are PivotDrill. Then before the workbook closes, the macro finds any sheet that starts with PivotDrill and deletes it.

The implementation does get a bit tricky because you essentially have to have two pieces of code. One piece goes in the Worksheet_BeforeDoubleClick event, whereas the other piece goes into the Workbook_BeforeClose event.

```
Private Sub Worksheet_BeforeDoubleClick(ByVal Target As Range,
    Cancel As Boolean)
```

```
'Step 1: Declare you Variables
    Dim pt As String


'Step 2: Exit if Double-Click did not occur on a PivotTable
    On Error Resume Next
    If IsEmpty(Target) And ActiveCell.PivotField.Name <> "" Then
    Cancel = True
    Exit Sub
    End If



'Step 3:  Set the PivotTable object
    pt = ActiveSheet.Range(ActiveCell.Address).PivotTable


'Step 4:  If Drilldowns are Enabled, Drill down
    If ActiveSheet.PivotTables(pt).EnableDrilldown Then
        Selection.ShowDetail = True

    ActiveSheet.Name = _
        Replace(ActiveSheet.Name, "Sheet", "PivotDrill")
    End If

End Sub
```

1. Step 1 starts by creating the pt object variable for your PivotTable.

2. Step 2 checks the double-clicked cell. If the cell is not associated with any PivotTable, the double-click event is cancelled.

3. If a PivotTable is indeed associated with a cell, Step 3 fills the pt variable with the PivotTable.

4. Finally, Step 4 checks the EnableDrillDown property. If it is enabled, you trigger the ShowDetail method. This outputs the drill-down details to a new worksheet.

   The macro follows the output and renames the output sheet so that the first ten characters are PivotDrill. You do this by using the Replace function. The Replace function replaces certain text in an expression with other text. In this case, you are replacing the word Sheet with PivotDrill: Replace(ActiveSheet.Name, "Sheet", "PivotDrill").

   Sheet1 becomes PivotDrill1, Sheet12 becomes PivotTrill12, and so on.

Next, the macro sets up the Worksheet_BeforeDoubleClick event. As the name suggests, this code runs when the workbook closes:

```
Private Sub Workbook_BeforeClose(Cancel As Boolean)


'Step 5:  Declare you Variables
    Dim ws As Worksheet


'Step 6:  Loop through worksheets
    For Each ws In ThisWorkbook.Worksheets


'Step 7:  Delete any sheet that starts with PivotDrill
        If Left(ws.Name, 10) = "PivotDrill" Then
            Application.DisplayAlerts = False
            ws.Delete
            Application.DisplayAlerts = True
        End If
    Next ws

End Sub
```

5. Step 5 declares the ws Worksheet variable. This is used to hold worksheet objects as you loop through the workbook.

6. Step 6 starts the looping, telling Excel you want to evaluate all worksheets in this workbook.

7. In the last step, you evaluate the name of the sheet that has focus in the loop. If the left ten characters of that sheet name are PivotDrill, you delete the worksheet. After all of the sheets have been evaluated, all drill-down sheets have been cleaned up and the macro ends.

How to use it

To implement the first part of the macro, you need to copy and paste it into the Worksheet_BeforeDoubleClick event code window. Placing the macro here allows it to run each time you double-click on the sheet:

1. **Activate the Visual Basic Editor by pressing Alt+F11.**

2. **In the Project window, find your project/workbook name and click the plus sign next to it in order to see all the sheets.**

3. Click on the sheet in which you want to trigger the code.

4. Select the BeforeDoubleClick event from the Event drop-down list box (see Figure 8-3).

5. Type or paste the code.

To implement this macro, you need to copy and paste it into the Workbook_BeforeClose event code window. Placing the macro here allows it to run each time you try to close the workbook:

1. Activate the Visual Basic Editor by pressing Alt+F11.

2. In the Project window, find your project/workbook name and click the plus sign next to it in order to see all the sheets.

3. Click ThisWorkbook.

4. Select the BeforeClose event in the Event drop-down list (see Figure 8-4).

5. Type or paste the code.

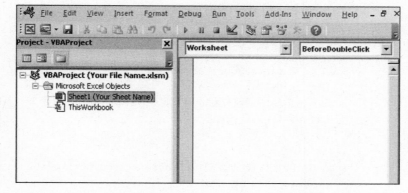

FIGURE 8-3:
Type or paste your code in the Worksheet_ BeforeDouble-Click event code window.

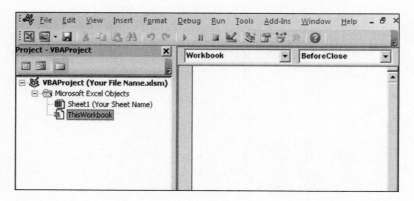

FIGURE 8-4:
Enter or paste your code in the Workbook_ BeforeClose event code window.

Printing a PivotTable for Each Report Filter Item

PivotTables provide an excellent mechanism to parse large data sets into printable files. You can build a PivotTable report, complete with aggregations and analysis, and then place a field (such as Region) into the report filter. With the report filter, you can select each data item at a time, and then print the PivotTable report.

The macro in this section demonstrates how to automatically iterate through all the values in a report filter and print.

How it works

In the Excel object model, the Report Filter drop-down list is known as the Page-Field. To print a PivotTable for each data item in a report filter, you need to loop through the PivotItems collection of the PageField object. As you loop, you dynamically change the selection in the report filter, and then use the ActiveSheet.Print-Out method to print the target range.

```
Sub Macro1()

'Step 1: Declare your Variables
    Dim pt As PivotTable
    Dim pf As PivotField
    Dim pi As PivotItem


'Step 2: Point to the PivotTable in the activecell
    On Error Resume Next
    Set pt = ActiveSheet.PivotTables(ActiveCell.PivotTable.Name)


'Step 3:  Exit if active cell is not in a PivotTable
    If pt Is Nothing Then
    MsgBox "You must place your cursor inside of a PivotTable."
    Exit Sub
    End If


'Step 4:  Exit if more than one page field
    If pt.PageFields.Count > 1 Then
    MsgBox "Too many Report Filter Fields. Limit 1."
```

```
      Exit Sub
      End If


'Step 5:  Start looping through the page field and its pivot
   items
      For Each pf In pt.PageFields
         For Each pi In pf.PivotItems


'Step 6:  Change the selection in the report filter
            pt.PivotFields(pf.Name).CurrentPage = pi.Name


'Step 7: Set Print Area and print
            ActiveSheet.PageSetup.PrintArea = pt.TableRange2.
   Address
            ActiveSheet.PrintOut Copies:=1


'Step 8: Get the next page field item
         Next pi
      Next pf

End Sub
```

1. For this macro, Step 1 declares three variables: pt as the memory container for the PivotTable, pf as a memory container for the page fields, and pi to hold each pivot item as you loop through the PageField object.

2. The active cell must be inside a PivotTable for this macro to run. The assumption is that when the cursor is inside a particular PivotTable, you want to perform the macro action on that pivot.

Step 2 sets the pt variable to name of the PivotTable on which the active cell is found. You do this by using the ActiveCell.PivotTable.Name property to get the name of the target pivot.

If the active cell is not inside of a PivotTable, the macro throws an error. This is why you use the On Error Resume Next statement. This tells Excel to continue with the macro if it encounters an error.

3. Step 3 checks to see whether the pt variable is filled with a PivotTable object. If the pt variable is set to Nothing, the active cell was not on a PivotTable, thus no PivotTable could be assigned to the variable. If this is the case, the user is notified via a message box, and then you exit the procedure.

4. Step 4 determines whether there is more than one report filter field. (If the count of PageFields is greater than 1, there is more than one report filter.) You do this check for a simple reason: If you have multiple report filter fields, you might wind up printing hundreds of pages. The macro stops with a message box if the PivotTable contains more than one report filter field. You can remove this limitation simply by deleting or commenting out Step 4 in the macro.

5. Step 5 starts two loops. The outer loop tells Excel to iterate through all the report filters. The inner loop tells Excel to loop through all the pivot items in the report filter that currently has focus.

6. For each pivot item, the macro captures the item name and uses it to change the report filter selection. This effectively alters the PivotTable report to match the pivot item.

7. Step 7 prints the active sheet and then moves to the next pivot item. After you have looped through all pivot items in the report filter, the macro moves to the next PageField. After all PageFields have been evaluated, the macro ends.

How to use it

You can implement this kind of macro in a standard module:

1. **Activate the Visual Basic Editor by pressing Alt+F11.**

2. **Right-click the project/workbook name in the Project window.**

3. **Choose Insert ⇨ Module.**

4. **Type or paste the code.**

Creating a New Workbook for Each Report Filter Item

PivotTables provide an excellent mechanism to parse large data sets into separate files. You can build a PivotTable report, complete with aggregations and analysis, and then place a field (such as Region) into the report filter. With the report filter, you can select each data item at a time, and then export the PivotTable data to a new workbook.

The macro in this section demonstrates how to automatically iterate through all the values in a report filter and export to a new workbook.

How it works

In the Excel object model, the Report Filter drop-down list is known as the Page-Field. To copy a PivotTable report for each data item in a report filter, the macro needs to loop through the PivotItems collection of the PageField object. As the macro loops, it must dynamically change the selection in the report filter, and then export the PivotTable report to a new workbook.

```
Sub Macro1()

'Step 1: Declare your Variables
    Dim pt As PivotTable
    Dim pf As PivotField
    Dim pi As PivotItem


'Step 2: Point to the PivotTable in the activecell
    On Error Resume Next
    Set pt = ActiveSheet.PivotTables(ActiveCell.PivotTable.Name)


'Step 3:  Exit if active cell is not in a PivotTable
    If pt Is Nothing Then
    MsgBox "You must place your cursor inside of a PivotTable."
    Exit Sub
    End If


'Step 4:  Exit if more than one page field
    If pt.PageFields.Count > 1 Then
    MsgBox "Too many Report Filter Fields. Limit 1."
    Exit Sub
    End If


'Step 5:  Start looping through the page field and its pivot
   items
    For Each pf In pt.PageFields
        For Each pi In pf.PivotItems


'Step 6:  Change the selection in the report filter
        pt.PivotFields(pf.Name).CurrentPage = pi.Name
```

```
'Step 7: Copy the data area to a new workbook
        pt.TableRange1.Copy

        Workbooks.Add.Worksheets(1).Paste
        Application.DisplayAlerts = False

        ActiveWorkbook.SaveAs _
        Filename:="C:\" & pi.Name & ".xlsx"
        ActiveWorkbook.Close
        Application.DisplayAlerts = True


'Step 8: Get the next page field item
        Next pi
    Next pf

End Sub
```

1. Step 1 declares three variables, pt as the memory container for the PivotTable, pf as a memory container for the page fields, and pi to hold each pivot item as the macro loops through the PageField object.

2. The active cell must be inside a PivotTable for this macro to run. The assumption is that when the cursor is inside a particular PivotTable, you want to perform the macro action on that pivot.

   Step 2 sets the pt variable to the name of the PivotTable in which the active cell is found. The macro does this by using the ActiveCell.PivotTable.Name property to get the name of the target pivot.

   If the active cell is not inside of a PivotTable, an error is thrown. This is why you use the On Error Resume Next statement. This tells Excel to continue with the macro if it encounters an error.

3. Step 3 checks to see whether the pt variable is filled with a PivotTable object. If the pt variable is set to Nothing, the active cell was not in a PivotTable, thus no PivotTable could be assigned to the variable. If this is the case, the macro notifies the user via a message box and then exits the procedure.

4. Step 4 determines whether there is more than one report filter field. If the count of PageFields is greater than 1, there is more than one report filter. You do this check for a simple reason: If you have multiple report filter fields, you might wind up creating hundreds of workbooks. The macro stops with a message box if the PivotTable contains more than one report filter field. You can remove this limitation simply by deleting or commenting out Step 4 in the macro.

5. Step 5 starts two loops. The outer loop tells Excel to iterate through all the report filters. The inner loop tells Excel to loop through all the pivot items in the report filter that currently has focus.

6. For each pivot item, Step 6 captures the item name and uses it to change the report filter selection. This effectively alters the PivotTable report to match the pivot item.

7. Step 7 copies TableRange1 of the PivotTable object. TableRange1 is a built-in range object that points to the range of the main data area for the PivotTable. You then paste the data into a new workbook and save it. Note that you need to change the save path to one that works in your environment.

8. Step 8 moves to the next pivot item. After the macro has looped through all pivot items in the report filter, the macro moves to the next PageField. After all PageFields have been evaluated, the macro ends.

How to use it

You can implement this kind of macro in a standard module:

1. **Activate the Visual Basic Editor by pressing Alt+F11.**
2. **Right-click the project/workbook name in the Project window.**
3. **Choose Insert ⇨ Module.**
4. **Type or paste the code.**

Resizing All Charts on a Worksheet

When building a dashboard, you often want to achieve some degree of symmetry and balance. This sometimes requires some level of chart size standardization. The macro in this section gives you an easy way to set a standard height and width for all your charts at once.

How it works

All charts belong to the ChartObjects collection. To take an action on all charts at one time, you simply iterate through all the charts in ChartObjects. Each chart in the ChartObjects collection has an index number that you can use to bring it into focus. For example, ChartObjects(1) points to the first chart in the sheet.

In this macro, you use this concept to loop through the charts on the active sheet with a simple counter. Each time a new chart is brought into focus, you change its height and width to the size you've defined.

```
Sub Macro1()

'Step 1: Declare your variables
    Dim i As Integer


'Step 2:  Start Looping through all the charts
    For i = 1 To ActiveSheet.ChartObjects.Count


'Step 3: Activate each chart and size
    With ActiveSheet.ChartObjects(i)
    .Width = 300
    .Height = 200
    End With


'Step 4:  Increment to move to next chart
    Next i

End Sub
```

1. Step 1 declares the variable i as an integer object used for a looping mechanism.

2. Step 2 starts the looping by setting i to count from 1 to the maximum number of charts in the ChartObjects collection on the active sheet. When the code starts, i initiates with the number 1. As you loop, the variable increments up one number until it reaches a number equal to the maximum number of charts on the sheet.

3. Step 3 passes i to the ChartObjects collection as the index number. This brings a chart into focus. You then set the width and height of the chart to the number you specify here in the code. You can change these numbers to suit your needs.

4. In Step 4, the macro loops back around to increment i up one number and get the next chart. After all charts have been evaluated, the macro ends.

How to use it

To implement this macro, you can copy and paste it into a standard module:

1. **Activate the Visual Basic Editor by pressing Alt+F11.**

2. **Right-click the project/workbook name in the Project window.**

3. **Choose Insert ⇨ Module.**

4. **Type or paste the code into the newly created blank module.**

Aligning a Chart to a Specific Range

Along with adjusting the size of our charts, many of us spend a good bit of time positioning them so that they align nicely in our dashboards. This macro helps easily snap your charts to defined ranges, getting perfect positioning every time.

How it works

Every chart has four properties that dictate its size and position. These properties are Width, Height, Top, and Left. Interestingly enough, every Range object has these same properties. So if you set a chart's Width, Height, Top, and Left properties to match that of a particular range, the chart essentially snaps to that range.

The idea is that after you have decided how you want your dashboard to be laid out, you take note of the ranges that encompass each area of your dashboard. You then use those ranges in this macro to snap each chart to the appropriate range. In this example, you adjust four charts so that their Width, Height, Top, and Left properties match a given range.

Note that you are identifying each chart with a name. Charts are, by default, named "Chart" and the order number they were added (Chart 1, Chart 2, Chart 3, and so on). You can see what each of your charts are named by clicking any chart, and then going up to the Ribbon and selecting Format ⇨ Selection Pane. This activates a task pane (shown in Figure 8–5) that lists all the objects on your sheet with their names.

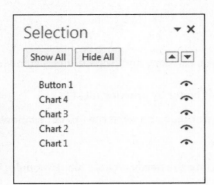

FIGURE 8-5:
The Selection
pane allows you
to see all of your
chart objects and
their respective
names.

You can use it to get the appropriate chart names for your version of this macro.

```
Sub Macro1()

Dim SnapRange As Range

Set SnapRange = ActiveSheet.Range("B6:G19")
    With ActiveSheet.ChartObjects("Chart 1")
     .Height = SnapRange.Height
     .Width = SnapRange.Width
     .Top = SnapRange.Top
     .Left = SnapRange.Left
    End With




Set SnapRange = ActiveSheet.Range("B21:G34")
    With ActiveSheet.ChartObjects("Chart 2")
     .Height = SnapRange.Height
     .Width = SnapRange.Width
     .Top = SnapRange.Top
     .Left = SnapRange.Left
    End With




Set SnapRange = ActiveSheet.Range("I6:Q19")
    With ActiveSheet.ChartObjects("Chart 3")
     .Height = SnapRange.Height
     .Width = SnapRange.Width
     .Top = SnapRange.Top
     .Left = SnapRange.Left
    End With
```

```
Set SnapRange = ActiveSheet.Range("I21:Q34")
   With ActiveSheet.ChartObjects("Chart 4")
    .Height = SnapRange.Height
    .Width = SnapRange.Width
    .Top = SnapRange.Top
    .Left = SnapRange.Left
   End With

End Sub
```

How to use it

To implement this macro, you can copy and paste it into a standard module:

1. **Activate the Visual Basic Editor by pressing Alt+F11.**
2. **Right-click the project/workbook name in the Project window.**
3. **Choose Insert ⇨ Module.**
4. **Type or paste the code into the newly created module.**

Creating a Set of Disconnected Charts

When you need to copy charts from a workbook and paste them elsewhere (another workbook, PowerPoint, Outlook, and so on), it's often best to disconnect them from the original source data. This way, you won't get any of the annoying missing link messages that Excel throws. This macro copies all of the charts in the active sheet, pastes them into a new workbook, and disconnects them from the original source data.

How it works

This macro uses the ShapeRange.Group method to group all the charts on the active sheet into one shape. This is similar to what you would do if you were to group a set of shapes manually. After the charts are grouped, you copy the group and paste it into a new workbook. You then use the BreakLink method to remove references to the original source data. When you do this, Excel hard-codes the chart data into array formulas.

```
Sub Macro1()

'Step 1:  Declare your variables
Dim wbLinks As Variant


'Step 2:  Group the charts, copy the group, and then ungroup
    With ActiveSheet.ChartObjects.ShapeRange.Group
    .Copy
    .Ungroup
    End With


'Step 3:  Paste into a new workbook and ungroup
    Workbooks.Add.Sheets(1).Paste
    Selection.ShapeRange.Ungroup


'Step 4: Break the links
    wbLinks = ActiveWorkbook.LinkSources(Type:=xlLinkType
    ExcelLinks)
    ActiveWorkbook.BreakLink Name:=wbLinks(1), _
                            Type:=xlLinkTypeExcelLinks

End Sub
```

1. Step 1 declares the wbLinks variant variable. The macro uses this in Step 4 to pass the link source when breaking the links.

2. Step 2 uses ChartObjects.ShapeRange.Group to group all the charts into a single shape. The macro then copies the group to the clipboard. After the group is copied, the macro ungroups the charts.

3. Step 3 creates a new workbook and pastes the copied group to Sheet 1. After the group has been pasted, you can ungroup so that each chart is separate again. Note that the newly created workbook is now the active object, so all references to ActiveWorkbook points back to this workbook.

4. Step 4 captures the link source in the wbLinks variable. The macro then tells Excel to break the links.

REMEMBER

Note that because this technique converts the chart source links to an array formula, this technique can fail if your chart contains too many data points. How many is too many? It can be different for every PC because it is limited by memory.

How to use it

To implement this macro, you can copy and paste it into a standard module:

1. **Activate the Visual Basic Editor by pressing Alt+F11.**

2. **Right-click the project/workbook name in the Project window.**

3. **Choose Insert ⇨ Module.**

4. **Type or paste the code into the newly created module.**

Printing All Charts on a Worksheet

To print a chart, you can click any embedded chart in your worksheet and then click Print. This prints the chart on its own sheet without any of the other data on the sheet. This sounds easy enough, but it can become a chore if you've got to do this for many charts. This macro makes short work of this task.

How it works

All charts belong to the ChartObjects collection. To take an action on all charts at one time, you simply iterate through all the charts in ChartObjects. Each chart in the ChartObjects collection has an index number that you can use to bring it into focus. For example, ChartObjects(1) points to the first chart in the sheet.

In this macro, you use this concept to loop through the charts on the active sheet with a simple counter. Each time a new chart is brought into focus, print it.

```
Sub Macro1()

'Step 1: Declare your variables
    Dim ChartList As Integer
    Dim i As Integer


'Step 2:  Start Looping through all the charts
    For i = 1 To ActiveSheet.ChartObjects.Count


'Step 3: Activate each chart and print
        ActiveSheet.ChartObjects(i).Activate
```

```
        ActiveChart.PageSetup.Orientation = xlLandscape
        ActiveChart.PrintOut Copies:=1


'Step 4:   Increment to move to next chart
    Next i

End Sub
```

1. Step 1 declares the variable i as an integer object used for a looping mechanism.

2. Step 2 starts the looping by setting i to count from 1 to the maximum number of charts in the ChartObjects collection on the active sheet. When the code starts, i initiates with the number 1. As you loop, the variable increments up one number until it reaches a number equal to the maximum number of charts on the sheet.

3. Step 3 passes i to the ChartObjects collection as the index number. This brings a chart into focus. You then use the ActiveChart.Printout method to trigger the print. Note that you can adjust the Orientation property to either xlLandscape or xlPortrait depending on what you need.

4. Step 4 loops back around to increment i up one number and get the next chart. After all charts have been evaluated, the macro ends.

How to use it

To implement this macro, you can copy and paste it into a standard module:

1. **Activate the Visual Basic Editor by pressing Alt+F11.**

2. **Right-click the project/workbook name in the Project window.**

3. **Choose Insert ⇨ Module.**

4. **Type or paste the code into the newly created module.**

Chapter **9**

Sending Emails from Excel

D id you know that you probably integrate Excel and Outlook all the time? It's true. If you've sent or received an Excel workbook through Outlook, you've integrated the two programs, albeit manually. This chapter shows you a few examples of how you can integrate Excel and Outlook in a more automated fashion.

The macros in this chapter automate Microsoft Outlook. For these macros to work, you need Microsoft Outlook installed on your system.

REMEMBER

Mailing the Active Workbook as an Attachment

The most fundamental Outlook task you can perform through automation is sending an email. In the sample code shown here, the active workbook is sent to two email recipients as an attachment.

REMEMBER

Some of you may notice that we are not using the SendMail command native to Excel. With the SendMail command, you can send simple email messages directly from Excel. However, the SendMail command is not as robust as Outlook automation. SendMail does not allow you to attach files, or use the CC and BCC fields in the email, which makes the technique that this macro uses a superior method.

How it works

Because this code runs from Excel, you need to set a reference to the Microsoft Outlook Object Library. You can set the reference by opening the Visual Basic Editor in Excel and choosing Tools➪References. Scroll down until you find the entry Microsoft Outlook *XX* Object Library, where the *XX* is your version of Outlook. Select the check box next to the entry.

```
Sub Macro1()

'Step 1:  Declare our variables
    Dim OLApp As Outlook.Application
    Dim OLMail As Object


'Step 2:  Open Outlook start a new mail item
    Set OLApp = New Outlook.Application
    Set OLMail = OLApp.CreateItem(0)
    OLApp.Session.Logon


'Step 3:  Build our mail item and send
    With OLMail
    .To = "admin@datapigtechnologies.com;
        mike@datapigtechnologies.com"
    .CC = ""
    .BCC = ""
    .Subject = "This is the Subject line"
    .Body = "Sample File Attached"
```

```
        .Attachments.Add ActiveWorkbook.FullName
        .Display
        End With



'Step 4:  Memory cleanup
    Set OLMail = Nothing
    Set OLApp = Nothing


End Sub
```

1. Step 1 declares two variables. OLApp is an object variable that exposes the Outlook Application object. OLMail is an object variable that holds a mail item.

2. Step 2 activates Outlook and starts a new session. Note that you use OLApp. Session.Logon to log on to the current MAPI session with default credentials. It also creates a mail item. This is equivalent to clicking the New Message button in Outlook.

3. Step 3 builds the profile of your mail item. This includes the To recipients, the CC recipients, the BCC recipients, the Subject, the Body, and the Attachments. This step notes that the recipients are entered in quotes and separates recipients with a semicolon. The standard syntax for an attachment is .Attachments.Add "File Path". Here in this code, you specify the current workbook's file path with the syntax ActiveWorkbook.Fullname. This sets the current workbook as the attachment for the email. When the message has been built, you use the .Display method to review the email. You can replace .Display with .Send to automatically fire the email without reviewing.

4. Releasing the objects assigned to your variables is generally good practice. This reduces the chance of any problems caused by rogue objects that may remain open in memory. As you can see in the code, you simply set the variables to Nothing.

How to use it

To implement this macro, copy and paste it into a standard module:

1. **Activate the Visual Basic Editor by pressing Alt+F11.**

2. **Right-click the project/workbook name in the Project window.**

3. **Choose Insert ⇨ Module.**

4. **Type or paste the code into the newly created module.**

Mailing a Specific Range as an Attachment

You may not always want to send your entire workbook through email. This macro demonstrates how to send a specific range of data rather than the entire workbook.

How it works

Because this code is run from Excel, you need to set a reference to the Microsoft Outlook Object Library. You can set the reference by opening the Visual Basic Editor in Excel and choosing Tools⇨References. Scroll down until you find the entry Microsoft Outlook *XX* Object Library, where the *XX* is your version of Outlook. Select the check box next to the entry.

```
Sub Macro1()

'Step 1:  Declare our variables
    Dim OLApp As Outlook.Application
    Dim OLMail As Object


'Step 2:  Copy range, paste to new workbook, and save it
    Sheets("Revenue Table").Range("A1:E7").Copy
    Workbooks.Add
    Range("A1").PasteSpecial xlPasteValues
    Range("A1").PasteSpecial xlPasteFormats
    ActiveWorkbook.SaveAs ThisWorkbook.Path & _
            "\TempRangeForEmail.xlsx"


'Step 3:  Open Outlook start a new mail item
    Set OLApp = New Outlook.Application
    Set OLMail = OLApp.CreateItem(0)
    OLApp.Session.Logon


'Step 4:  Build our mail item and send
    With OLMail
        .To = "admin@datapigtechnologies.com;" _
            mike@datapigtechnologies.com"
        .CC = ""
        .BCC = ""
        .Subject = "This is the Subject line"
```

```
      .Body = "Sample File Attached"
      .Attachments.Add (ThisWorkbook.Path & _
            "\TempRangeForEmail.xlsx")
      .Display
      End With



'Step 5:  Delete the temporary Excel file
      ActiveWorkbook.Close SaveChanges:=True
      Kill ThisWorkbook.Path & "\TempRangeForEmail.xlsx"



'Step 6:  Memory cleanup
      Set OLMail = Nothing
      Set OLApp = Nothing

End Sub
```

1. Step 1 declares two variables. OLApp is an object variable that exposes the Outlook Application object. OLMail is an object variable that holds a mail item.

2. Step 2 copies a specified range and pastes the values and formats to a temporary Excel file. The macro then saves that temporary file, giving it a file path and filename.

3. Step 3 activates Outlook and starts a new session. Note that you use OLApp. Session.Logon to log on to the current MAPI session with default credentials. You also create a mail item. This is equivalent to clicking the New Message button in Outlook.

4. Step 4 builds the profile of the mail item. This includes the To recipients, the CC recipients, the BCC recipients, the Subject, the Body, and the Attachments. This step notes that the recipients are entered in quotes and separates recipients by a semicolon. Here in this code, you specify your newly created temporary Excel file path as the attachment for the email. When the message has been built, you use the .Display method to review the email. You can replace .Display with .Send to automatically fire the email without reviewing.

5. You don't want to leave temporary files hanging out there, so after the email has been sent, Step 5 deletes the temporary Excel file you created.

6. It is generally good practice to release the objects assigned to your variables. This reduces the chance of any problems caused by rogue objects that may remain open in memory. In Step 6, you simply set the variables to Nothing.

How to use it

To implement this macro, copy and paste it into a standard module:

1. Activate the Visual Basic Editor by pressing Alt+F11.
2. Right-click the project/workbook name in the Project window.
3. Choose Insert ⇨ Module.
4. Type or paste the code into the newly created module.

Mailing a Single Sheet as an Attachment

This example demonstrates how to send a specific worksheet of data rather than the entire workbook.

How it works

Because this code is run from Excel, you need to set a reference to the Microsoft Outlook Object Library. You can set the reference by opening the Visual Basic Editor in Excel and choosing Tools ⇨ References. Scroll down until you find the entry Microsoft Outlook *XX* Object Library, where the *XX* is your version of Outlook. Place a check in the check box next to the entry.

```
Sub Macro1()

'Step 1:  Declare our variables
    Dim OLApp As Outlook.Application
    Dim OLMail As Object


'Step 2:  Copy Worksheet, paste to new workbook, and save it
    Sheets("Revenue Table").Copy
    ActiveWorkbook.SaveAs ThisWorkbook.Path & _
        "\TempRangeForEmail.xlsx"


'Step 3:  Open Outlook start a new mail item
    Set OLApp = New Outlook.Application
    Set OLMail = OLApp.CreateItem(0)
    OLApp.Session.Logon
```

```
'Step 4:  Build our mail item and send
    With OLMail
    .To = "admin@datapigtechnologies.com;
          mike@datapigtechnologies.com"
    .CC = ""
    .BCC = ""
    .Subject = "This is the Subject line"
    .Body = "Sample File Attached"
    .Attachments.Add (ThisWorkbook.Path &
          "\TempRangeForEmail.xlsx")
    .Display
    End With


'Step 5:  Delete the temporary Excel file
    ActiveWorkbook.Close SaveChanges:=True
    Kill ThisWorkbook.Path & "\TempSheetForEmail.xlsx"


'Step 6:  Memory cleanup
    Set OLMail = Nothing
    Set OLApp = Nothing

End Sub
```

1. Step 1 declares two variables. OLApp is an object variable that exposes the Outlook Application object. OLMail is an object variable that holds a mail item.

2. Step 2 copies the specified sheet and pastes the values and formats to a temporary Excel file. You then save that temporary file, giving it a file path and filename.

3. Step 3 activates Outlook and starts a new session. Note that you use OLApp. Session.Logon to log on to the current MAPI session with default credentials. You also create a mail item. This is equivalent to clicking the New Message button in Outlook.

4. Step 4 builds the profile of the mail item. This includes the To recipients, the CC recipients, the BCC recipients, the Subject, the Body, and the Attachments. The recipients are entered in quotes and separated by a semicolon. In this code, you specify your newly created temporary Excel file path as the attachment for the email. When the message has been built, you use the .Display method to review the email. You can replace .Display with .Send to automatically fire the email without reviewing.

5. You don't want to leave temporary files hanging out there, so after the email has been sent, you delete the temporary Excel file you created.

6. It is generally good practice to release the objects assigned to your variables. This reduces the chance of any problems caused by rogue objects that may remain open in memory. As you can see in the code, you simply set the variables to Nothing.

How to use it

To implement this macro, copy and paste it into a standard module:

1. **Activate the Visual Basic Editor by pressing Alt+F11.**
2. **Right-click the project/workbook name in the Project window.**
3. **Choose Insert ⇨ Module.**
4. **Type or paste the code into the newly created module.**

Sending Mail with a Link to Your Workbook

Sometimes, you don't need to send an attachment at all. Instead, you simply want to send an automated email with a link to a file. This macro does just that.

REMEMBER

Your users or customers need at least read access to the network or location tied to the link.

How it works

Keep in mind that because this code is run from Excel, you need to set a reference to the Microsoft Outlook Object Library. You can set the reference by opening the Visual Basic Editor in Excel and choosing Tools ⇨ References. Scroll down until you find the entry Microsoft Outlook *XX* Object Library, where the *XX* is your version of Outlook. Select the check box next to the entry.

```
Sub Macro1()

'Step 1:  Declare our variables
    Dim OLApp As Outlook.Application
    Dim OLMail As Object
```

```
'Step 2:  Open Outlook start a new mail item
    Set OLApp = New Outlook.Application
    Set OLMail = OLApp.CreateItem(0)
    OLApp.Session.Logon


'Step 3:  Build our mail item and send
    With OLMail
    .To = "admin@datapigtechnologies.com;
        mike@datapigtechnologies.com"
    .CC = ""
    .BCC = ""
    .Subject = "Monthly Report Email with Link"
    .HTMLBody = _
    "<p>Monthly report is ready. Click the link to get
        it.</p> " & _
    "<p><a href=" & Chr(34) &
        "Z:\Downloads\MonthlyReport.xlsx" & _
    Chr(34) & ">Download Now</a></p>"
    .Display
    End With


'Step 4:  Memory cleanup
    Set OLMail = Nothing
    Set OLApp = Nothing

End Sub
```

1. Step 1 declares two variables. OLApp is an object variable that exposes the Outlook Application object. OLMail is an object variable that holds a mail item.

2. Step 2 activates Outlook and starts a new session. Note that you use OLApp. Session.Logon to log on to the current MAPI session with default credentials. This step also creates a mail item. This is equivalent to clicking the New Message button in Outlook.

3. Step 3 builds the profile of your mail item. This includes the To recipients, the CC recipients, the BCC recipients, the Subject, and the HTMLBody. To create the hyperlink, you need to use the HTMLBody property to pass HTML tags. You can replace the file path address shown in the macro with the address for your file. Note that this macro is using the .Display method, which opens the email for review. You can replace .Display with .Send to automatically fire the email without reviewing.

4. It is generally good practice to release the objects assigned to your variables. This reduces the chance of any problems caused by rogue objects that may remain open in memory. In Step 4, you simply set the variables to Nothing.

How to use it

To implement this macro, copy and paste it into a standard module:

1. Activate the Visual Basic Editor by pressing Alt+F11 on your keyboard.

2. Right-click the project/workbook name in the Project window.

3. Choose Insert ⇨ Module.

4. Type or paste the code into the newly created module.

Mailing All Email Addresses in Your Contact List

Ever need to send out a mass mailing such as a newsletter or a memo? Instead of manually entering each of your contacts' email addresses, you can run the following procedure. This procedure sends out one email, automatically adding all the email addresses in your contact list to the email.

How it works

Because this code is run from Excel, you need to set a reference to the Microsoft Outlook Object Library. You can set the reference by opening the Visual Basic Editor in Excel and choosing Tools ⇨ References. Scroll down until you find the entry Microsoft Outlook *XX* Object Library, where the *XX* is your version of Outlook. Select the check box next to the entry.

```
Sub Macro1()


'Step 1:  Declare our variables
    Dim OLApp As Outlook.Application
    Dim OLMail As Object
    Dim MyCell As Range
    Dim MyContacts As Range
```

```
'Step 2:  Define the range to loop through
    Set MyContacts = Sheets("Contact List").Range("H2:H21")


'Step 3:  Open Outlook
    Set OLApp = New Outlook.Application
    Set OLMail = OLApp.CreateItem(0)
    OLApp.Session.Logon


'Step 4:  Add each address in the contact list
    With OLMail

        For Each MyCell In MyContacts
        .BCC = .BCC & Chr(59) & MyCell.Value
        Next MyCell

        .Subject = "Sample File Attached"
        .Body = "Sample file is attached"
        .Attachments.Add ActiveWorkbook.FullName
        .Display

    End With


'Step 5:  Memory cleanup
    Set OLMail = Nothing
    Set OLApp = Nothing

End Sub
```

1. Step 1 declares four variables: OLApp is an object variable that exposes the Outlook Application object. OLMail is an object variable that holds a mail item. MyCell is an object variable that holds an Excel range. MyContacts is an object variable that holds an Excel range.

2. Step 2 points the MyContacts variable to the range of cells that contains your email addresses. This is the range of cells you loop through to add email addresses to your email.

3. Step 3 activates Outlook and starts a new session. Note that you use OLApp. Session.Logon to log on to the current MAPI session with default credentials. You also create a mail item. This is equivalent to clicking the New Message button in Outlook.

4. Step 4 builds the profile of your mail item. Note that you are looping through each cell in the MyContacts range and adding the contents (which are email

addresses) to the BCC. Here, you are using the BCC property rather than To or CC so that each recipient gets an email that looks as though it was sent only to him. Your recipients won't be able to see any of the other email addresses because the addresses have been sent with BCC (Blind Courtesy Copy). Note also that this macro is using the .Display method, which opens the email for review. You can replace .Display with .Send to automatically fire the email without reviewing.

5. It is generally good practice to release the objects assigned to your variables. This reduces the chance of any problems caused by rogue objects that may remain open in memory. In Step 5, you simply set the variables to Nothing.

How to use it

To implement this macro, copy and paste it into a standard module:

1. **Activate the Visual Basic Editor by pressing Alt+F11 on your keyboard.**
2. **Right-click the project/workbook name in the Project window.**
3. **Choose Insert ⇨ Module.**
4. **Type or paste the code into the newly created module.**

Saving All Attachments to a Folder

You may often find that certain processes lend themselves to the exchange of data via email. For example, you may send out a budget template for each branch manager to fill out and send back to you via email. Well, if there are 150 branch members, it could be a bit of a pain to download all those email attachments.

The following procedure demonstrates one solution to this problem. In this procedure, you use automation to search for all attachments in the inbox and save them to a specified folder.

How it works

Because this code is run from Excel, you need to set a reference to the Microsoft Outlook Object Library. You can set the reference by opening the Visual Basic Editor in Excel and choosing Tools ⇨ References. Scroll down until you find the entry Microsoft Outlook *XX* Object Library, where the *XX* is your version of Outlook. Select the check box next to the entry.

```
Sub Macro1()

'Step 1:  Declare our variables
    Dim ns As Namespace
    Dim MyInbox As MAPIFolder
    Dim MItem As MailItem
    Dim Atmt As Attachment
    Dim FileName As String


'Step 2:  Set a reference to our inbox
    Set ns = GetNamespace("MAPI")
    Set MyInbox = ns.GetDefaultFolder(olFolderInbox)


'Step 3:  Check for messages in our inbox; exit if none
    If MyInbox.Items.Count = 0 Then
    MsgBox "No messages in folder."
    Exit Sub
    End If


'Step 4:  Create directory to hold attachments
    On Error Resume Next
    MkDir "C:\Temp\MyAttachments\"


'Step 5:  Start to loop through each mail item
    For Each MItem In MyInbox.Items


'Step 6:  Save each attachment then go to the next attachment
    For Each Atmt In MItem.Attachments
    FileName = "C:\Temp\MyAttachments\" & Atmt.FileName
    Atmt.SaveAsFile FileName
    Next Atmt


'Step 7:  Move to the next mail item
    Next MItem
```

```
'Step 8:  Memory cleanup
    Set ns = Nothing
    Set MyInbox = Nothing

End Sub
```

1. Step 1 declares five variables. ns is an object used to expose the MAPI namespace. MyInbox is used to expose the target mail folder. MItem is used to expose the properties of a mail item. Atmt is an object variable that holds an Attachment object. FileName is a string variable that holds the name of the attachment.

2. Step 2 sets the MyInbox variable to point to the inbox for the default mail client.

3. Step 3 performs a quick check to make sure there are actual messages in the inbox. If no messages are found, the macro exits the procedure with a message box stating that there are no messages.

4. Step 4 creates a directory to hold the attachments you find. Although you could use an existing directory, using a directory dedicated specifically for the attachments you bring down is usually best. Here, you are creating that directory on the fly. Note you are using On Error Resume Next. This ensures that the code does not error out if the directory you are trying to create already exists.

5. Step 5 starts the loop through each mail item in the target mail folder.

6. Step 6 ensures that each mail item you loop through gets checked for attachments. As you loop, each attachment you find gets saved into the specified directory you created.

7. Step 7 loops back to Step 5 until there are no more mail items to go through.

8. Releasing the objects assigned to your variables is good general practice. This reduces the chance of any problems caused by rogue objects that may remain open in memory. Step 8 simply sets the variables to Nothing.

How to use it

To implement this macro, copy and paste it into a standard module:

1. **Activate the Visual Basic Editor by pressing Alt+F11.**

2. **Right-click the project/workbook name in the Project window.**

3. **Choose Insert ⇨ Module.**

4. **Type or paste the code into the newly created module.**

Saving Certain Attachments to a Folder

The previous procedure showed how to use automation to search for all attachments in your inbox and save them to a specified folder. However, in most situations, you probably only want to save certain attachments; for example, those attached to emails that contain a certain Subject. This example demonstrates how to check for certain syntax and selectively bring down attachments.

How it works

Because this code is run from Excel, you need to set a reference to the Microsoft Outlook Object Library. You can set the reference by opening the Visual Basic Editor in Excel and choosing Tools⇨References. Scroll down until you find the entry Microsoft Outlook *XX* Object Library, where the *XX* is your version of Outlook. Select the check box next to the entry.

```
Sub Macro1()

'Step 1:  Declare our variables
    Dim ns As Namespace
    Dim MyInbox As MAPIFolder
    Dim MItem As Object
    Dim Atmt As Attachment
    Dim FileName As String
    Dim i As Integer


'Step 2:  Set a reference to our inbox
    Set ns = GetNamespace("MAPI")
    Set MyInbox = ns.GetDefaultFolder(olFolderInbox)


'Step 3:  Check for messages in our inbox; exit if none
    If MyInbox.Items.Count = 0 Then
    MsgBox "No messages in folder."
    Exit Sub
    End If


'Step 4:  Create directory to hold attachments
    On Error Resume Next
    MkDir "C:\OffTheGrid\MyAttachments\"
```

```
'Step 5:  Start to loop through each mail item
    For Each MItem In MyInbox.Items


'Step 6:  Check for the words Data Submission in Subject line
    If InStr(1, MItem.Subject, "Data Submission") < 1 Then
    GoTo SkipIt
    End If



'Step 7:  Save each with a log number; go to the next
          attachment
    i = 0
    For Each Atmt In MItem.Attachments
    FileName = _
    "C:\Temp\MyAttachments\Attachment-" & i & "-" &
          Atmt.FileName
    Atmt.SaveAsFile FileName
    i = i + 1
    Next Atmt



'Step 8:  Move to the next mail item
SkipIt:
    Next MItem



'Step 9:  Memory cleanup
    Set ns = Nothing
    Set MyInbox = Nothing

End Sub
```

1. Step 1 declares six variables. ns is an object used to expose the MAPI
   namespace. MyInbox is used to expose the target mail folder. MItem is used to
   expose the properties of a mail item. Atmt is an object variable that holds an
   Attachment object. FileName is a string variable that holds the name of the
   attachment. i is an integer variable used to ensure each attachment is saved as
   a unique name.

2. Step 2 sets the MyInbox variable to point to the inbox for your default mail
   client.

3. Step 3 performs a quick check to make sure there are actual messages in your inbox. If no messages are found, it exits the procedure with a message box stating that there are no messages.

4. Step 4 creates a directory to hold the attachments you find. Note that it uses On Error Resume Next. This ensures that the code does not error out if the directory you are trying to create already exists.

5. Step 5 starts the loop through each mail item in the target mail folder.

6. In Step 6, you use the Instr function to check whether the string "Data Submission" is in the Subject line of the email. If that string does not exist, you don't care about any attachments to that message. Therefore, you force the code to go to the SkipIt reference (in Step 8). Because the line of code immediately following the SkipIt reference is essentially a Move Next command, this effectively tells the procedure to move to the next mail item.

7. Step 7 loops through and saves each attachment into the specified directory you created. Note that you are adding a running integer to the name of each attachment. This is to ensure that each attachment is saved as a unique name, helping to avoid overwriting attachments.

8. Step 8 loops back to Step 5 until there are no more mail items to go through.

9. Releasing the objects assigned to your variables is generally good practice. This reduces the chance of any problems caused by rogue objects that may remain open in memory. In Step 9, you simply set the variables to Nothing.

How to use it

To implement this macro, copy and paste it into a standard module:

1. Activate the Visual Basic Editor by pressing Alt+F11.

2. Right-click the project/workbook name in the Project window.

3. Choose Insert ➪ Module.

4. Type or paste the code into the newly created module.

Chapter **10**

Wrangling External Data with Macros

External data is exactly what it sounds like: data that isn't located in the Excel workbook in which you're operating. Some examples of external data sources are text files, CSV files, Access tables, and even SQL Server tables.

There are numerous ways to get data into Excel. In fact, between the functionality found in the UI and the VBA/code techniques, there are too many techniques to focus on in one chapter. Instead, then, this chapter focuses on a handful of techniques that you can implement in most situations and that don't come with a lot of pitfalls and gotchas.

Working with External Data Connections

Every Excel workbook has the ability to store syntax that allows the workbook to pull in data from external databases, files, and websites. This ability is made possible by Excel's External Data Connection feature. You can create any number of data connections in order to retrieve the needed external data.

This next section walks you through the ins and outs of working with external data connections.

Manually creating a connection

Excel has made it easy to manually connect to external data sources such as Microsoft Access, SQL Server, or any other ODBC connection you regularly use. For example, you can connect to an Access database by following these steps:

TIP

Feel free to follow along by using the Facility Services.accdb Access database found on book's website, which you can access at www.dummies.com/go/excelmacros. The DynamicDataConnection.xlsm file contains the sample macros found in this section.

1. **Open a new Excel workbook and click the Data tab on the Ribbon.**

2. **In the Get External Data group, select the From Microsoft Access icon.**

The Select Data Source dialog box opens, as shown in Figure 10-1. If the database from which you want to import data is local, browse to the file's location and select it. If your target Access database resides on a network drive at another location, you need the proper authorization to select it.

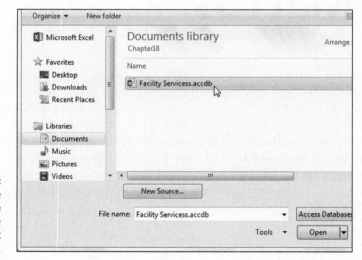

FIGURE 10-1:
Choose the source database that contains the data you want imported.

3. **Navigate to your sample database and click Open.**

4. **Click OK.**

The Select Table dialog box shown in Figure 10-2 opens. This dialog box lists all the available tables and queries in the selected database.

The Select Table dialog box contains a column called Type. There are two types of Access objects you can work with: views and tables. View indicates that the dataset listed is an Access query, and Table indicates that the dataset is an

Access table. In this example, Sales_By_Employee is actually an Access query. This means that you import the results of the query. This is true interaction at work; Access does all the back-end data management and aggregation, and Excel handles the analysis and presentation.

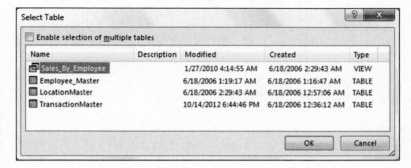

FIGURE 10-2:
Select the Access object you want to import.

5. **Select your target table or query and click OK.**

REMEMBER

In cases when your Access database is password protected, Step 3 activates a series of Data Link Properties dialog boxes asking for credentials (that is, username and password). Most Access databases don't require logon credentials, but if your database does require a username and password, type them in the Data Link Properties dialog box.

The Import Data dialog box shown in Figure 10-3 opens. Here you define where and how to import the table. You have the option of importing the data into a Table, a PivotTable Report, a PivotChart, or a Power View Report. You also have the option of creating only the connection, making the connection available for later use.

Note that if you choose PivotChart or PivotTable Report, the data is saved to a pivot cache without writing the actual data to the worksheet. Thus your PivotTable can function as normal without you having to import potentially hundreds of thousands of data rows twice (once for the pivot cache and once for the spreadsheet).

6. **Select Table as the output view and define cell A1 as the output location, as shown in Figure 10-3.**

7. **Click OK.**

Your reward for all your work is a table (see Figure 10-4) which contains the imported data from your Access database.

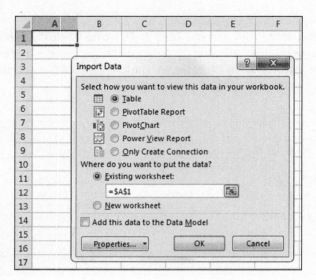

FIGURE 10-3:
Choosing how
and where
to view your
Access data.

	A	B	C	D	
1	Region ▼	Market ▼	Branch_Number ▼	Employee_Number ▼	La
2	MIDWEST	TULSA	401612	1336	RA
3	MIDWEST	TULSA	401612	1336	RA
4	MIDWEST	TULSA	401612	60224	HE
5	MIDWEST	TULSA	401612	60224	HE
6	MIDWEST	TULSA	401612	55662	W
7	MIDWEST	TULSA	401612	60224	HE
8	MIDWEST	TULSA	401612	1336	RA
9	MIDWEST	TULSA	401612	55662	W
10	MIDWEST	TULSA	401612	55662	W
11	MIDWEST	TULSA	401612	1336	RA
12	MIDWEST	TULSA	401612	55662	W
13	MIDWEST	TULSA	401612	55662	W

FIGURE 10-4:
Data imported
from Access.

The incredibly powerful thing about importing data this way is that it's refresh-able. That's right. If you import data from Access using this technique, Excel creates a table that you can update by right-clicking it and selecting Refresh from the pop-up menu, as shown in Figure 10-5. When you update your imported data, Excel reconnects to your Access database and imports the data again. As long as a connection to your database is available, you can refresh with a mere click of the mouse.

Again, a major advantage to using the Get External Data group is that you can establish a refreshable data connection between Excel and Access. In most cases, you can set up the connection one time and then just update the data connection when needed. You can even record an Excel macro to update the data on some trigger or event, which is ideal for automating the transfer of data from Access.

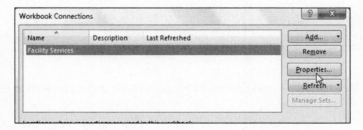

FIGURE 10-5:
As long as a
connection to
your database is
available, you
can update your
table with the
latest data.

Manually editing data connections

Once you have a connection, you can use the connection properties to point to another database table or query. You can even write your own SQL statements. *SQL* (Structured Query Language) is the language that relational database systems (such as Microsoft Access) use to perform various tasks. You can pass instructions right from Excel by using SQL statements. This can give you more control over the data you pull into your Excel model.

Although a detailed discussion of SQL is beyond the scope of this book, let's step a bit outside our comfort zone and edit our external data connection using a simple SQL statement to pull in a different set of data.

1. **Go to the Data tab on the Ribbon and select Connections. This activates the Workbook Connections dialog box shown in Figure 10-6.**

FIGURE 10-6:
Choose the
Properties button
for the connection
you want to
change.

2. **Choose the connection you want to edit and then click the Properties button.**

3. **The Connection Properties dialog box opens. Here, you can click the Definition tab (see Figure 10-7).**

4. **Change the Command Type property to SQL and then enter your SQL statement. In this case, you can enter:**

```
SELECT * FROM [Sales_By_Employee]
WHERE ([Market] = 'Tulsa')
```

This statement tells Excel to pull in all records from the Sales_By_Employee table where the Market equals Tulsa.

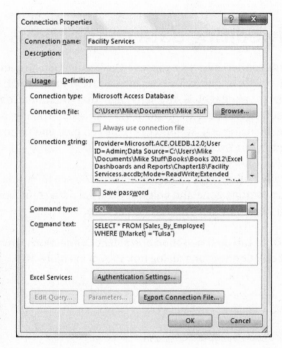

FIGURE 10-7:
On the Definitions tab, select the SQL command type and enter your SQL statement.

5. **Click OK to confirm your changes and close the Connection Properties dialog box.**

Excel immediately triggers a refresh of your external connection, bringing in your new data.

Using Macros to Create Dynamic Connections

By now, you should have noticed that you haven't used any macros yet. So far, you have simply hard-coded the criteria for your connection. For example, in

Figure 10-7, Tulsa is specified directly into the SQL statement WHERE clause. This obviously would cause the data being returned to always be data for Tulsa.

But what if you wanted to select a market and have the SQL statement to dynamically change to respond to your selection? Well, you can use a bit of VBA to change the SQL statement on the fly. Follow these steps:

1. Designate a cell in your worksheet that will catch the dynamic selection for your criteria.

For example, in Figure 10-8, cell C2 will be the place that users can select a market. You would typically give users a way to select criteria with either a Combo Box or a Data Validation list.

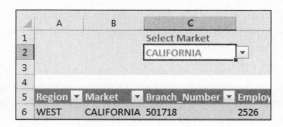

FIGURE 10-8:
Designate a cell that will trap the criteria selection.

2. Open the Workbook Connections dialog box by clicking the Connections command on the Data tab.

Take note of the name for the connection you want to dynamically change. In Figure 10-9, you see the connection name is Facility Services.

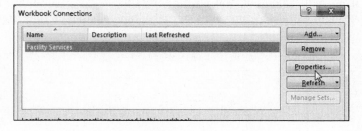

3. Close the Workbook Connections dialog box and press Alt+F11 on your keyboard. This takes you to the Visual Basic Editor.

4. In the Visual Basic Editor, choose Insert ⇨ Module from menu bar.

5. Enter the following code in the newly created module:

```
Sub RefreshQuery()

ActiveWorkbook.Connections( _
"Facility Services").OLEDBConnection.CommandText = _
"SELECT * FROM [Sales_By_Employee] WHERE [Market] = '" & _
 Range("C2").Value & "'"

ActiveWorkbook.Connections("Facility Services").Refresh

End Sub
```

This code creates a new macro called RefreshQuery. This macro uses the Workbook.Connections collection to change the attributes of the specified connection. In this case, you want to change the CommandText property of the Facility Services connection.

The command text is essentially the SQL Statement you want the connection to use when connecting to the data source. In this example, the command text selects from the [Sales_By_Employee] table and sets the criteria for the [Market] field to the value in cell C2. The code then refreshes the Facility Services connection.

6. Close the Visual Basic Editor and place a new command button on your worksheet. To do this, click the Developer tab, select the Insert drop-down, and add a Button Form control.

7. Assign the newly created RefreshQuery macro to the command button.

If all went smoothly, you have a nifty mechanism that allows for the dynamic extraction of data from your external database based on the criteria you specified (see Figure 10-10).

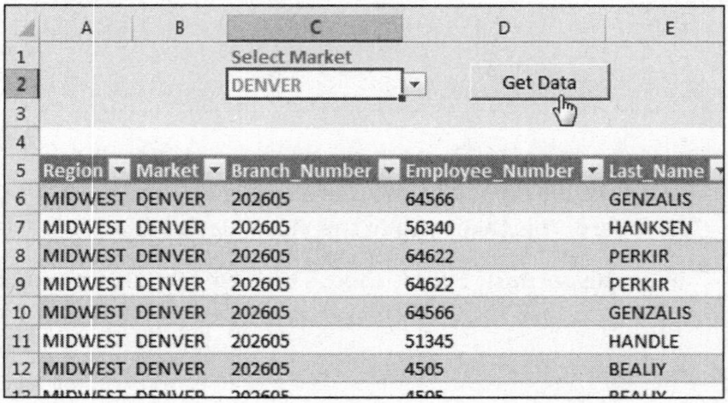

FIGURE 10-10: You now have an easy-to-use mechanism to pull external data for a specified market.

Iterating through All Connections in a Workbook

You can also use the Workbook.Connections collection to iterate through all the connection objects in a workbook and examine or modify their properties. For example, say you have a workbook with multiple external data connections. You can use this macro to populate a worksheet with a list of all connection objects in the current workbook, along with their associated connection strings and command texts:

```
Sub ListConnections()

'Step 1:  Declare your variables
Dim i As Long
Dim Cn As WorkbookConnection

'Step 2:  Add a worksheet with header for
    'Connection Name, Connection String, and Command Text
Worksheets.Add
With ActiveSheet.Range("A1:C1")
.Value = Array("Cn Name","Connection String","Command Text")
.EntireColumn.AutoFit
End With

'Step 3: Iterate through each connection and write the
'needed properties to the newly created worksheet.
For Each Cn In ThisWorkbook.Connections
i = i + 1

Select Case Cn.Type
Case Is = xlConnectionTypeODBC

With ActiveSheet
.Range("A1").Offset(i,0).Value=Cn.Name
.Range("A1").Offset(i,1).Value=Cn.ODBCConnection.Connection
.Range("A1").Offset(i,2).Value=Cn.ODBCConnection.CommandText
End With

Case Is = xlConnectionTypeOLEDB

With ActiveSheet
.Range("A1").Offset(i,0).Value=Cn.Name
.Range("A1").Offset(i,1).Value=Cn.OLEDBConnection.Connection
```

```
      .Range("A1").Offset(i,2).Value=Cn.OLEDBConnection.CommandText
   End With

   End Select

   Next Cn
End Sub
```

1. Step 1 declares two variables: an integer variable that ensures the data for each connection string is written on its own row, and a Workbook Connection object used to expose the properties you are looking for.

2. In Step 2 you add a new worksheet along with column headers for each connection property you want to document.

3. Step 3 iterates through all the connections in the workbook, outputting the specified properties for each connection. Note that you are testing to check the kind of connection currently in focus. There are two types of connections: xlConnectionTypeODBC and xlConnectionTypeOLEDB. Because the syntax for getting their properties are slightly different, you need to test to check which type you are working with.

TIP

A working version of this macro is available at www.dummies.com/go/excelmacros in the **Dynamic Data Connection.xlsm** file for this chapter.

Using ADO and VBA to Pull External Data

Another technique for working with external data is to use VBA with ADO (ActiveX Data Objects). Using the combination of ADO with VBA allows you to work with external data sets in memory. This comes in handy when you need to perform complex, multilayered procedures and checks on external data sets, but you don't want to create workbook connections or return those external data sets to the workbook.

REMEMBER

When working with complex Excel workbooks that pull data from external sources, you will periodically encounter code (written by others) that utilizes ADO. It's important you recognize and understand the basics of ADO so you can deal with this kind of code. The next few sections walk you through some of the fundamental concepts of ADO and show you how to construct your own ADO procedures to pull data. Keep in mind that ADO programming is a broad topic that cannot be fully covered here. If you find that you need to work extensively with ADO and external data in your Excel application, you'll probably want to invest in one or more books that cover this topic in detail.

Understanding ADO syntax

When trying to grasp the basics of ADO, it helps to think of ADO as a tool that will help you accomplish two tasks: connect to a data source and specify the dataset to work with. The following section explores the fundamental syntax you need to know in order to do just that.

The connection string

The first thing you must do is connect to a data source. To do this, you must give VBA few pieces of information. This information is passed to VBA in the form of a connection string. Here is an example connection string that points to an Access database:

```
"Provider=Microsoft.ACE.OLEDB.12.0;" & _
"Data Source= C:\MyDatabase.accdb;" & _
"User ID=Administrator;" & _
"Password=AdminPassword"
```

Don't be intimidated by all the syntax here. A connection string is fundamentally nothing more than a text string that holds a series of variables (also called arguments), which VBA uses to identify and open a connection to a data source. Although connection strings to either Access or Excel can get pretty fancy with a myriad of arguments and options, there are only a handful of commonly used arguments that novices of ADO should focus on: Provider, Data Source, Extended Properties, User ID, and Password.

>> **Provider:** The Provider argument tells VBA what type of data source you are working with. When using Access or Excel as the data source, the Provider syntax will read: Provider=Microsoft.ACE.OLEDB.12.0.

>> **Data Source:** The Data Source argument tells VBA where to find the database or workbook that contains the data needed. With the Data Source argument, you pass the full path of the database or workbook. For example: Data Source=C:\Mydirectory\MyDatabaseName.accdb.

>> **Extended Properties:** The Extended Properties argument is typically used when connecting to an Excel workbook. This argument tells VBA that the data source is something other than a database. When working with an Excel workbook, this argument would read: Extended Properties=Excel 12.0.

>> **User ID:** The User ID argument is optional and only used if a user ID is required to connect to the data source: User Id=MyUserId.

>> **Password:** The Password argument is optional and only used if a password is required to connect to the data source: Password=MyPassword.

Take a moment now to re-examine the syntax previously shown. You can easily pick out the arguments in the connection string.

```
"Provider=Microsoft.ACE.OLEDB.12.0;" & _
"Data Source= C:\MyDatabase.accdb;" & _
"User ID=Administrator;" & _
"Password=AdminPassword"
```

Declaring a Recordset

In addition to building a connection to your data source, you need to define the data set you need to work with. In ADO, this dataset is referred to as the Recordset. A Recordset object is essentially a container for the records and fields returned from the data source. The most common way to define a Recordset is to open an existing table or query using the following arguments:

```
Recordset.Open Source, ConnectString, CursorType, LockType
```

>> The **Source** argument specifies the data to be extracted. This is typically a table, query, or an SQL statement that retrieves records.

>> The **ConnectString** argument specifies the connection string used to connect to your chosen data source.

>> The **CursorType** argument defines how a Recordset allows you to move through the data to be extracted. In terms of pulling external data into Excel, the setting for this argument is adOpenForwardOnly. This CursorType is the most efficient type because it only allows you to move through the Recordset one way: from beginning to end. This is ideal for reporting processes where data only needs to be retrieved.

>> The **LockType** argument lets you specify whether the data returned by the Recordset can be changed. This argument is typically set to adLockReadOnly (the default setting) to indicate that there is no need to edit the data returned. Alternatively, this argument can be set to adLockOptimistic which allows for the free editing of the data returned (in the Recordset, not the source database).

The following shows the syntax for declaring a Recordset and opening the Products table:

```
MyRecordset.Open "Products", _
MyConnection, adOpenForwardOnly, adLockReadOnly
```

Using ADO in a macro

With these basic ADO fundamentals under your belt, you're ready to create your own ADO procedure. But before you do anything with ADO, you need to first set a reference the ADO object library. Just as Excel has its own set of VBA objects, properties, and methods, so does ADO. Because Excel does not inherently know the ADO object model, you need to point Excel to the ADO reference library.

1. **Open a new Excel workbook and open the Visual Basic Editor.**

2. **Once you are in the Visual Basic Editor, go up to the application menu and choose Tools ➪ References. This opens the References dialog box shown in Figure 10-11.**

3. **Scroll down until you locate the latest version of the Microsoft ActiveX Data Objects Library.**

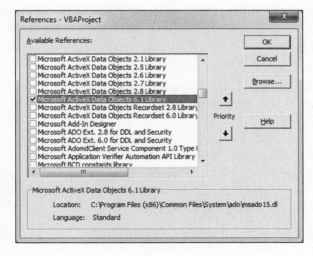

FIGURE 10-11: Select the latest version of the Microsoft ActiveX Data Objects Library.

It's normal to have several versions of the same library displayed in the References dialog box, and generally best to select the latest version available. Note that versions after 2.8 are called Microsoft ActiveX Data Objects Recordset Library.

4. **Click OK to confirm your selection.**

You can open the References dialog box again to ensure that your reference is set. You will know that your selection took effect when the Microsoft ActiveX Data Objects Library appears at the top of the References dialog box with a check next to it.

REMEMBER

The references you set in any given workbook or database are not applied at the application level. This means that you will need to repeat these steps with each new workbook or database you create.

Now you can bring together what you just learned in a macro. The following example uses ADO to connect to an Access database and retrieve the Products table:

```
Sub GetAccessData()

'Step 1:  Declare your variables
    Dim MyConnect As String
    Dim MyRecordset As ADODB.Recordset


'Step 2:  Define your connection string and open recordset
    MyConnect = "Provider=Microsoft.ACE.OLEDB.12.0;" & _
                "Data Source= C:\MyDir\MyDatabaseName.accdb"

    Set MyRecordset = New ADODB.Recordset

    MyRecordset.Open "LocationMaster", _
    MyConnect, adOpenStatic, adLockReadOnly

'Step 3:  Copy data from recordset to spreadsheet
    Sheets("MySheetName").Range("A2").CopyFromRecordset _
    MyRecordset


'Step 4:  Add data labels and
    With ActiveSheet.Range("A1:C1")
        .Value = Array("Product", "Description", "Segment")
        .EntireColumn.AutoFit
    End With

End Sub
```

1. Step 1 declares two variables: a string variable to hold the connection string, and a Recordset object to hold the results of the data pull. In this example, the variable called MyConnect holds the connection string identifying the data source. Meanwhile, the variable called MyRecordset holds the data returned by the procedure.

2. In Step 2, you define the connection string for the ADO procedure. In this scenario, you are connecting to the MyDatabaseName.accdb file found in the

C:\MyDir\ directory. Once you have defined your data source, you can open your Recordset and use MyConnect to return static read-only data.

3. Step 3 uses Excel's CopyFromRecordset method to get the data out of the RecordSet and into your spreadsheet. This method requires two pieces of information: the location of the data output and the Recordset object that holds the data. In this example, you are copying the data in the MyRecordset object onto the sheet called MySheetName (starting at cell A2).

4. Interestingly enough, the CopyFromRecordset method does not return column headers or field names. This forces one final action (Step 4) where you add column headers by simply defining them in an array and writing them to the active sheet.

With ADO and VBA, you can build all the necessary components one time in a nicely packaged macro, and then simply forget about it. As long as the defined variables in your code (that is, the data source path, the Recordset, the output path) do not change, then your ADO-based procedures require virtually zero maintenance.

A working version of this macro is available at www.dummies.com/go/excelmacros in the **Dynamic Data Connection.xlsm** file for this chapter.

Working with text files

VBA contains a number of statements that allow for manipulation of files. These input/output (I/O) statements give you much more control over files than Excel's normal text file import and export options.

Opening a text file

The VBA Open statement opens a file for reading or writing. Before you can read from or write to a file, you must open it.

The VBA Open statement is not the same as the Open method of the Workbook object. VBA's Open statement has its own set of arguments (shown as follows in bold). Here is the required syntax for the Open statement:

```
Open [pathname] For [mode] As [#]filenumber
```

>> **pathname**: The pathname part of the Open statement simply contains the name and path (the path is optional) of the file to be opened.

>> **mode**: The mode part of the Open statement specifies if and how the file can be edited or written to. This argument is a required field that can be any one of the following:

Append: This mode allows the file to be read and the data to be appended to the end of the file.

Input: This mode allows the file to be read but not written to.

Output: This mode always creates a new file that can be read and written to.

Binary: A random-access mode that allows data to be read or written to on a byte-by-byte basis.

Random: A random-access mode that allows data to be read or written in units determined by an optional reclength argument of the Open statement.

>> **filenumber**: This required argument is a file number ranging from 1 to 511. You can use the FreeFile function to get the next available file number.

In the following example, you are using the Open statement to open a text file called MyFile as a read-only file designated as file #1:

```
Open "myfile.txt" For Input As #1
```

Reading the opened text file

After a text file has been opened, you will typically want to either read the file or write to the file.

There are three ways you can tell VBA to read a text file. These statements are used for reading data from a sequential text file:

>> **Input:** Reads a specified number of characters from a file.

>> **Input #:** Reads data as a series of variables, with variables separated by a comma.

>> **Line Input #:** Reads a complete line of data (delineated by a carriage return character, a linefeed character, or both).

Two statements are used for writing data to your opened text file:

>> **Write #:** Writes a series of values, with each value separated by a comma and enclosed in quotes.

>> **Print #:** Writes a series of values, with each value separated by a tab character.

A practical example: Logging workbook usage in a text file

If you're completely confused, don't worry. Things should clear up with a practical example. Say you want to log each time Excel is opened. You can create a macro that writes data to a text file every time Excel is opened and closed.

For this example to work reliably, the macro must be located in a workbook that's opened every time you start Excel. Storing the macro in your Personal Macro Workbook is an excellent choice.

The Personal Macro Workbook is loaded whenever you start Excel. In the VBE Project window, it is named personal.xlsb.

1. Activate the Visual Basic Editor by pressing Alt+F11 on your keyboard.

2. In the Project window, find the personal.xlb project/workbook name and click the plus sign next to it in order to see all the sheets in the Project window.

3. Click ThisWorkbook.

4. Select the Open event in the Event dropdown.

5. Type or paste the following code:

```
Private Sub Workbook_Open()

Open Application.DefaultFilePath & _
"\excelusage.txt" For Append As #1

Print #1, "Excel Started " & Now

Close #1

End Sub
```

TIP

A working version of this macro is available at www.dummies.com/go/excelmacros in the **Excel Usage Log.xlsm** file for this chapter.

This macro first opens a text file called excelusage.txt in your Windows Documents directory (Application.DefaultFilePath). If the text file does not exist, Excel creates it. Once the text file is open, this macro appends a new line containing the current date and time and might look something like this:

```
Excel Started 12/5/2016 2:37:13 PM
```

A practical example: Importing a text file to a range

The example in this section opens and reads the TextFile.CSV (found with the sample files for this chapter at www.dummies.com/go/excelmacros). It then stores the values beginning at the active cell in the active worksheet. The code reads each character and essentially parses the line of data, ignoring quote characters and looking for commas to delineate the columns.

TIP

A working version of this macro is available at www.dummies.com/go/excelmacros in the **Import Text File.xlsm** file for this chapter.

```
Sub ImportRange()

    Dim ImpRng As Range
    Dim Filename As String
    Dim r As Long, c As Integer
    Dim txt As String, Char As String * 1
    Dim Data
    Dim i As Integer

    Set ImpRng = ActiveCell
    On Error Resume Next
    Filename = Application.ThisWorkbook.Path & "\textfile.csv"

    Open Filename For Input As #1
    If Err <> 0 Then
        MsgBox "Not found: " & Filename, vbCritical, "ERROR"
        Exit Sub
    End If
    r = 0
    c = 0
    txt = ""

    Application.ScreenUpdating = False

    Do Until EOF(1)
        Line Input #1, Data
        For i = 1 To Len(Data)
            Char = Mid(Data, i, 1)
            If Char = "," Then 'comma
                ActiveCell.Offset(r, c) = txt
                c = c + 1
                txt = ""
```

```
        ElseIf i = Len(Data) Then 'end of line
            If Char <> Chr(34) Then txt = txt & Char
            ActiveCell.Offset(r, c) = txt
            txt = ""
        ElseIf Char <> Chr(34) Then
            txt = txt & Char
        End If
    Next i
    c = 0
    r = r + 1
Loop

Close #1
Application.ScreenUpdating = True

End Sub
```

REMEMBER

The preceding procedure works with most data, but it has a flaw: It doesn't handle data that contains a comma or a quote character. But commas resulting from formatting are handled correctly (they're ignored). In addition, an imported date will be surrounded by number signs: for example, #2016-12-12#.

5
Part of Tens

Take a look at a few tricks that help you more efficiently use the Visual Basic Editor.

Discover some of the debugging tips for avoiding errors in your VBA code.

Learn how to most effectively use the Excel Help system when searching for VBA help.

Gain insight into some of the resources available online to further your macro skills.

Chapter **11**

Ten Handy Visual Basic Editor Tips

f you're going to be spending time working with macros in the Visual Basic Editor, then why not take advantage of a few of the built-in tools that will make your job easier? Whether you're a fresh-faced analyst new to programming, or a jaded veteran living on Mountain Dew and sunflower seeds, these tips will greatly improve your macro programming experience.

Applying Block Comments

Placing a single apostrophe in front of any line of code effectively tells Excel to skip that line of code. This is called commenting out code. Most programmers use the single apostrophe to create comments or notes within the code (see Figure 11-1).

```
'Declare your Variables
    Dim ws As Worksheet

'Avoid Error if no formulas are found
    On Error Resume Next

'Start looping through worksheets
    For Each ws In ActiveWorkbook.Worksheets

'Select cells and highlight them
    With ws.Cells.SpecialCells(xlCellTypeFormulas)
    .Interior.ColorIndex = 36
    End With

'Get next worksheet
    Next ws
```

FIGURE 11-1:
A single apostrophe in front of any line turns that line into a comment.

It's sometimes beneficial to comment out multiple lines of code. This way, you can test certain lines of code while telling Excel to ignore the commented lines.

Instead of spending time commenting out one line at a time, you can use the Edit toolbar to comment whole blocks of code.

You can activate the Edit toolbar by going to the VBE menu and choosing View ⇨ Toolbars ⇨ Edit.

The idea is to select the lines of code you want commented out and then click the Comment Block icon on the Edit toolbar (see Figure 11-2).

Apply Comment   Remove Comment

FIGURE 11-2:
The Edit toolbar allows you to select entire blocks of code, then apply comments to all the lines at once.

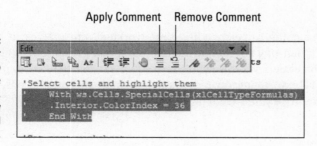

REMEMBER

You can ensure the Edit toolbar is always visible by dragging it up to the VBE menu. It anchors itself to the location you choose.

Copying Multiple Lines of Code at Once

You can copy entire blocks of code by highlighting the lines you need, and then holding down the Ctrl key on your keyboard while dragging the block where you need it. This is an old Windows trick that works even when you drag across modules.

You'll know you are dragging a copy when your cursor shows a plus symbol next to it, as shown in Figure 11-3.

```
'Define the target Range.
    Set MyRange = ActiveSheet.UsedRange

'Start reverse looping through the range.
    For iCounter = MyRange.Columns.Count To 1 Step -1

'If entire column is empty then delete it.
        If Application.CountA(Columns(iCounter).EntireColumn) = 0 Then
        Columns(iCounter).Delete
        End If
```

FIGURE 11-3: Holding down the Ctrl key while dragging code creates a copy of that code to where you point your cursor.

Jumping between Modules and Procedures

Once your cache of macro code starts to grow, it can be a pain to move quickly between modules and procedures. You can ease the pain by using a few hot keys.

Press **Ctrl+Tab** to move quickly between modules.

Press **Ctrl+Page Up** and **Ctrl+Page Down** to move between procedures within a module.

Teleporting to Your Functions

When reviewing a macro, you may sometimes encounter a variable or function name that is obviously pointing to some other piece of code. Instead of scouring through all the modules to find where that function or variable name comes from, you can simply place your cursor on that function/variable name and press Shift+F2.

As Figure 11-4 illustrates, you will instantly be teleported to the origin of that function or variable name.

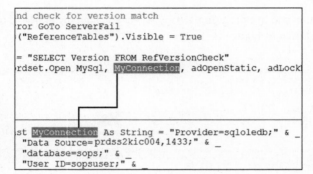

FIGURE 11-4:
Pressing Shift+F2
with your cursor
on a function or
variable name
will take you to it.

```
nd check for version match
ror GoTo ServerFail
("ReferenceTables").Visible = True

= "SELECT Version FROM RefVersionCheck"
rdset.Open MySql, MyConnection, adOpenStatic, adLock

st MyConnection As String = "Provider=sqloledb;" & _
  "Data Source=prdss2kic004,1433;" & _
  "database=sops;" & _
  "User ID=sopsuser;" & _
```

Pressing Ctrl+Shift+F2 takes you back to where you started.

Staying in the Right Procedure

When your modules contain multiple procedures, it can get difficult to scroll through a particular procedure without inadvertently scrolling into another procedure. You will often find yourself scrolling up, then down, trying to get back into the correct piece of code.

To avoid this nonsense, you can use the Procedure View button on the lower left-hand corner of the VBE (see Figure 11-5). Clicking this button limits scrolling to only the procedure you're in.

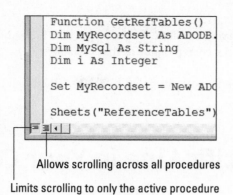

```
Function GetRefTables()
Dim MyRecordset As ADODB.
Dim MySql As String
Dim i As Integer

Set MyRecordset = New ADO

Sheets("ReferenceTables")
```

FIGURE 11-5:
Use the
Procedure View
button to limit
scrolling to just
the active
procedure.

Allows scrolling across all procedures

Limits scrolling to only the active procedure

Stepping through Your Code

VBA offers several tools to help you "debug" your code. In programming, the term debugging means finding and correcting possible errors in code.

One of the more useful debugging tools is the ability to step through your code one line at a time. When you step through code, you are literally watching as each line executes.

To step through your code, place your cursor anywhere within your macro and then press the F8 key on your keyboard. This places your macro into debug mode.

The first line of code highlights and a small arrow appears on the code window's left margin (see Figure 11-6). Press F8 again to execute the highlighted line of code and move to the next line. You can keep pressing F8 to watch each line execute until the end of the macro.

```
'Declare your variables.
    Dim MyRange As Range
    Dim iCounter As Long

'Define the target Range.
    Set MyRange = ActiveSheet.UsedRange

'Start reverse looping through the range.
    For iCounter = MyRange.Columns.Count To 1 Step -1
        iCounter = 12
'If entire column is empty then delete it.
        If Application.CountA(Columns(iCounter).EntireColumn) = 0 Then
        Columns(iCounter).Delete
        End If



'Step 5: Increment the counter down
    Next iCounter
```

FIGURE 11-6:
Press the F8 key
on your keyboard
to step through
each line of your
macro at your
own pace.

As a bonus, while stepping through the code, you can hover over any string or integer variable to see the current value of that variable.

To get out of debug mode, you can go up to the VBE menu and choose Debug ⇨ Step Out.

Stepping to a Specific Line in Your Code

In the last example, you saw how you can step through your code by placing your cursor anywhere within your macro and then pressing the F8 key on your keyboard. This puts your macro into debug mode, highlighting the first line of code and placing a small arrow in the left margin of the code window.

This is great, but what if you want to start stepping through your code at a specific line? Well, you can do just that by simply moving the arrow!

When a line of code is highlighted in debug mode, you can click and drag the arrow in the left margin of the code window upward or downward, dropping it at whichever line of code you want to execute next (see Figure 11-7).

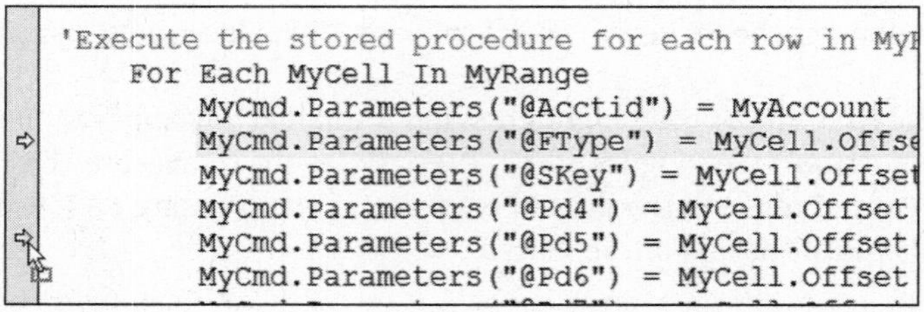

FIGURE 11-7:
You can click and drag the yellow arrow while stepping through your code.

```
'Execute the stored procedure for each row in My
    For Each MyCell In MyRange
        MyCmd.Parameters("@Acctid") = MyAccount
        MyCmd.Parameters("@FType") = MyCell.Offse
        MyCmd.Parameters("@SKey") = MyCell.Offset
        MyCmd.Parameters("@Pd4") = MyCell.Offset
        MyCmd.Parameters("@Pd5") = MyCell.Offset
        MyCmd.Parameters("@Pd6") = MyCell.Offset
```

Stopping Your Code at a Predefined Point

Another useful debugging tool is the ability to set a breakpoint in your code. When you set a breakpoint, your code runs as normal and then halts at the line of code you defined as the breakpoint.

This debugging technique comes in handy when you want to run tests on small blocks of code at a time. For example, if you suspect there may be an error in your macro but you know that the majority of the macro runs without any problems, you can set a breakpoint starting at the suspect line of code then run the macro. When the macros reaches your breakpoint, execution halts. At this point, you can then press the F8 key on your keyboard to watch as the macro runs one line at a time.

To set a breakpoint in your code, place your cursor where you want the breakpoint to start, and then press the F9 key on your keyboard. As Figure 11-8 demonstrates, VBA clearly marks the breakpoint with a dot in the code window's left margin, and the code line itself is shaded maroon.

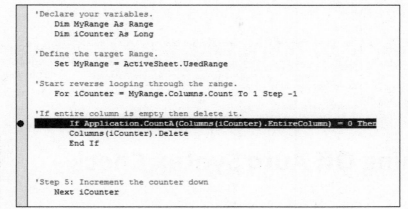

```
'Declare your variables.
    Dim MyRange As Range
    Dim iCounter As Long

'Define the target Range.
    Set MyRange = ActiveSheet.UsedRange

'Start reverse looping through the range.
    For iCounter = MyRange.Columns.Count To 1 Step -1

'If entire column is empty then delete it.
        If Application.CountA(Columns(iCounter).EntireColumn) = 0 Then
            Columns(iCounter).Delete
        End If



'Step 5: Increment the counter down
    Next iCounter
```

FIGURE 11-8:
A breakpoint is marked by a dot in the left margin along with shaded text.

REMEMBER

Hitting a breakpoint effectively puts your macro into debug mode. To get out of debug mode, you can go up to the VBE menu and choose Debug⇨ Step Out.

Seeing the Beginning and End of Variable Values

If you hover over a string or integer variable in VBA while in debug mode, you can see the value of that variable in a tooltip. This allows you to see the values being passed in and out of variables — very useful.

However, these tooltips can hold only 77 characters (including the variable name). This basically means if the value in your variable is too long, it gets cut off.

To see the last 77 characters, simply hold down the Ctrl key on your keyboard while you hover.

Figure 11-9 demonstrates what the tooltip looks like when hovering over a variable in debug mode.

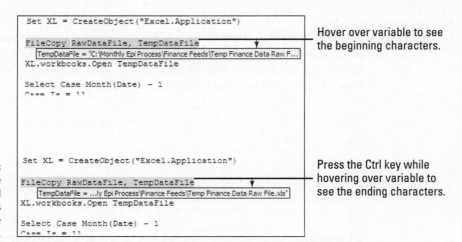

Hover over variable to see the beginning characters.

FIGURE 11-9:
Showing the beginning and ending characters in a variable tooltip.

```
Set XL = CreateObject("Excel.Application")

FileCopy RawDataFile, TempDataFile
    TempDataFile = ...ly Epi Process\Finance Feeds\Temp Finance Data Raw File.xls"
XL.workbooks.Open TempDataFile

Select Case Month(Date) - 1
Case To = 11
```

Press the Ctrl key while hovering over variable to see the ending characters.

Turning Off Auto Syntax Check

Often times, while working on some code, you find that you need to go to another line to copy something. You're not done with the line — you just need to leave it for a second. But VBE immediately stops you in your tracks with an error message, similar to the one shown in Figure 11-10, warning you about something you already know.

These message boxes force you to stop what you're doing to acknowledge the error by clicking the OK button, not pressing. After a half-day of these abrupt message boxes, you'll be ready to throw your computer against the wall.

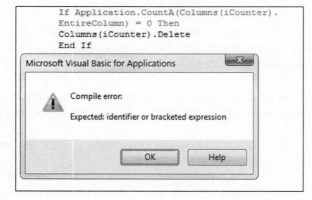

FIGURE 11-10:
Leaving a line of code unfinished, even for a second, results in a jarring error message.

Well, you can save your computer and your sanity by turning off Auto Syntax Check. Go up to the VBE menu and choose Tools ⇨ Options.

The options dialog box activates, exposing the Editor tab shown in Figure 11-11. Uncheck the Auto Syntax Check option to stop these annoying error messages.

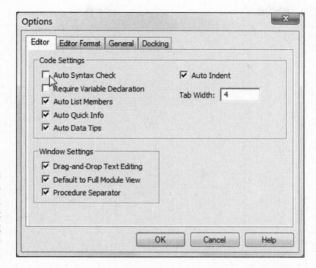

FIGURE 11-11:
Uncheck the Auto Syntax Check option to prevent warning messages while coding.

Don't worry about missing a legitimate mistake. Your code still turns red if you goof up, providing a visual indication that something is wrong.

Chapter **12**

Ten Places to Turn for Macro Help

No one is going to be a macro expert in one day. VBA is a journey of time and practice. The good news is that plenty of resources are out there that can help you on your path. In this chapter, you'll discover ten of the most useful places to turn to when you need an extra push in the right direction.

Let Excel Write the Macro for You

One of the best places to get macro help is the Macro Recorder in Excel. When you record a macro with the Macro Recorder, Excel writes the underlying VBA for you. After recording, you can review the code; see what the recorder is doing, and then try to turn the code it creates into something more suited to your needs.

For example, say you need a macro that refreshes all the PivotTables in your workbook and clears all the filters in each PivotTable. Writing this macro from a blank canvas would be a daunting task. Instead, you can start the Macro Recorder and record yourself refreshing all the PivotTables and clearing all the filters. Once you've stopped recording, you can review the macro and make any changes you deem necessary.

Use the VBA Help Files

To a new Excel user, the Help system may seem like a clunky add-in that returns a perplexing list of topics that has nothing to do with the original topic of the search. The truth is, however, once you learn how to use the Excel Help system effectively, it's often the fastest and easiest way to get extra help on a topic.

You just need to remember two basic tenants of the Excel Help system:

>> **Location matters when asking for help.** In Excel, there are actually two Help systems: one providing help on Excel features, and another providing help on VBA programming topics. Instead of doing a global search with your criteria, Excel throws only your search criteria that is relevant to your current location against the Help system. This essentially means that the help you get is determined by the area of Excel in which you're working. So, if you need help on a topic that involves macros and VBA programming, you'll need to be in the VBA Editor while performing your search. This ensures that you perform your keyword search on the correct Help system.

>> **Online help is better than offline help.** When you search for help on a topic, Excel checks to see if you're connected to the Internet. If you are, Excel returns help results based on online content from Microsoft's website. If you aren't, Excel uses the Help files stored locally with Microsoft Office. One way to maximize the help you get in Excel is to use the online help. Online help is generally better than offline help because the content you find with online help is often more detailed and includes updated information, as well as links to other resources not available offline.

Pilfer Code from the Internet

The dirty secret about programming in the Internet age is that there is no original code out there anymore. All the macro syntax that will ever be needed has been documented somewhere on the Internet. In many ways, programming has become less about the code one creates from scratch, and more about how to take existing code and apply it creatively to a particular scenario.

If you are stuck trying to create a macro for a particular task, fire up your favorite online search engine and simply describe the task you are trying to accomplish. For the best results, enter "Excel VBA" before your description.

For example, if you are trying to write a macro that deletes all blank rows in a worksheet, search for "Excel VBA delete blank rows in a worksheet." You can bet two months' salary that someone out there on the Internet has already tackled the same problem. Nine times out of ten, you will find some example code that will give you the nugget of information you need to jump-start some ideas for building your own macro.

Leverage User Forums

If you find yourself in a bind, you can post your question in a forum to get customized guidance based on your scenario.

User forums are online communities that revolve around a particular topic. In these forums, you can post questions and have experts offer advice on how to solve particular problems. The folks answering the questions are typically volunteers who have a passion for helping the community solve real-world challenges.

There are many forums dedicated to all things Excel. To find an Excel forum, enter the words "Excel Forum" in your favorite online search engine.

Here are a few tips for getting the most out of user forums:

> Always read and follow the forum rules before you get started. These rules often include advice on posting questions and community etiquette guidelines.

> Use concise and accurate subject titles for your questions. Don't create forum questions with vague titles like "Need advice," or "Please Help."

> Keep the scope of your questions as narrow as possible. Don't ask questions like "How do I build an invoicing macro in Excel?"

Be patient. Remember the folks answering your questions are volunteers who typically have day jobs. Give the community some time to answer your question.

Check back often. After posting your question, you may receive requests for more details about your scenario. Do everyone a favor and return to your posting to either review the answers or respond to follow-up questions.

Thank the expert who answered your question. If you receive an answer that helps you, take a moment to post a thank you to the expert who helped you out.

Visit Expert Blogs

A few dedicated Excel gurus share their knowledge through blogs. These blogs are often treasure troves of tips and tricks, offering nuggets that can help build up your skills. Best of all, they are free!

Although these blogs will not necessarily speak to your particular needs, they offer articles that advance your knowledge of Excel and can even provide general guidance on how to apply Excel in practical business situations.

Here is a list of a few of the best Excel blogs on the Internet today:

ExcelGuru: Ken Puls is a Microsoft Excel MVP who shares knowledge at his blog, `www.excelguru.ca/blog`. In addition to his blog, Ken offers several learning resources for advancing your knowledge in Excel.

Chandoo.org: Purna "Chandoo" Duggirala is a Microsoft Excel MVP out of India, who burst onto the scene in 2007. His innovative blog (`http://chandoo.org/`) offers many free templates and articles aimed at "making you awesome in Excel."

Contextures: Debra Dalgleish is a Microsoft Excel MVP and the owner of one of the most popular Excel sites, `www.contextures.com`. With an alphabetized list of over 350 Excel topics, you're sure to find something that will interest you.

DailyDose: Dick Kusleika is the owner of the longest running Excel blog, `www.dailydoseofexcel.com`. He is the king of Excel VBA blogging with over ten years' worth of articles and examples.

MrExcel: Bill Jelen is the larger-than-life ambassador of Excel. This long-time Excel MVP offers over a thousand free videos and a huge library of training resources on his site: `www.mrexcel.com`

Mine YouTube for Video Training

Some of us learn better if we watch a task being done. If you find that you absorb video training better than online articles, consider mining YouTube. There are dozens of channels run by amazing folks who have a passion for sharing knowledge. You'll be surprised at how many free high-quality video tutorials you'll find.

Go to www.YouTube.com and search for the words "Excel VBA."

Attend Live and Online Training Classes

Live and online training events are an awesome way to absorb Excel knowledge from a diverse group of people. Not only is the instructor feeding you techniques, but the lively discussions during the class offer a wealth of ideas and new tips that you probably never thought of before. If you thrive on the energy of live training events, then consider searching for Excel classes.

Here are a few sites that provide excellent instructor-led Excel courses:

```
http://academy.excelhero.com/excel-hero-academy-tuition

http://chandoo.org/wp/vba-classes

https://exceljet.net
```

Learn from the Microsoft Office Dev Center

The Microsoft Office Dev Center is a site dedicated to helping new developers get a quick start in programming Office products. You can get to the Excel portion of this site by going to https://msdn.microsoft.com/en-us/library/office/fp179694.aspx.

Although the site can be a bit difficult to navigate, it's worth a visit to see all the free resources, including sample code, tools, step-by-step instructions, and much more.

Dissect the Other Excel Files in your Organization

Like finding gold in your backyard, the existing files in your organization are often a treasure trove for learning. Consider cracking open those Excel files that contain macros, and have a look under the covers. See how others in your organization use macros. Try going through the macros line-by-line and see if you can spot new techniques.

You could find a few new tricks you never thought of. You may even stumble upon entire chunks of useful code you can copy out and implement in your own workbooks.

Ask Your Local Excel Genius

Do you have an Excel genius in your company, department, organization, or community? Make friends with that person today. What you have there is your own personal Excel forum.

Most Excel experts love sharing their knowledge, so don't be afraid to approach your local Excel guru to ask questions or seek out advice on how to tackle certain macro problems.

Chapter **13**

Ten Ways to Speed Up Your Macros

As your macros become increasingly robust and complex, you may find they lose performance. When discussing macros, the word performance is usually synonymous with speed. Speed is how quickly your VBA procedures perform their intended tasks.

There are steps you can take to improve the performance of your macros. In this chapter, you find ten ways you can help keep your Excel macros running at their optimum performance level.

Halt Sheet Calculations

Did you know that each time a cell that affects any formula in your spreadsheet is changed or manipulated, Excel recalculates the entire worksheet? In worksheets that have a large amount of formulas, this behavior can drastically slow down your macros.

If your workbook is formula intensive, you may not want Excel to trigger a recalculation every time your macro alters a cell value. You can use the Application. Calculation property to tell Excel to switch to manual calculation mode. When a workbook is in manual calculation mode, the workbook does not recalculate until you explicitly trigger a calculation by pressing the F9 key on your keyboard.

Turning off the automatic calculation behavior of Excel can dramatically speed up your macro. The idea is to place Excel into manual calculation mode, run your code, and then switch back to automatic calculation mode.

```
Sub Macro1()

Application.Calculation = xlCalculationManual

'Place your macro code here

Application.Calculation = xlCalculationAutomatic

End Sub
```

Setting the calculation mode back to xlCalculationAutomatic automatically triggers a recalculation of the worksheet. So there is no need to press the F9 key on your keyboard after your macro runs.

Depending on the task at hand, you may actually need calculations to be performed during the running of your macro, in which case you would not want to evoke manual calculation mode. Be sure to think about your specific scenario and determine what will happen when calculations are turned off while your macro runs.

Disable Sheet Screen Updating

You may notice that when your macros run, your screen does a fair amount of flickering. This flickering is Excel trying to redraw the screen in order to show the current state the worksheet is in. Unfortunately, each time Excel redraws the screen, it takes up memory resources. In most cases, you don't need Excel using up resources to redraw the screen each time your macro performs some action.

In addition to setting the calculation mode to manual, you can use the Application. ScreenUpdating property to disable any screen updates until your macro has completed. This saves time and resources, allowing your macro to run a little faster. Once you macro code is done running, you can turn screen updating back on.

```
Sub Macro1()

Application.Calculation = xlCalculationManual
Application.ScreenUpdating = False

'Place your macro code here

Application.Calculation = xlCalculationAutomatic
Application.ScreenUpdating = True

End Sub
```

TIP

After you set the ScreenUpdating property back to True, Excel automatically triggers a redraw of the screen.

Turn Off Status Bar Updates

At the bottom of the Excel window, you see the Excel status bar. The status bar normally displays the progress of certain actions in Excel. For example, if you copy/paste a range, Excel shows the progress of that operation in the status bar. Oftentimes, the action is performed so fast, you don't see the status bar progress. However, if your macro is working with lots of data, the status bar takes up some resources.

It's important to note that turning off screen updating is separate from turning off the status bar display. That is to say, the status bar continues to be updated even if you disable screen updating. You can use the Application.DisplayStatusBar property to temporarily disable any status bar updates, further improving the performance of your macro.

```
Sub Macro1()

Application.Calculation = xlCalculationManual
Application.ScreenUpdating = False
Application.DisplayStatusBar = False

'Place your macro code here

Application.Calculation = xlCalculationAutomatic
Application.ScreenUpdating = True
Application.DisplayStatusBar = True

End Sub
```

Tell Excel to Ignore Events

As discussed in Chapter 3, you can implement macros as event procedures, telling Excel to run certain code when a worksheet or workbook changes.

Sometimes, standard macros make changes that will actually trigger an event procedure. For example, say you have a Worksheet_Change event implemented for Sheet1 of your workbook. Any time a cell or range is altered, the Worksheet_Change event fires.

So if you have a standard macro that manipulates several cells on Sheet1, each time a cell on that sheet is changed, your macro has to pause while the Worksheet_Change event runs. You can imagine how this behavior would slow down your macro.

You can add another level of performance-boosting by using the EnableEvents property to tell Excel to ignore events while your macro runs.

Simply set the EnableEvents property to False before running your macro. Once your macro code is done running, you can set the EnableEvents property back to True.

```
Sub Macro1()

Application.Calculation = xlCalculationManual
Application.ScreenUpdating = False
Application.DisplayStatusBar = False
Application.EnableEvents = False

'Place your macro code here

Application.Calculation = xlCalculationAutomatic
Application.ScreenUpdating = True
Application.DisplayStatusBar = True
Application.EnableEvents = True

End Sub
```

WARNING

Although disabling events can indeed speed up your macros, you may actually need some events to trigger while your macro runs. Be sure to think about your specific scenario and determine what will happen if your worksheet or workbook events are turned off while your macro runs.

Hide Page Breaks

Another opportunity for a performance boost can be found in page breaks. Each time your macro modifies the number of rows, modifies the number of columns, or alters the page setup of a worksheet, Excel is forced to take up time recalculating where the page breaks are shown on the sheet.

You can avoid this by simply hiding the page breaks before starting your macro.

Set the DisplayPageBreaks sheet property to False in order to hide page breaks. If you want to continue to show page breaks after your macro runs, you can set the DisplayPageBreaks sheet property back to True.

```
Sub Macro1()

Application.Calculation = xlCalculationManual
Application.ScreenUpdating = False
Application.DisplayStatusBar = False
Application.EnableEvents = False
Activesheet.DisplayPageBreaks = False

'Place your macro code here

Application.Calculation = xlCalculationAutomatic
Application.ScreenUpdating = True
Application.DisplayStatusBar = True
Application.EnableEvents = True
Activesheet.DisplayPageBreaks = True

End Sub
```

Suspend PivotTable Updates

If your macro manipulates PivotTables that contain large data sources, you may experience poor performance when doing things like dynamically adding or moving pivot fields. This is because each change you make to the structure of the PivotTable requires Excel to recalculate the values in the PivotTable for each pivot field your macro touches.

You can improve the performance of your macro by suspending the recalculation of the PivotTable until all your pivot field changes have been made. Simply set the

PivotTable.ManualUpdate property to True to defer recalculation, run your macro code, and then set the PivotTable.ManualUpdate property back to False to trigger the recalculation.

```
Sub Macro1()

ActiveSheet.PivotTables("PivotTable1").ManualUpdate=True

'Place your macro code here

ActiveSheet.PivotTables("PivotTable1").ManualUpdate=False

End Sub
```

Steer Clear of Copy and Paste

It's important to remember that while the Macro Recorder saves time by writing VBA code for you, it does not always write the most efficient code. A prime example of this is how the Macro Recorder captures any copy-and-paste action you perform while recording.

If you were to copy cell A1 and paste it into cell B1 while recording a macro, the Macro Recorder would capture this:

```
Range("A1").Select

Selection.Copy

Range("B1").Select

ActiveSheet.Paste
```

While this code indeed copies from cell A1 and pastes into B1, it forces Excel to utilize the clipboard which adds a kind of middle man where there does not need to be one.

You can give your macros a slight boost by cutting out the middle man and performing a direct copy from one cell to a destination cell. This alternative code uses the Destination argument to bypass the clipboard and copy the contents of cell A1 directly to cell B1.

```
Range("A1").Copy Destination:=Range("B1")
```

If you only need to copy values (not formatting or formulas), you can improve performance even more by avoiding the Copy method altogether. Simply set the value of the destination cell to the same value found in the source cell. This method is approximately 25 times faster than using the Copy method.

```
Range("B1").Value = Range("A1").Value
```

If you need to copy only the formulas from one cell to another (not values or formatting), you can set the formula of the destination cell to the same formula contained in the source cell.

```
Range("B1").Formula = Range("A1").Formula
```

Use the With Statement

When recording macros, you often manipulate the same object more than once. For example, your code may change the formatting of cell A1 so that it is underlined, italicized, and formatted bold. If you were to record a macro when applying these formatting options to cell A1, you would get something like this:

```
Range("A1").Select
Selection.Font.Bold = True
Selection.Font.Italic = True
Selection.Font.Underline = xlUnderlineStyleSingle
```

Unfortunately, this code is not as efficient as it could be because it forces Excel to select and then change each property separately.

You can save time and improve performance by using the With statement to perform several actions on a given object in one shot.

The With statement utilized in this example tells Excel to apply all the formatting changes at one time:

```
With Range("A1").Font

.Bold = True
.Italic = True
.Underline = xlUnderlineStyleSingle

End With
```

Getting into the habit of chunking actions into With statements not only keeps your macros running faster, but it also helps to more easily read your macro code.

Don't Explicitly Select Objects

If you were to record a macro while entering the value 1000 in cell A1 for multiple sheets, you would end up with code that looks similar to this:

```
Sheets("Sheet1").Select
Range("A1").Select
ActiveCell.FormulaR1C1 = "1000"

Sheets("Sheet2").Select
Range("A1").Select
ActiveCell.FormulaR1C1 = "1000"

Sheets("Sheet3").Select
Range("A1").Select
ActiveCell.FormulaR1C1 = "1000"
```

As you can see, the Macro Recorder is fond of using the Select method to explicitly select objects before taking actions on them. While this code will run fine, it is not all that efficient. It forces Excel to take the time to explicitly select each object being manipulated.

There is generally no need to select objects before working with them. In fact, you can dramatically improve macro performance by not using the Select method.

After recording your macros, make it a habit to alter the generated code to remove the Select methods. In this case, the optimized code would look like this. Note that nothing is being selected. The code simply uses the object hierarchy to apply the needed actions.

```
Sheets("Sheet1").Range("A1").FormulaR1C1 = "1000"
Sheets("Sheet2").Range("A1").FormulaR1C1 = "1000"
Sheets("Sheet3").Range("A1").FormulaR1C1 = "1000"
```

Avoid Excessive Trips to the Worksheet

Another way to speed up your macros is to limit the amount of times you reference worksheet data in your code. It is always less efficient to grab data from the worksheet than from memory. That is to say, your macros run much faster if they do not have to repeatedly interact with the worksheet.

For example, this simple code forces VBA to continuously return to Sheets("Sheet1"). Range("A1") to get the number needed for the comparison being performed in the If statement:

```
For ReportMonth = 1 To 12

    If Range("A1").Value = ReportMonth Then
    MsgBox 1000000 / ReportMonth
End If

Next ReportMonth
```

A much more efficient way is to save the value in Sheets("Sheet1").Range("A1") into a variable called MyMonth. This way, the code references the MyMonth variable rather than the worksheet.

```
Dim MyMonth as Integer
MyMonth = Range("A1").Value

For ReportMonth = 1 To 12
If MyMonth = ReportMonth Then
MsgBox 1000000 / ReportMonth
End If

Next ReportMonth
```

Index

Symbols
& (ampersand), 158
* (asterisk), 100
@ symbol, 153
\ (back slash), 100
: (colon), 100
" (double quote), 100
/ (forward slash), 82, 100
> (greater than), 100
< (less than), 100
| (pipe), 100
? (question mark), 100
_ (underscore), 35

A
absolute references, recording macros
   with, 14–17
activating
  Edit toolbar (VBE), 254
  Visual Basic (VB) Editor, 3, 12, 29
ActiveCell.PivotTable.Name property, 182, 184,
   187, 190, 193, 195, 201, 204
ActiveChart.Printout method, 212
ActiveSheet.PrintOut method, 200–201
ActiveSheet.UsedRange, 160
ActiveX controls, 23
ActiveX Data Objects (ADO), 240–249
Add method, 60, 86
adding
  text to left/right of cells, 156–158
  VBA modules, 32–33
  worksheets, 85–86
addresses, mailing to contact list, 222–224
adjusting pivot data field titles, 181–183
ADO (ActiveX Data Objects), 240–249
aligning charts to specific ranges, 207–209

alphabetical order, sorting fields in, 189–191
ampersand (&), 158
Application object, 44
Application.DisplayStatusBar property, 271
Application.ScreenUpdating property, 270–271
applying
  block comments, 254–255
  custom sort to data items, 191–192
  number formatting to data items, 185–189
  pivot field restrictions, 194–196
  PivotTable restrictions, 192–194
ASCII code, 159, 182
assigning macros to buttons and
   form controls, 22–23
asterisk (*), 100
@ symbol, 153
Atmt variable, 226, 228
attachment
  mailing active workbook as an, 214–215
  mailing single sheets as an, 218–220
  mailing specific ranges as an, 216–218
  saving to folders, 224–226, 227–229
Auto Data Tips option (Editor tab), 39
Auto Indent setting (Editor tab), 39
Auto List Members option (Editor tab), 39
Auto Quick Info option (Editor tab), 39
Auto Syntax Check
  option (Editor tab), 38
  turning off, 260–261
AutoFilter function, 165–167, 170
AutoFilterMode property, 165–168, 170
automatic calculations, turning off, 269–270
automating
  defined, 1
  reporting. *See* reporting
AutoSort method, 190
avoiding Select method, 276

replacing blank cells with values, 154–156

report filter

  creating workbooks for each, 202–205

  printing PivotTables for each, 200–202

reporting

  adjusting pivot data field titles, 181–183

  aligning charts to specific ranges, 207–209

  applying custom sort to data items, 191–192

  applying number formatting to data items, 185–189

  applying pivot field restrictions, 194–196

  applying PivotTable restrictions, 192–194

  automatically deleting PivotTable drill-down sheets, 196–199

  creating PivotTable inventory summaries, 177–180

  creating sets of disconnected charts, 209–211

  creating workbooks for each report filter item, 202–205

  one-touch, 27–28

  printing charts on worksheets, 211–212

  printing PivotTables for each report filter item, 200–202

  refreshing PivotTables in workbooks, 176–177

  resizing charts on worksheets, 205–207

  setting data items to sum, 183–185

  sorting fields in alphabetical order, 189–191

Require Variable Declaration option (Editor tab), 38–40

resizing charts on worksheets, 205–207

resources. *See also* blogs, expert

  Chandoo.org, 267

  Cheat sheet, 4

  Excel Hero Academy, 267

  Exceljet, 267

  Microsoft Office Dev Center, 267

  sample files, 3

  updates, 4

  Web extras, 4

  YouTube, 267

restrictions

  applying pivot field, 194–196

  applying PivotTable, 192–194

Right function, 150, 153

rows. *See also* columns

  copying to new workbooks, 167–168

  deleting blank, 125–127

  finding blank, 133–136

  hiding, 162–165

  highlighting, 110–112

  inserting blanks in ranges, 122–124

  selecting blank, 133–136

  unhiding, 124–125

S

sample files (website), 3

Save method, 63

SaveAs method, 61

SaveCopyAs method, 83

saving

  attachments to folders, 224–226, 227–229

  workbooks before closing, 64–66

  workbooks when cells changed, 61–63

ScreenUpdating property, 271

ScrollArea property, 129

security, in Excel 2010, 19–20

Select Case statement, 64–65

Select Data Source dialog box, 232

Select method, 276

Select Table dialog box, 232–233

selecting

  blank rows/columns, 133–136

  formulas in workbooks, 131–133

  named ranges, 118–120

  ranges, 116–118

sending

  emails. *See* emails

  mail with a link to your workbook, 220–222

SendMail command, 214

setting

  breakpoints in code, 258–259

  data items to sum, 183–185

setup, of trusted locations, 20–21

ShapeRange.Group method, 209

Dedication

For my family.

Author's Acknowledgments

My deepest thanks to everyone who helped bring this book to fruition. And a thank you to Mary, who will open this book long enough to read the dedication and acknowledgments.

About the Author

Mike Alexander is a Microsoft Certified Application Developer (MCAD) with over 15 years' experience consulting and developing Office solutions. He is the author of over a dozen books on business analysis using Microsoft Excel and Access. He has been named Microsoft Excel MVP for his contributions to the Excel community. Visit Mike at DataPigTechnologies.com where he offers free Excel and Access training.

Publisher's Acknowledgments

Executive Editor: Katie Mohr
Development Editor/Copy Editor: Scott Tullis
Technical Editor: Mike Talley
Editorial Assistant: Serena Novosel
Sr. Editorial Assistant: Cherie Case

Production Editor: Magesh Elangovan
Project Manager: Maureen Tullis
Cover Image: iStockphoto